Life

SECOND EDITION

**NATIONAL
GEOGRAPHIC**

L E A R N I N G

PAUL DUMMETT

JOHN HUGHES

HELEN STEPHENSON

Australia · Brazil · Mexico · Singapore · United Kingdom · United States

Contents

Listening	Reading	Critical thinking	Speaking	Writing
three people talking about important relationships in their lives an excerpt from a radio program about animal friendships	an article about millennials an article about immigrant families in New York	evaluating conclusions	friendships differences between generations family influences	text type: an informal email writing skill: greetings and endings
an interview with a film critic an interview with a professional photographer	an incredible story of a Formula 1 racing driver an article about the Brothers Grimm	the main message	a key moment the stories pictures tell storytelling	text type: a story writing skill: using descriptive words
three people making predictions about the future an interview from a radio program about 3D printing	a lecture about overpopulation an article about appropriate technology	supporting examples	predictions the future technological solutions	text type: short email requests writing skill: being polite
a conversation about two people who are creative in their free time an excerpt from a radio program about what's happening in Melbourne	an article about unusual street art an article about how music helps us	identifying opinions	art and music participation in the arts music playlists	text type: an online review writing skill: personalizing your writing
someone talking about the development of the Belo Monte dam in Brazil an interview with a journalist about social development in southern India	an article about urban development in Dubai an article about the teenage mind	ways of arguing	changes in your town or city a happy community stages of life	text type: an opinion essay writing skill: linking words
someone describing their stay at a mountainside guesthouse an interview about volunteer vacations	a blog post about vacations at home an excerpt from a travel magazine about unusual hotels	analyzing tone	planning a staycation a volunteer vacation ideas for an unusual hotel	text type: a letter/ email of complaint writing skill: formal language

Listening	Reading	Critical thinking	Speaking	Writing
someone describing the customs on the Tokyo subway an excerpt from a radio program about the diet of the indigenous people of northern Alaska	an article about the "tiger mother" approach to parenting a blog about personal space and turn-taking	questions and answers	traditional rules of behavior food and eating habits turn-taking in conversations	text type: a description writing skill: adding detail
someone talking about an unusual mural eight explorers describing superpowers they wish they had	an article about the first human computers an article about Madagascar's unique environment	emotive language	ambitions wishes strong feelings	text type: an online comment writing skill: giving vivid examples
a radio news report about the parents of Chinese university students three good-news stories reported on the television news	an article about an iconic image an article about the power of the press	different perspectives	something true that happened to you good-news stories the media	text type: a news article writing skill: using quotations
a description of a mahout's job someone talking about an extraordinary career a description of a man with an unusual talent	an article about an extraordinary career an article about a woman who was king	examining the evidence	a career path superhuman abilities job descriptions	text type: a personal profile writing skill: using *with*
a parent talking about a children's museum a talk by a psychologist on memory	an article about an innovative school an article about how animals think	explaining ideas	learning experiences making excuses types of learner	text type: an email about a misunderstanding writing skill: linking contrasting ideas
two people talking about the standard of living an interview with a professor about the growing service economy	an article about Norway's riches an article about a new business trend	opinion words	the economy in your country getting things done new business ideas	text type: a short report writing skill: key phrases in report writing

Life around the world—in 12 videos

Unit 7 Eating insects

Discover why eating insects could be good for you, and why one man is on a mission to change our tastes.

Unit 1 Lady Liberty and Ellis Island

The gateway for immigrants to the United States.

Unit 3 3D-printed prosthetic limbs

Discover how 3D printing is revolutionizing prosthetics.

Den
UK

Unit 12 The Farmery

Learn about how one farm is trying to do things differently to benefit the local community.

USA

Unit 4 Making plants into art

Learn about the work of the topiary artist Pearl Fryar.

Unit 2 How not to climb a mountain

A climber talks about how one climb went wrong.

Paraguay

Unit 11 Paraguay shaman

Find out why it's essential to record plants from the rain forests of Paraguay before they disappear.

Unit 5 Scandinavian mega-bridge

Find out about the challenges behind the construction of the Øresund Bridge, which links Denmark and Sweden.

den

Egypt

Japan

Thailand

Unit 8 What would you do if money didn't matter?

A Zen philosopher explains how we can follow our dreams.

Unit 6 The unexpected beauty of traveling solo

What one man discovered while making a journey on his own.

Tonga

Unit 10 Queen of Egypt

The history of the most famous Egyptian queen—Cleopatra.

Unit 9 News: the weird and the wonderful

Two good-news stories: one about the "kindness" of the humpback whale, and one about a man with an amazing ability.

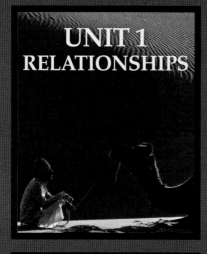

**UNIT 1
RELATIONSHIPS**

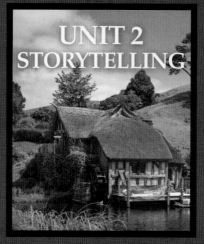

**UNIT 2
STORYTELLING**

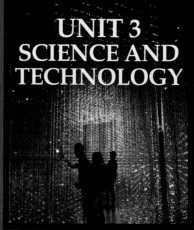

**UNIT 3
SCIENCE AND
TECHNOLOGY**

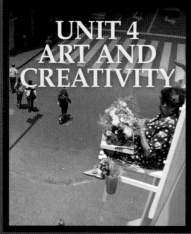

**UNIT 4
ART AND
CREATIVITY**

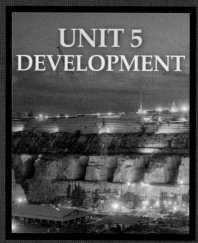

**UNIT 5
DEVELOPMENT**

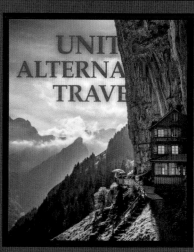

**UNIT 6
ALTERNATIVE
TRAVEL**

**UNIT 7
CUSTOMS AND
BEHAVIOR**

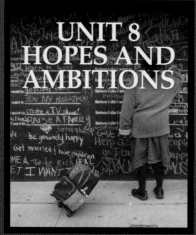

**UNIT 8
HOPES AND
AMBITIONS**

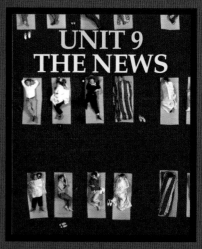

**UNIT 9
THE NEWS**

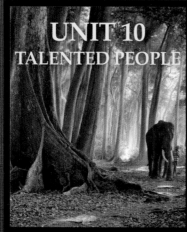

**UNIT 10
TALENTED PEOPLE**

**UNIT 11
KNOWLEDGE
AND LEARNING**

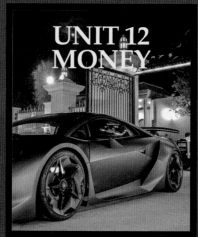

**UNIT 12
MONEY**

Unit 1 Relationships

A camel and his driver take a break in the desert, Rajasthan, India.

1 Work in pairs. Look at the photo and the caption. Circle the phrase you think best describes the photo.

| a faithful companion | blood relatives | a strong bond |
| a passing acquaintance | mutual respect | an odd couple |

2 ▶1 Listen to three people talking about important relationships in their lives. Write the number of the speaker (1, 2, and 3) next to the person they are talking about.

| brother-in-law ____ | colleague ____ | roommate ____ |
| grandparent ____ | husband ____ | old friend ____ |

3 Work in pairs. Look at these sayings about relationships (a–d) and discuss the questions (1–3).

a "Blood is thicker than water."
b "A friend in need is a friend indeed."
c "Like father, like son."
d "No man is an island."

1 What does each saying mean? Can you think of any examples from your or someone else's experience that show these sayings are true?
2 Do you have any similar sayings in your language?
3 What other sayings are there about relationships in your language? Can you translate them?

Suryia the orangutan and Roscoe the dog at a South Carolina sanctuary for endangered animals

1a Unlikely friends

Vocabulary describing character

1 Work in pairs. Look at the adjectives in the box below and discuss:

1 which adjectives are positive, which are negative, and which could be either.
2 which make pairs of opposites.
3 which adjectives you think describe you.

considerate	dependable	energetic	playful
laid-back	outgoing	selfish	
serious	shy	unreliable	

Listening

2 Work in pairs. Look at the photo and say:

1 where these animals are normally found (in a zoo, as pets, in the wild).
2 what the characteristics of each animal are.

3 ▶2 Work in pairs. Listen to an excerpt from a radio program. What unlikely things do Suryia and Roscoe do together?

4 ▶2 Listen again. Work in pairs and answer the questions.

1 What is uncommon between different species?
2 How do dogs usually feel about apes?
3 How is Suryia's character described?
4 What shared need is met in their relationship?

Grammar present tenses: simple, continuous, and perfect

▶ **PRESENT TENSES: SIMPLE, CONTINUOUS, and PERFECT**

Simple present
*Suryia **lives** with his keepers.*
*Most dogs **avoid** apes.*
*Each day, the dog **comes** into the compound.*

Present continuous
*It's clear they **are having** the time of their lives.*
*His understanding of the dog **is growing** day by day.*
*This week, we**'re looking** at animal friendships.*

Present perfect (simple and continuous)
*The story of Suryia **has attracted** a lot of interest.*
*They **have recognized** a basic social need in each other.*

*Recently, he **has been spending** time with a local dog.*
*They**'ve been doing** this every day since they first met.*

For more information and practice, see page 156.

5 Look at the grammar box. Match the tenses with the uses below. Write SP for simple present, PC for present continuous, and PP for present perfect.

1 for something happening at or around the time of speaking, including changing situations ____
2 for something seen as permanent or unchanging, including facts or habits and routines ____
3 for something that started in the past and continues into the present; or for a past event that has an impact on the present ____

6 Work in pairs. Match each sentence in the grammar box with the specific uses described in Exercise 5.

Suryia lives with his keepers. = a fact

7 Look at the examples of the present perfect in the grammar box. Which form (simple or continuous) generally expresses or emphasizes prolonged or repeated activity? _____

8 Circle the correct options to complete the text about animal friendships.

Lately, there ¹ *are / have been* a number of videos on YouTube showing unlikely animal friends. Lots of people ² *discuss / have been discussing* a particular video that shows a dog making friends with an elephant. Elephants often ³ *show / are showing* concern for other elephants in their social group, but this video shows an extraordinary scene where the elephant becomes upset when the dog gets injured. The dog ⁴ *has recovered / has been recovering* now, and the two animals are always together. The question scientists ⁵ *now ask / are now asking* is: Is this behavior normal, or do we just want it to be? No one ⁶ *has provided / has been providing* a definite answer, but it seems some animals are just naturally sociable. Others, like giant pandas, ⁷ *live / are living* more independent and solitary lives.

9 Complete the sentences (1–7). Use the correct present tense of the verbs in parentheses. Use contractions where possible.

1 I _____ (live) with my friend Ezra at the moment, but each of us also _____ (have) our own group of friends that we hang out with.
2 We're not close friends—we _____ (just / take) French class together for the past year.
3 Lara and I went on a trip to Peru ten years ago, and we _____ (be) friends ever since. We keep up with each other through social media.
4 Oh, do you _____ (know) Tom, too? He and I _____ (know) each other since elementary school. We should all meet up some time.
5 Kate is a really dependable friend. She _____ (always / stand) by me when I've needed help.

6 Colin and I _____ (write) a book together at the moment.
7 I get along very well with Marco, even though we _____ (never / see) each other socially.

Vocabulary friendships: phrasal verbs

10 Find these phrasal verbs in Exercise 9:

- one with the verb *get*
- one with the verb *stand*
- one with the verb *hang*
- two with the particle *up*

Work in pairs. Discuss what each phrasal verb means.

11 Complete these sentences with the correct phrasal verbs from Exercises 9 and 10.

1 We come from different backgrounds, but we _____ really well.
2 We don't have to do anything special. It would just be nice to _____ together for a while.
3 They _____ their friendship through frequent phone calls.
4 Why don't we _____ for dinner tonight?
5 Some friends are great to have fun with, but real friends are the ones who _____ you when things aren't going so well.

Speaking myLife

12 Think about one of your friends and make notes on these points.

- how you met and how long you've been friends
- where and how often you see them
- their current work or studies
- their personality and why you like them
- what things you usually do together or have done recently

13 Work in pairs. Describe your friend to your partner. Ask and answer questions to get more information. Discuss how your friendships are similar or different.

*Jana **is** one of my oldest friends. We met at a party, and we've **known** each other for ten years …*

1b The selfie generation

Reading

1 Work in pairs. Look at the photo. Discuss these questions.

   1 What does the photo show?
   2 Is this situation familiar to you?

2 Work in pairs. Discuss what you know about national parks. Then read the article. Did you learn anything new?

3 Read the article again. Find examples of the way millennials and baby boomers are different in each of these areas.

   • relationship with the outdoors
   • relationship with technology

4 Work in pairs. Why do you think the different generations (Casey's and his father's) differ in their attitudes toward the areas discussed in Exercise 3?

Wordbuilding forming adjectives

> ▶ **WORDBUILDING** forming adjectives
>
> There are various suffixes in English that are commonly used to form adjectives: *-ful*, *-ish*, *-ent*, *-ious*, *-ive*.
> act → active, study → studious
>
> For more practice, see Workbook page 11.

5 Look at the wordbuilding box. Find adjectives in the article that come from these root words.

beauty	glory	anxiety	mass	mind

6 Form adjectives from these words (1–6) by using the correct suffix and making any other necessary changes.

  1 ambition _____   4 help _____
  2 child _____   5 decide _____
  3 respect _____   6 success _____

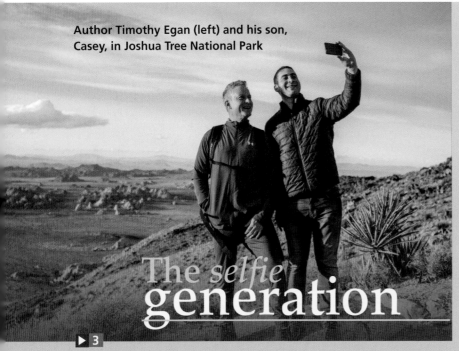

Author Timothy Egan (left) and his son, Casey, in Joshua Tree National Park

The *selfie* generation

▶ 3

We're standing at Lees Ferry, Arizona—the launch point for a four-day raft trip through the Grand Canyon, one of the world's most beautiful places.

"Darn! No service."

5 That's a good thing, I tell my son, Casey. Yes? Well, no. He's a millennial, mid-20s. I'm a baby boomer. My generation loves the national parks. His generation will have to save them.

Growing up in the West, I loved the outdoors. My folks never had a lot of money, but we were rich, my mother said: All of this glorious public land was

ours to enjoy. My wife and I raised our two kids
10 to love the parks as well. But in Casey, I sensed a lack of interest. And in that, he is not alone—I have noticed a similar apathy among other people his age.

"Young people," Jonathan Jarvis, director of
15 the National Park Service, told me, "are more separated from the natural world than perhaps any generation before them." Jarvis has been saying this for a couple of years. A large majority of millennials—71 percent—said they would be
20 "very uncomfortable" on a one-week vacation without connectivity. For boomers, the figure was 33 percent.

On our first day on the river, Casey and I were anxious. But soon, we couldn't wait for the
25 next rapids. We took breaks along the shore, exploring some wildflowers here, a massive natural amphitheater there. In the evening, we spread out sleeping bags and watched the day slip away. It was sublime.

30 But still, Casey and I experienced a bit of internet withdrawal. We should try to be mindful, I suggested. Stare at the stars. Drift. "I get it," said Casey, "this thing about being disconnected. But … everyone I know likes to share—publicly—
35 what we're doing. … If you can't share it now, is it really happening? Just a thought."

Grammar simple past and present perfect

▶ **SIMPLE PAST and PRESENT PERFECT**

Simple past
When she **was** little, she **agreed** with all my opinions.

Present perfect (simple and continuous)
Bella **has been studying** English for five years.
In spoken English, she **has overtaken** her parents.
She **has** already, in her short life, **learned** much more about the outside world than they have.

For more information and practice, see page 156.

7 Look at the grammar box. Circle the correct options to complete these sentences.

1 The *simple past / present perfect* expresses a connection between the past and the present.
2 The *simple past / present perfect* refers to something at a specific time in the past.
3 We generally use adverbials of finished time (e.g., *some time ago, when I was a child, in 2015*) with the *simple past / present perfect*.
4 We generally use adverbials of unfinished time (e.g., *until now, so far this year, since 2015*) with the *simple past / present perfect*.

8 Work in pairs. Look at the example below. Then underline two other sentences with the simple past and two sentences with the present perfect in the article. Say which tense is used and why.

*Growing up in the West, I **loved** the outdoors.* [= simple past to describe something at a specific time in the past]

9 Pronunciation auxiliary verbs *have* and *has*

▶ 4 Listen to how the auxiliary verbs *have* and *has* are pronounced in the present perfect sentences you underlined in the article. Then listen again and repeat.

10 Complete the conversation below between a parent (P) and a child (C). Use the simple past or the present perfect (simple and continuous) form of the verbs in parentheses.

P: ¹_____ (you / do) your math homework yet—the homework you ²_____ (not / do) yesterday?

C: Yes, it ³_____ (be) easy.

P: Oh, OK. What about your project on Mexican food? The one you ⁴_____ (ask) me about a few days ago?

C: I'm working on it now. I ⁵_____ (look) for up-to-date information on the internet all morning.

P: Well, I ⁶_____ (not / eat) Mexican food recently, but I'm good at searching the internet. I'll give you a hand.

C: Thanks, but I ⁷_____ (already / arrange) to meet Sam and work on it with him.

11 Look at the conversation in Exercise 10 again. Underline the time expressions that helped you choose the right tense. Then complete the chart below with the expressions you underlined.

Simple past	last week, in the past, in 2016, ¹_____ , ²_____
Present perfect simple	ever, so far, just, over the past three months, this year, since I was a child, ³_____ , ⁴_____ , ⁵_____
Present perfect continuous	just, over the past three months, this year, ⁶_____

12 Work in pairs. Act out two similar conversations between a parent and a child. Use these opening lines.

1 P: Have you cleaned your room yet?
2 P: Have you eaten any vegetables or fruit today?

13 Circle the correct options to complete these sentences. Then work in pairs to discuss which statements you agree with.

1 "Children *grew up / have been growing up* faster over the last twenty years."
2 "All the new technology that kids use nowadays *left / has left* the older generation behind."
3 "My grandparents' generation *probably worked / have probably worked* harder than we do, but they *didn't have / haven't had* as much fun."
4 "Some of my parents' generation *already retired / have already retired* with good pensions."
5 "When I was young, I *rebelled / have been rebelling* against my parents because they *were / have been* very strict."

Speaking *my*Life

14 Make a list of the differences between your parents' lives and your own. Think about the areas below or your own ideas. Then work in pairs and discuss which generation you think has had a better life.

- upbringing and school
- work opportunities
- free time
- standard of living

*My parents **had** a much freer childhood than I **did**. The outside world **has become** a more dangerous place …*

1c Bloodlines

Reading

1 Work in pairs. Discuss these questions.

- Why do you think people emigrate to other countries?
- What difficulties do immigrants face when they settle in a new country?

2 Read the article about immigrants in New York. Then cover the text and try to remember these details from Richard and Tanja's stories.

1 where their ancestors originally came from
2 what Richard and Tanja's jobs are now
3 how coming from immigrant families has influenced them

3 Read the article again. According to the writer, are these sentences true (T) or false (F)?

1	Many immigrants in Queens feel attached to their new country.	T	F
2	Tomas had a good relationship with his stepmother.	T	F
3	Tomas met his brother in New York one day by accident.	T	F
4	Tanja's mother was able to balance her job with being involved with Tanja's education.	T	F
5	Tanja has chosen a similar career to her parents.	T	F

4 Find these phrases in the article. Work with a partner to discuss what you think they mean.

1 a **melting pot** (paragraph 1)
2 **their** ancestral **roots** (paragraph 2)
3 **seek his fortune** (paragraph 3)
4 a **strong work ethic** (paragraph 4)

Critical thinking evaluating conclusions

5 What conclusions do you think the author wanted you to draw after reading the article? Check (✓) your answers.

☐ Immigration has benefited America.
☐ Immigrants have a stronger connection to their original country than their new home.
☐ It is important for descendants of immigrants to be aware of their family history.
☐ Immigrant families have a strong motivation to work hard and make a good life for themselves.
☐ Many immigrants struggle to adapt to their new home because of cultural differences.

6 Work in pairs. Where in the text did you find evidence to draw the conclusions in Exercise 5? Which do you think is the author's main conclusion? Why?

Word focus *sense*

7 Look at the expression in **bold** from the article. Then circle the best options to complete the sentences (1–5).

*... all of us have a strong **sense of belonging** to ...*

1 It doesn't *have / make* any sense to emigrate if you are happy where you are.
2 Most people want a secure job. It's *common / usual* sense.
3 She's got a great sense of *humor / comedy*.
4 My parents did a lot for me, so I feel a sense of *necessity / duty* to take care of them now.
5 I always get lost in big cities. I have a terrible sense of *direction / location*.

Speaking [myLife]

8 Work in pairs. Look at the questionnaire below. Take turns asking and answering the questions with your partner. Does family have a strong influence in your lives?

HOW DOES FAMILY SHAPE YOU?

1 Do you think you have a close family?

2 How much time do you spend with family:
- out of a sense of duty?
- because you want to?

3 Is family a consideration for you in choosing where to live?

4 How aware are you of your family's history?

5 Is there a "head" of the family? How important is it to have this person's approval?

6 Who in your family do you particularly admire? Why?

7 Has your family influenced your academic choices or your chosen career path?

8 When seeking advice, do you usually ask your friends or your family?

BLOOD LINES

▶ 5

1 The USA, as a whole, is well-known for being a melting pot of different ethnic groups and cultures. This diversity is particularly evident in Queens, New
5 York. Here, second-generation Puerto Ricans live alongside third-generation Greeks and first-generation Koreans, all united by a feeling of pride in their American identity.

2 10 However, they are also proud of something that fascinates us all: their ancestral roots. These days, tracing back your family tree as far as you can is a popular hobby, but what
15 really interests these families is their recent history: how their grandparents and great-grandparents arrived in America, why they emigrated, and how they—their descendants—can
20 best honor their memory. Here are two Queens residents' stories.

Richard, 38

3 My great-grandfather Tomas was a builder by trade—like me. He came to America from Poland when he was fifteen. His mother had become
25 ill and died, and his father decided to remarry. Tomas didn't like his new stepmother, so he ran away to Belgium, where he boarded a ship to America. Arriving in America with nothing, he got a job on the railroads in California. Then one day, by chance, he saw an announcement in a newspaper. It was from his brother in New York who had also come to
30 America to seek his fortune and was now looking for Tomas. Tomas got in touch, and the two had an emotional reunion in New York. Tomas settled in the city, and the two brothers worked in construction. This is the story that my grandmother has passed down to us, to my parents, and all my aunts and uncles. She is an amazing woman—the one who holds us all together.
35 This has meant that all of us have a strong sense of belonging to a group that has struggled and fought together to succeed.

Tanja, 29

4 I'm a first-generation American. Both my parents came here from Jamaica. My dad was a nurse in Jamaica, but he had an ambition to be a doctor in the
40 US. When he first came here, he studied during the day and worked at night. Both my parents have a strong work ethic. My mom has always worked as a nurse, but at the same time has always been very involved in my life, helping with my studies and following my career with interest. I've followed my parents into the medical profession, and now I'm working as a doctor at
45 the Mount Sinai Hospital in Queens. I don't know if that kind of dedication is genetic or just something that you learn from your parents, but that desire to get ahead … I've certainly inherited it. The great thing about America is that it gives you the opportunity to live out your dreams, too.

1d What's up?

Real life meeting people

1 Work in pairs. Which phrases would you use to:

a greet someone for the first time?
b greet someone you know in a formal context?
c greet a close friend?

> How are things?   How do you do?
> How are you?   How's it going?
> Nice to meet you.

2 ▶ 6 Listen to a conversation between two friends, Tom and Greta. Work in pairs and answer the questions.

1 What have Tom and Greta been doing since they last met?
2 What future arrangement do they make?

3 ▶ 6 Listen to the conversation again. Circle the expressions for meeting people that the speakers use.

> ### ▶ MEETING PEOPLE
>
> How are things?
> How's everything going?
> What have you been up to?
>
> I'm doing fine, thanks.
> Not bad.
> Busy as ever.
> I just got a new job.
> I've been studying for my law exams.
>
> You're looking good.
> It obviously suits you.
>
> How's she doing?
> She was asking about you the other day.
> Please give her my best wishes.
> Say hello to her for me.
>
> Well, I should probably go and …
> Sorry, I'm in kind of a hurry.
> I don't mean to be rude, but I need to …
> It was really nice to see you.
> It was great to see you.
> Good luck with …

4 Work in pairs. Which of the expressions that you circled in Exercise 3 match these functions (1–4)?

1 how Greta asks Tom for his news
2 what Tom says about Greta's appearance
3 how Greta describes her life
4 what Greta says about Amanda, their mutual friend

5 Pronunciation word boundaries

a ▶ 7 Common expressions are often said quickly, so the word boundaries become more difficult to hear. Listen to eight expressions and write expressions 5–8.

1 How are things?
2 How's everything going?
3 What's up?
4 I haven't seen you for a really long time.
5 _____
6 _____
7 _____
8 _____

b Work in pairs. Practice saying the eight expressions in Exercise 5a in the same way that you heard them.

6 Imagine you are in a large shopping mall. Walk around and "bump into" other people you know. Find out what each person has been doing, and make a future arrangement with them. Then move on until you bump into someone else.

1e News from home

Writing an informal email

1 Work in pairs. When you send news or communicate with friends in other cities or countries, how do you usually communicate (letter, email, social media, etc.)? Why?

2 Work in pairs. Read the email from Mateo to his friend Fergus. Where is Mateo, and what is he doing there?

3 How are these things (1–4) expressed in the email? Discuss with a partner.

1 sending good wishes   3 giving news
2 asking for news   4 suggesting a meeting

4 Look at the differences between formal and informal written English. Then work in pairs and find examples of informal language in the email.

Informal	Formal
Contractions (e.g., *isn't*)	Uncontracted forms (e.g., *is not*)
Informal linking words (e.g., *so, but*)	Formal linking words (e.g., *therefore, however*)
Conversational words (e.g., *get, nice*)	More formal vocabulary (e.g., *receive, pleasant*)
Idiomatic expressions (e.g., *it's no big deal*)	Conventional language (e.g., *it is not important*)

5 **Writing skill greetings and endings**

Look at the greetings and endings below. Circle the phrases that are appropriate for an informal email to a friend or relative.

All my love	Best wishes	Dear Mr. Lee
Respectfully	Hi John	All the best
Love	Dear Sir/Madam	Yours sincerely

Dear Fergus,

I hope all's well with you. I've been meaning to write with my news for ages, but my work takes up a lot of my time. I've been thinking about you all, and I'm getting very homesick. But I have to remind myself of why I'm here—to get experience as a freelance journalist and photographer.

I'm now in Sri Lanka visiting some tea plantations and talking to people about how their lives have changed in the last twenty years or so. The countryside here is amazing. At the moment, I'm in the hills just outside Kandy. It's so lush and green here, you wouldn't believe it. I'm trying to get an interview with one of the plantation owners so I can write an article for a magazine. Fingers crossed!

My plan is to stay here until the end of September, and then get a plane back to Buenos Aires so that I can go and talk to some publishers about my work. It would be great to get together with you then. How's the family? Has Sarah found a job yet? Send everyone my love. I'll write again soon.

All the best,

Mateo

---

6 Imagine you have been away from home studying or working in another country. Write an email to a friend or family member back home. Include these elements.

- A greeting
- Giving your news
- Asking for their news
- Suggesting meeting when you return
- Good wishes and an ending

7 Exchange emails with a partner. Use these questions to check your partner's email.

- Did their email include all the elements listed in Exercise 6?
- Is the use of tenses correct?
- Is the style appropriate (informal)?
- Did the email use an appropriate greeting and ending?

1f Lady Liberty and Ellis Island

The Statue of Liberty, New York City, USA

Before you watch

1 Work in pairs. Read the description of the video below and answer these questions.

   1 Why was the island closed to visitors?
   2 Who are we going to hear speaking on the video?

> *December 26, 2013:* Ellis Island has recently reopened to visitors, following significant damage from Hurricane Sandy. Stewards[1] and visitors describe the importance of the island to them.

2 Key vocabulary

a Work in pairs. Read the sentences (1–5). The words in **bold** are used in the video. Guess the meaning of the words.

   1 There are a lot of new houses in the town, but there is no **infrastructure** to support them.
   2 The building is basically in good condition, but it needs some **renovation**.
   3 It takes four weeks to **process** a new passport application.
   4 Seeing the families greet each other after so long apart was a very **moving** sight.
   5 I have **faith** in people to do the right thing.

b Write the words in **bold** in Exercise 2a next to their definitions (a–e).

   a deal with using an official procedure
      _____
   b the process of repairing and improving a structure _____
   c a strong belief in someone or something
      _____
   d communication systems and facilities that support an area _____
   e producing strong emotion _____

While you watch

3 ▢◀ **1.1, 1.2, 1.3** Watch Parts 1–3 of the video. Work in pairs and answer the questions.

   1 Who came to Ellis Island in the past?
   2 Who visits it today? Why?

4 ▢◀ **1.1** Watch Part 1 of the video again. Then answer the questions with a partner.

   1 How does David Luchsinger describe himself? Complete the phrase "the last _____ ."
   2 Apart from being a steward, what is David's personal connection to Ellis Island?
   3 What were immigrants asked to do with their bags after arriving at Ellis Island?
   4 What record is David proud of?

5 ▢◀ **1.2** Watch Part 2 of the video again. Match each quote (1–4) with the correct speaker.

   1 "I don't know that our generation would be as gutsy as they were, to come."   ○   ○ Peter
   2 "I got emotional when I saw [the Statue of Liberty] for the first time."   ○   ○ Judith
   3 "Right here—at Ellis Island—this is where my family became American."   ○   ○ Raea
   4 "Our ancestors came over in 1914 from Lithuania."   ○   ○ Pablo

6 ▢◀ **1.3** Watch Part 3 of the video again. Circle the correct options to complete the sentences.

   1 At its busiest point, Ellis Island processed over 12,000 immigrants *a day / a month*.
   2 Now, in the summer months, Ellis Island receives *over / up to* 22,000 visitors per day.
   3 Hurricane Sandy destroyed the *infrastructure / renovated buildings*.
   4 The stewards saw the storm as an opportunity to improve the *park / statue*.

After you watch

7 Vocabulary in context

a ▢◀ **1.4** Watch the clips from the video. Choose the correct meaning of the words and phrases.

b Complete these sentences in your own words. Then share your sentences with a partner.

   1 My … means the world to me.
   2 I showed up late for …
   3 It was very gutsy of … to …

8 Think of two monuments or places of national interest in your country. Then work in pairs and ask and answer these questions.

   1 What is the name of the monument or place?
   2 How would you describe it? Do you like it, and have you visited it?

9 Prepare a brief guide for immigrants to your country. Write down at least six key points. Include things like local eating habits, cultural habits, and advice on transportation.

10 Work in groups. Compare your ideas from Exercise 9. Do you think it would be difficult for someone new to adapt to life in your country? Why or why not?

> **¹steward** (n) /ˈstjuːərd/ a person employed to look after a particular place

Grammar

1 Circle the correct verb forms to complete the text about changing trends in family structures.

When we talk about family, we [1] *need / are needing* to make a distinction between extended family and nuclear family. The nuclear family is the parents and children. The extended family [2] *means / is meaning* all the people who are related to us by blood or by marriage: aunts, uncles, grandparents, in-laws, etc. In the West, the importance of the extended family [3] *has decreased / has been decreasing* for some time. In the past, we [4] *relied / have relied* on extended family to help with childcare or to look after us in old age. [5] *We've shared / We shared* living space and household chores, and so our living costs [6] *have been / were* lower. But now, more and more people [7] *chose / are choosing* to live in nuclear families, and so the economics [8] *have changed / changed*. The older generation says that we [9] *are losing / lose* our traditional family values. But there's an economic issue, too: We [10] *have lost / lost* a valuable support network that was free of charge.

2 Work in pairs. Answer the questions.

1 What is the difference between a nuclear family and an extended family?
2 What benefits of an extended family does the writer mention?

3 >> MB Work in pairs. Answer these questions.

1 Can you explain your choice of tense for items 2–8 in Exercise 1?
2 What other time phrases would fit grammatically instead of *for some time* (item 3) and *in the past* (item 4)?

I CAN	
use present tenses	☐
use simple past and present perfect	☐

Vocabulary

4 Complete the words and phrases in **bold** to make definitions of different relationships. Someone who:

1 you go on a trip with is a **travel com**_____ .
2 you and another friend both know is a _____**ual friend**.
3 you share an apartment with is a **room**_____ .
4 you know but who is not a close friend is an _____**tance**.
5 you are related to by birth is a **b**_____ **relative**.

5 >> MB Work in pairs. Using the words and phrases in **bold** in Exercise 4, describe someone:

1 who you hang out with regularly.
2 who you haven't kept up with.
3 whose house you visit regularly.

6 >> MB Work in pairs. Look at the list of adjectives below.

considerate	shy	energetic	playful	laid-back
outgoing	selfish	dependable	unreliable	serious

1 Which adjectives describe the animals on page 10? Why?
2 Choose three adjectives to describe three of your relatives. Tell your partner and give an example to illustrate each adjective.

I CAN	
describe friends and relatives	☐

Real life

7 Complete the phrases using a preposition or particle.

__1__ **L:** Hello, Jim. How are you?
____ **L:** Yeah, that'd be nice. I'm [1] _____ kind of a hurry now, but I'll call you.
____ **L:** I've been working in New York [2] _____ the past month.
____ **L:** Oh, well, please give her my best wishes.
____ **L:** Thanks. You, too. How's Sarah doing?
____ **J:** Yes, do. And good luck [3] _____ your work in New York.
____ **J:** She's fine. Still studying hard.
____ **J:** That's exciting. You're looking good.
____ **J:** I will. Maybe we can all get [4] _____ some time soon.
____ **J:** Great, thanks, Laura. It's been ages. What have you been [5] _____ to?

8 Number the sentences from Exercise 7 in the correct order (1–10) to form a conversation between Laura (L) and Jim (J).

I CAN	
have conversations with someone I meet	☐

Unit 2 Storytelling

A watermill in New Zealand, used as a movie location

FEATURES

1 Work in pairs. Look at the photo and the caption. What kind of movie do you think this is a location for? Give reasons.

2 Look at the pairs of adjectives (1–4). Match each pair with the type of movie it best describes.

Adjectives	Type of movie
1 funny, touching	thriller/adventure
2 creepy, scary	romantic comedy
3 fast-moving, gripping	horror
4 original, imaginative	science fiction/fantasy

3 ▶8 Work in pairs. Listen to a conversation about a movie adaptation of a book. How did the director manage to make a successful movie from the book?

4 ▶8 Listen to the conversation again. Complete these phrases with the adjectives you hear.

1 a very _Original_ imaginary world
2 the dark, _Scary_ mountains
3 the story is very _fast moving_ and _gripping_

5 Work in pairs. Tell your partner what type(s) of movie you generally like and why. Give examples.

2a A key moment

Vocabulary describing stories

1 Match the words in list A with the words in list B that have a similar meaning.

A	B
1 main characters	time and place
2 plot	central ideas
3 setting	key players
4 themes	important event
5 key moment	story

2 Work in pairs. Think of a movie or TV drama that you have seen recently and answer the questions.

1 What was the setting, and who were the main characters?
2 What was the basic plot? Was there a particular key moment in the story?

3 Complete the description of the movie *Rush*. Use words from list A in Exercise 1.

FROM THE DIRECTOR OF
APOLLO 13 AND **A BEAUTIFUL MIND**

"AN INSPIRATIONAL FILM
MAGNIFICENT"
★★★★★
GO

"BREAKNECK THRILLS
UNMISSABLE"
★★★★
DAILY STAR

"TENSE AND
THRILLING"
★★★★★
TIME OUT
TOTAL FILM

A FILM BY RON HOWARD

CHRIS HEMSWORTH · DANIEL BRÜHL · OLIVIA WILDE · ALEXANDRA MARIA LARA

RUSH

BASED ON THE INCREDIBLE TRUE STORY

IN CINEMAS SEPTEMBER 13TH

The ¹ _____plot_____ of *Rush*, which is based on real events, focuses on the rivalry between two ² _main characters_: Formula 1 racing drivers James Hunt of Great Britain and Niki Lauda of Austria. The movie's ³ _themes_ are danger, drama, and the mutual respect of competitors. The ⁴ _Key moment_ in the movie comes with Lauda's accident in 1976 and his amazing fight to recover from it.

Reading

4 Work in pairs. Read the account below of the key moment in the movie *Rush* and answer the questions.

1 Why did Lauda want the race at the Nürburgring to be stopped?
2 What was the cause of Lauda's accident?
3 What were the consequences of the accident for Lauda and for the race?

A KEY **MOMENT**

▶ 9

It was July 1976, and Niki Lauda was leading the world Formula 1 championship. The next race was the German Grand Prix at the Nürburgring—an old, long track that ran through the Eifel Mountains. The
5 track was narrow, bumpy, and in poor condition, and many people—including Lauda—considered it unsafe. A few days before the race, Lauda had tried to get the race stopped at a meeting of the drivers, but James Hunt had argued for it to go
10 ahead and had won by one vote.

So, on August 1st at 1:00 p.m., the cars set off—Hunt from first position and Lauda from second. It had been raining during the morning, and parts of the track were still wet. But as the race progressed,
15 the track began to dry, and the drivers came into the pits to change their wet-weather tires.

Lauda had lost time by driving more slowly in the difficult conditions, but now, on his new dry-weather tires, he began to push harder. Halfway
20 around the track, he came out of a left-hand corner too fast and lost control of his car. It hit a bank on the far side of the road, bounced back, and immediately burst into flames. There were few safety marshals at this part of the track, but
25 fortunately, other drivers were following Lauda's car. Three of them stopped and ran to help. They managed to pull Lauda free, but by then he had been sitting trapped in the intense heat for over a minute. Eventually, a helicopter arrived and
30 transported Lauda to the hospital. He had suffered extreme burns and was fighting for his life.

Meanwhile, the organizers restarted the race, which Hunt went on to win. Amazingly, just six weeks later, after serious plastic surgery, Lauda got
35 back into his racing car at the Italian Grand Prix and finished fourth. As for the old Nürburgring, that was the last Formula 1 race held there.

Grammar narrative past tenses

> ▶ **NARRATIVE PAST TENSES**
>
> **Simple past**
> He **came** out of a left-hand corner too fast and **lost** control of his car.
> … an old, long track that **ran** through the Eifel Mountains.
>
> **Past continuous**
> It was July 1976, and Niki Lauda **was leading** the world Formula 1 championship.
>
> **Past perfect**
> A few days before, Lauda **had tried** to get the race stopped.
>
> **Past perfect continuous**
> It **had been raining** during the morning, and parts of the track were still wet.
>
> For more information and practice, see page 158.

5 Look at the grammar box. Match the tenses with the uses below. Write SP for simple past, PC for past continuous, PP for past perfect, and PPC for past perfect continuous.

   a to describe an action that started and finished at a specific time in the past; or to describe a general state in the past ____

   b to describe something that happened before the main event(s) or story in the past ____

   c to describe an activity in progress in the past, which is a background to the main story or to an event within it ____

   d to describe an activity in progress up to the main event(s) in the past; emphasizes the duration of the past activity ____

6 Work in pairs. Cover the account of the key moment on page 22. Can you retell the story of what happened to Niki Lauda?

7 Circle the correct options to complete the story of Niki Lauda and James Hunt.

> Niki Lauda and James Hunt had very different approaches to life. They both
> [1] *were driving / drove* hard, but Hunt liked to play hard, too. Often, while Lauda
> [2] *was preparing / had prepared* carefully the night before a race, Hunt was out at a nightclub. Both men [3] *knew / had known* that danger was a part of the attraction of motor racing for fans, but Lauda [4] *was refusing / refused* to take unnecessary risks. That's why people were so amazed when he
> [5] *was returning / returned* to the track six weeks after he [6] *lay / had been lying* in the hospital, fighting for his life.

8 Pronunciation /æ/, /ʌ/, and /ɒ/

a ▶ **10** Listen to the vowel sounds in these simple past verbs and past participles. Then listen again and repeat.

/æ/ crashed, ran, sat
/ʌ/ run, stuck, suffered
/ɒ/ got, lost, stopped

b ▶ **11** Work in pairs. What are the simple past and past participle forms of these verbs? Listen and check.

become	begin	drink	forget
shine	sing	go	win

9 ▶ **12** Complete this story using the correct past tense of the verbs in parentheses. Then listen and check your answers.

Mr. Charles Everson and his wife Linda
[1] _____ (drive) home one Sunday when a cow [2] _____ (fall) from the sky and [3] _____ (land) on the hood of their van. The cow—which [4] _____ (escape) from a local farm—[5] _____ (graze) all morning near the edge of a cliff, when it slipped and [6] _____ (plunge) seventy meters to the road below. The Eversons weren't hurt, but the cow wasn't so lucky—it [7] _____ (have) to be put to sleep.

Speaking myLife

10 Work in pairs. Read this story about a key moment in two people's lives. Discuss how you think the story continues and ends. Write at least five more sentences using the correct past tenses.

> In 2010, TV viewers around the world watched as, one by one, 33 Chilean copper miners emerged into the sunlight. For 69 days, the miners had been trapped in a hole 450 meters below the surface after part of the mine had collapsed. Melanie Mayer was one of the people who was watching the news at her home in Germany. As the sixteenth miner, Daniel Herrera, came out, it was love at first sight for Melanie. …

11 ▶ **13** Work with another pair. Take turns telling your version of the story. Then listen and compare your stories to the version you hear.

12 Work in pairs. Describe a key moment in your life. Talk about the events before and after it.

2b Visual storytelling

Schoolboys, Muscat, Oman

Lifejackets, Lesbos, Greece

Vocabulary communication

1 Work in pairs. Match the verbs in the box with the nouns (a–g) to make collocations. There is sometimes more than one answer.

| bring | engage | express | tell |
| reach | share | present | |

a _____ a story
b _____ an idea
c _____ information
d _____ your audience
e _____ a photo
f _____ a story to life
g _____ an emotion

▶ **WORDBUILDING collocations**

In English, some words go naturally together, e.g., we say **make a mistake** (NOT *do a mistake*). This is called "collocation." Often, more than one verb can collocate with a particular noun.
tell a story, *share a story*

For more practice, see Workbook page 19.

2 Work in pairs. Look at the two photos on the left and answer these questions.

1 What do you think each photo aims to do? Use a collocation from Exercise 1 to describe this.
2 Which photo had a greater impact on you? Why?

Listening

3 ▶ **14** Listen to an interview with a professional photographer, Olaf Paulsen. Work in pairs and answer the questions.

1 According to Olaf Paulsen, what is "visual storytelling"?
2 Why does he think it has become such a popular form of storytelling?
3 What does he say is the message or story behind the two photos on the left?

4 ▶ **14** Are the sentences true (T) or false (F)? Listen again and check your answers.

1 Paulsen thinks that a good photographer is a storyteller.   T   F

2 According to Paulsen, a good photo is one that can engage you emotionally.   T   F

3 Anyone can take a photo, but only a professional photographer can tell a visual story.   T   F

4 The lifejackets on the beach is an example of a photo that tells a big story.   T   F

Grammar the passive

▶ THE PASSIVE

Active
People **present** a lot of factual information visually now.
Recently, people **have called** you a "visual storyteller."
In the past, publishers **used** photos in magazines.
I acted like a magazine **had paid** me to do a job.
Anyone **can share** stories from anywhere in the world.

Passive
A lot of factual information **is presented** visually now.
Recently, you**'ve been called** a "visual storyteller."
In the past, photos **were used** in magazines.
I acted like I **had been paid** by a magazine to do a job.
Stories **can be shared** by anyone from anywhere in
the world.

For more information and practice, see page 158.

5 Look at the grammar box. Circle the correct options
to complete the sentences (1–4).

1 The *subject* / *object* of the active verb is the
subject / *object* of the passive verb.
2 We form the passive with the verb *be* +
present / *past* participle.
3 In passive sentences, the person or thing doing
the action (the agent) is introduced with *by* / *with*.
4 In passive sentences, you *always* / *don't always*
have to mention the agent.

6 Pronunciation weak forms in passive verbs

a ▶ **15** Listen to the passive sentences in the
grammar box. In each **bold** phrase, notice the
unstressed auxiliary verb and the stressed main verb.

b ▶ **16** Work in pairs. Read these sentences aloud
with the same stress patterns in the passive verbs.
Then listen and compare.

1 The story was first published in 2012.
2 She has been given permission to tell her story.
3 More photos are being shared online.
4 It will be seen by people all over the world.
5 The joy of the moment is captured wonderfully.

7 Rewrite the paragraph below about infographics.
Use the passive form of the verbs in **bold**. Make any
other changes and include the agent if necessary.

In infographics, people **combine** data and images to
communicate information. We **can present** the data
using numbers or words. William Playfair probably
created the first infographics in his 1786 book,
A Commercial and Political Atlas of England. However,
people **have called** Edward Tufte—a teacher at
Princeton University—the true father of the modern
infographic. He **published** his first book,
Visual Display, in 1982.

8 Circle the best option (a or b) to complete the text.
Sometimes both options are possible.

Photo sharing and visual storytelling has
increased greatly in the last twenty years. One
reason for this is the rise of blogging and of social
networking sites like Facebook. [1] _____
in 2004. [2] _____ in the 1990s, but blogging
didn't really take off until the mid-2000s. But
perhaps the most important factor in the rise
of visual storytelling was the invention of the
smartphone. Before the smartphone, most
photos were taken with a separate camera,
before [3] _____ onto a computer. With a
smartphone, [4] _____ in a message, a blog,
or on their Facebook page.

[1] a They launched Facebook
b Facebook was launched
[2] a A few people were already writing blogs
b Blogs were already being written by a few
people
3 a were uploaded
b being uploaded
4 a the user can easily insert a photo
b a photo can easily be inserted

Speaking ⬛ *my* Life

9 Complete these questions about photos, using active
or passive verbs.

1 Where _____ (this photo / take)?
2 What _____ (show) in the photo?
3 What story _____ (the photo / tell)?
4 What emotions or ideas _____
(express) in the photo?

10 Look at the two photos below and work in pairs.

Student A: Look at the notes on page 153 about
photo A.

Student B: Look at the notes on page 154 about
photo B.

Take turns asking and answering the questions in
Exercise 9 about each photo.

2c Once upon a time …

Reading

1 Work in pairs. What were your favorite stories or picture books as a child? Discuss what they were about and why you still remember them.

2 Read the article about the Brothers Grimm and their book of fairy tales. Then cover the article and tell your partner what you remember about the following:

1 where and when the brothers lived
2 where the stories came from
3 what the brothers' interest in writing the stories was
4 why people still like the stories

3 Work in pairs. Read the article again and answer the questions.

1 How did the Brothers Grimm first become interested in fairy tales?
2 What did the early editions of their book lack?
3 What did the early editions contain that is unusual for a book of fairy tales?
4 How were the stories useful to parents?
5 What element of the stories do some parents not like so much?
6 What does the phrase *a rags to riches story* (line 50) mean?

4 The writer uses various words and expressions associated with fairy tales. Underline words and expressions in the text that mean:

1 a long time ago (paragraph 1) *once upon a time* ✓
2 the opposite of heroes (paragraph 1) *villains* ✓
3 distant countries (paragraph 1) *faraway lands* ✓
4 the lesson to be learned (paragraph 5) *moral* ✓
5 a woman (often bad) who does magic *witch* ✓ (paragraph 6)
6 for the rest of time (paragraph 7) *ever after* ✓ *(para siempre)*

Word focus *keep*

5 Work in pairs. Complete these phrases from the article with the word *keep*. Discuss what each phrase means.

1 keep each other _____ (paragraph 4)
2 keeping _____ (paragraph 5)
3 keep your _____ (paragraph 5)

6 Look at these other phrases with *keep*. Work in pairs. Discuss what each phrase means.

1 Please **keep an eye on** the time. We can't leave any later than ten-thirty.
2 I wouldn't tell him your news just yet, if I were you. He's not very good at **keeping secrets**.
3 Technology is moving so fast these days. It's difficult to **keep track of** all the changes.
4 I think it's a good idea to **keep a diary** when you are traveling, to look back on later. *record.*

Critical thinking **the main message**

7 Look at sentences a–c. Which do you think is the main message of the article? Circle your answer.

a The Brothers Grimm chose classic stories that they knew would be popular with future generations, especially children.
b In carefully recording traditional stories, the Brothers Grimm produced a wonderful book that is popular with children and adults today.
c The Brothers Grimm produced an academic book about the history of German folktales, and the lives of storytellers.

8 Work in pairs. Where in the article can you find evidence for these ideas?

1 The author of the article thinks that the Grimms' story collection is great.
2 The story collection was not very popular initially, but it is now.
3 In the beginning, the brothers' interest was only in preserving the stories.

Writing and speaking myLife

9 Think of a traditional story or fairy tale. Make notes about the basic plot, setting, and main characters of the story. Include a moral if you like. Then think about how you could put the story into a modern setting.

10 Work in pairs. Tell each other your modern version of the traditional story. Did your partner's story have a moral? If so, what was it?

Once upon a time...

▶ 17

1 Once upon a time in Germany, there lived two brothers who loved a good story—one with magic, danger, royalty, and villains. At school, they met a wise man who led them to a treasure—a library of old books with tales more
5 enchanting than any they had ever heard. Inspired, the brothers began collecting their own stories, listening to the folktales people told them. Soon, they produced their own treasure—a book of fairy tales that would fascinate millions in faraway lands for generations to come.

2 10 The Brothers Grimm—Jacob and Wilhelm—named their story collection *Children's and Household Tales* and published it in Germany in 1812. The collection has since been translated into more than 160 languages, from Inupiat in the Arctic to Swahili in Africa. In Japan,
15 there are two theme parks devoted to the tales. In the United States, the Grimms' collection has helped to turn Disney into a media giant.

3 The humble Grimms would have been embarrassed by such fame. During their lifetime, the story collection
20 sold only a few copies in Germany, and the early editions were not even aimed at children. They had no illustrations, and scholarly[1] footnotes[2] took up almost as much space as the tales themselves, Jacob and Wilhelm Grimm viewed themselves as students of local
25 folklore[3] who were trying to preserve the stories of oral storytellers.

4 As in many other countries, storytelling had been popular in Germany long before the Grimms' time. During long winter nights, people would keep each
30 other entertained with tales of adventure, romance, and magic. To write their stories, the Grimms interviewed about forty such storytellers.

5 Although the brothers claimed that they were just keeping records of tales, Wilhelm continued to improve
35 and reshape the stories up to the final edition of 1857. In an effort to make the stories more acceptable to children's parents, he stressed the moral of each tale. The collection, he said, should be used as "a manual of manners": keep your promises, don't talk to strangers,
40 work hard, obey your parents.

6 However, the unpleasant details of the stories were often left untouched. The cruel treatment of children (Hansel and Gretel are put in a cage by a witch and then fattened for eating) and the violent punishments handed out to
45 the stories' villains (in the original *Snow White*, the evil stepmother is forced to dance in red-hot iron shoes until she drops dead) are still too much for some parents.

7 So why are the stories still so popular? Some suggest that it is because they are about our struggle for happiness:
50 *Cinderella* is a classic "rags to riches" story, where a poor young girl finds her wealthy prince; *Beauty and the Beast* is about a girl with such a loving nature that she sees past the monstrous looks and bad temper of the Beast to find the good in him. Grimms'
55 tales were part of a storytelling tradition—not just in Germany but worldwide—which often gave people an escape from the hard realities of daily life, and hope for a better future. But as for the brothers themselves, they just wished to retell these exciting stories accurately. In
60 doing so, they ensured that Grimms' fairy tales would live happily ever after.

---

[1] **scholarly** (adj) /ˈskɒlərli/ connected with academic study
[2] **footnote** (n) /ˈfʊtˌnəʊt/ a note at the bottom of a page that gives more information
[3] **folklore** (n) /ˈfəʊkˌlɔːr/ traditional stories and beliefs from a particular community

2d What a nightmare!

Real life reacting to stories

1 Work in pairs. What kinds of everyday things can often go wrong? (e.g., losing a phone, missing a bus, burning dinner, spilling coffee)

2 ▶ 18 Look at the excerpts below from six personal accounts of things that went wrong. Work in pairs. Discuss what you think happened next. Then listen and compare.

1 The bus broke down on the highway, so we were all left waiting until help could arrive.
2 My pants got caught on the door handle, and as I walked away, they ripped.
3 I bent my house key trying to force it into the door lock, and when I tried to straighten the key, it snapped.
4 The elevator got stuck between the eighteenth and nineteenth floors, and two people completely panicked.
5 The tires on my bike were all worn out, and when I hit a bump in the road, one of them popped.
6 My computer froze while I was working.

3 ▶ 18 Look at the expressions below for reacting to stories. Can you remember which expressions were used in the conversations in Exercise 2? Discuss with a partner and circle your answers. Then listen to the conversations again and check.

> ### ▶ REACTING TO STORIES
>
> **Sympathizing when something bad has happened**
> Oh, no!
> How embarrassing!
> Oh, that's really awkward.
> Poor you!
> What a nightmare!
> Really? That's odd.
>
> **Commenting on a good outcome to a bad situation**
> That must have been a relief.
> That was smart.
> That was good thinking.
> That was lucky.
>
> **Talking about similar experiences**
> I can sympathize with that.
> Yeah, I think I would have done the same thing.
> Yeah, a similar thing happened to me once.
> Yeah, I once had the same experience.

4 Pronunciation linking and elision

a ▶ 19 Listen to these responses. Notice how the underlined sounds are either linked as in *been a* or elided as in *what did*, where the *t* of *what* disappears. Repeat each phrase.

1 That must have been a relief. (linked)
2 So what did you do? (elided)

b ▶ 20 Work in pairs. Underline the sounds in these sentences that you think are linked or elided. Then listen and check. Practice saying the sentences.

Linked

1 What a nightmare!
2 Poor you!
3 How embarrassing!
4 Really? That's odd.

Elided

5 That was good thinking.
6 A similar thing happened to me once.

5 Choose one of the following topics and prepare to tell a short story about something that happened to you. Then work in pairs. Take turns telling your stories and reacting.

• a time you were lost or stranded
• something embarrassing that happened to you
• a minor accident you had
• a computer problem
• a situation where something broke or got stuck

2e A real-life drama

Writing a story

1 Read the paragraph below from a story about two men walking in the Amazon rain forest in Peru. Work in pairs. Answer these questions.

1 What happened to Rowan?
2 Why did Chris feel anxious?

2 Work in pairs. Number these events in the order in which they actually happened (1–6). Why do you think the writer starts the story when Rowan cries out?

_____ Rowan cried out.
_____ Rowan's foot got caught in something.
_____ Rowan was moaning about his sore feet.
_____ Chris and Rowan were walking through the jungle.
_____ Chris went back to help Rowan.
_____ Chris saw that it was an animal trap.

> "I can't move," cried Rowan. "My foot's stuck in something—it's really painful!" Chris knew that Rowan was struggling. He had been moaning all day about his sore feet, and they had only covered a kilometer in the last half an hour. Chris was also tired from hiking through the thick jungle, but he was anxious to return to camp before it got dark. They weren't carrying many supplies with them, and neither had eaten anything for at least three hours. "It's probably just a thorn bush or something," he said encouragingly, as he walked back slowly to see what the problem was. "Reach down and try to free your foot." But as Chris got closer, he could see that it wasn't a bush that had caught Rowan, but a metal animal trap that had clamped itself firmly to his right ankle.

3 Writing skill using descriptive words

a Work in pairs. Look at the highlighted words and phrases in the story. Which describe movement, and which describe a way of speaking?

b Work in pairs. Look at the words and phrases in **bold** in the sentences below (1–8). Try to figure out their meaning from the context. Then check in a dictionary.

Speaking
1 "Help!" she **screamed**. "That man running away has just stolen my wallet!"
2 They continued on their way, but Jake could tell that Jess was unhappy because she kept **muttering** under her breath.
3 He **mumbled** something about it being unfair, but I couldn't catch his exact words.
4 "OK. Let's try your way then," she **said with a sigh**. She had lost the energy to argue.

Moving
5 We **moved cautiously** along the narrow path, conscious of the steep drop to our left.
6 When he heard the car arrive, he **leapt** to his feet and ran to the door.
7 She **tripped** on a rock and almost fell, but then regained her balance.
8 She **turned anxiously** toward the door, wondering whether she should enter.

4 Look at the main events of a story on page 153. Then write the story in full, using this checklist.

- Start the story at its most dramatic point.
- Use the correct past tenses when you describe events.
- Use some descriptive verbs and adverbs, but don't overuse them!

5 Exchange stories with a partner. Did your partner use the checklist in Exercise 4? Whose version of the story do you like better? Why?

Climber Cedar Wright prepares
for a rock climb.

Before you watch

1 Key vocabulary

Work in pairs. Look at the diagram below. Explain in your own words these features of a mountain.

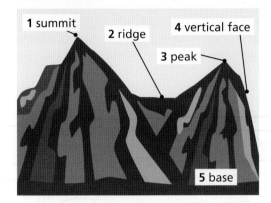

1 summit
2 ridge
4 vertical face
3 peak
5 base

2 Work in pairs. Look at the title of the video and the list of possible mistakes (a–c). Then think of two more possible mistakes.

a The climbers chose a mountain that was too difficult for them.
b The climbers attempted to do the climb in bad weather.
c The climbers took the wrong equipment.

While you watch

3 ▶ 2.1 Work in pairs. Watch the video of Cedar Wright and Alex Honnold climbing Middle Palisade Mountain in the Sierra Nevada in the USA. What mistake did they make?

4 ▶ 2.1 Watch the video again. Circle the correct options to complete the sentences.

1 Middle Palisade is a *10,000-foot / 14,000-foot* peak.
2 Wright and Honnold *had / hadn't* read a description of how to climb the mountain.
3 While climbing, they thought they might be on the wrong *mountain / route*.
4 They discovered their mistake when they saw the *summit register / real summit in the distance*.
5 To reach the real summit, they had to *avoid / walk along* a dangerous ridge.
6 The climb took them *eight / twelve* hours in total.

5 ▶ 2.1 What did Cedar Wright say about their experience? Watch the video again and complete these sentences with the words he uses.

1 Wright and Honnold thought the peak they were looking at was Middle Palisade because it was "the _____ mountain here."
2 The climb up the peak was "kind of _____ ."
3 On their way to the top, they "were _____ all the summit registers."
4 The ridge they had to go along looked like "death on a _____ ."
5 The rock was peeling off "like sheets of _____ ."
6 At the end of the climb, they were "completely _____ ."
7 Although the climb was horrible, Wright's conclusion was "_____ times! You should totally do it!"

After you watch

6 Vocabulary in context

a ▶ 2.2 Watch the clips from the video. Choose the correct meaning of the words and phrases.

b Complete these sentences in your own words. Then share your sentences with a partner.

1 The house was in a bad condition. The paint was peeling off … and the …
2 I was very ill-prepared for …
3 For our summer vacation, we are heading to …

7 Work in pairs. Retell the story from the video, using these prompts (1–8) to help you. Take turns describing the events.

1 climb—Middle Palisade
2 description—phones
3 tough—wrong route
4 top—summit register
5 realize—mistake
6 walk—ridge
7 rock—peel off
8 arrive—twelve hours

8 Look at these situations (1–4). Imagine what could go wrong. Write two possibilities for each situation. Then compare your ideas with a partner. Which do you think would be the worst mistake? Why?

1 You are starting evening classes in English at a local college.
You go to the wrong room, and you realize five minutes into the lesson it is a French class.
2 You are going to the wedding of an old friend. You take a card and a present with you.
3 You are driving to a job interview. You leave the house in good time.
4 You are giving a presentation at work. You use audiovisual equipment in your presentation.

UNIT 2 REVIEW AND MEMORY BOOSTER

Grammar

1 Complete the story using the correct past tense form of the verbs in parentheses. Use both active and passive forms.

Most people have heard of Richard Branson—head of the Virgin Group. But not many people know about his love of April Fools' jokes.* In 2011, an article ¹_____ (be / publish) on the Virgin website announcing that Branson ²_____ (just / buy) the planet Pluto. In 2013, he ³_____ (claim) that his company ⁴_____ (work) for some time on a glass-bottomed plane, so passengers could look down at the scenery while they ⁵_____ (fly). The story ⁶_____ (be / pick up) by several media agencies. Branson even ⁷_____ (play) an April Fools' joke on the British police. In 1989, police officers ⁸_____ (be / call) to a field near London, where several people ⁹_____ (report) seeing a UFO. When the officers ¹⁰_____ (arrive), they were shocked to see a silver flying saucer in the field. (In fact, it was a hot air balloon that ¹¹_____ (be / make) to look like a UFO.) They were even more surprised when a figure in a silver suit, who looked like an alien, ¹²_____ (step) out of it!

> * April Fools' Day is celebrated every year on April 1st by playing practical jokes.

2 >> **MB** Work in pairs. Identify the four passive verbs in the story in Exercise 1. Discuss why passive forms are used rather than active forms.

3 >> **MB** Write two sentences about something that happened to you last week. Read the sentences to your partner and ask each other questions.

A: I was late to class on Wednesday.
B: Why were you late?

I CAN	
use narrative past tenses	☐
use active and passive forms	☐

Vocabulary

4 Circle the correct options to complete the description of a movie.

Bridge of Spies is a ¹ *gripped / gripping* thriller directed by Steven Spielberg. The ² *setting / stage* is Berlin in the 1960s, and the ³ *theme / plot* is based on true events. The story is ⁴ *said / told* from the point of view of the main character. Spielberg is amazing at ⁵ *bringing / fetching* a story to life and ⁶ *sharing / engaging* his audience.

5 >> **MB** Look at the photo and work in pairs.

What do you remember about this story? Use appropriate adjectives to describe it.

I CAN	
describe stories	☐

Real life

6 >> **MB** Work in pairs. Take turns being Student A and Student B.

Student A: Make statements about these things to elicit the responses in the box below.

- my phone
- my vacation
- my new boss
- my jacket

Student B: Respond to Student A's story using as many expressions from the box as possible.

> How embarrassing!   Oh, no!
> Really? That's odd.   That must have been a relief.
> That was good thinking.
> Yeah, I think I would have done the same thing.

A: I lost my phone at work.
A: So I put up a "lost" notice.

B: Oh, no!
B: That was good thinking.

I CAN	
react to stories	☐

Unit 3 Science and technology

"Crystal Universe," from the Future World
Exhibition at the ArtScience Museum, Singapore

FEATURES

1 Work in pairs. How much do you depend on technology in your day-to-day life? How affected will you be if you lose your phone, or if your computer crashes?

2 Work in pairs. Look at the photo and the caption. Which of these areas of technology is represented in the photo? In which area do you think the main breakthrough of the next fifty years will come?

artificial intelligence	communications	energy use
medicine	space exploration	transportation

3 ▶ 21 Work in pairs. Read these statements from three people making predictions about the future. What reasons do you think they will give for their predictions? Listen and check.

1 I expect that most of my generation will live to be around 100 years old.
2 I think in the future, people will be interacting with intelligent machines even more than they do now.
3 I think science will be able to find a solution to global warming.

4 Which of the predictions in Exercise 3 do you think will come true? Discuss with your partner.

Is technology the answer?

So, I think I'll begin … Today, we're going to look at overpopulation: why it's a growing problem, and what solution we might find for it in the future. Overpopulation, simply put, is a situation where there
5 are more people than there are resources—food, water, land, energy—to support them. When an area becomes overpopulated, one or more of the following things will happen: Some people will go hungry; pollution will increase; unemployment will rise; and people might
10 even begin to fight over the limited resources.

But overpopulation is an issue that divides opinion. Some say that population has to be controlled. The American biologist Paul Ehrlich wrote in his 1968 book, *The Population Bomb*, that medical science had
15 advanced too far and we were keeping too many people alive. He predicted that, as a result, millions of people would starve to death. The population has doubled since then to seven billion and—at the current rate—is going to reach nine billion by 2050. Mass
20 starvation hasn't happened, though, because in the 1970s and 1980s, scientists developed better seeds and pesticides to increase food production. That is why other experts in the scientific community say that people will always find a technological solution to overpopulation.
25 They say that we are about to enter an even more productive era of safer and cheaper food with the help of biotechnology and nanotechnology.

The real question is: Have we now reached a point where we cannot simply rely on science to provide
30 the answers? Do we, instead, have to start reducing our consumption? I'm visiting various cities in Europe next month to speak to groups who are researching this approach. The problem, as the eighteenth-century English economist Thomas Malthus pointed out, is that
35 people are basically lazy. They won't act unless they have to. Malthus claimed that the population will continue to grow until war, disease, or famine arrive to stop it. (I'll give you the references to his and Ehrlich's work at the end of my lecture.) …

Reading

1 Work in groups. Look at the photo above. Which of these problems does it illustrate?

congestion	epidemics	overpopulation
pollution	poverty	starvation

2 Read the excerpt above from a lecture about overpopulation. Match the opinions (1–3) with the correct person or group (a–c).

1 People will only act to deal with a problem when there is no other option.
2 Many people are going to die because there is not enough food for the growing population.
3 Science and technology will find answers to the problem of overpopulation.

a Paul Ehrlich _2_
b Thomas Malthus _1_
c Other experts in the scientific community _3_

(N) famine starvation

3 According to the excerpt above, are these sentences true (T) or false (F)?

1 One possible consequence of overpopulation is conflict between people. **(T)** F
2 Paul Ehrlich had an optimistic view of the future. T **(F)**
3 The global population will rise to nine billion by 2050. **(T)** F
4 Thomas Malthus believed that human society could never be perfected because humans are, by nature, lazy. **(T)** F

4 Pronunciation /r/ and /t/ in American English

a ▶ 23 Listen to these words from the lecture. How does the speaker pronounce the letters *r* and *t*?

water	energy	limited	starve
better	more	visiting	cities

b ▶ 24 Listen and complete these phrases said by another American speaker with the words you hear.

1. _____ billion
2. an _____ site
3. a _____-_____ birthday
4. great _____
5. another _____

Grammar future forms

> ### ▶ FUTURE FORMS
>
> **Predictions**
> 1. *Some people **will go** hungry; pollution **will increase**.*
> 2. *People **might begin** to fight over the limited resources.*
> 3. *At the current rate, the population **is** probably **going to** reach nine billion by 2050.*
> 4. *We **are about to enter** an era of safer and cheaper food.*
>
> **Plans and arrangements**
> 5. *Today, **we're going to look** at overpopulation.*
> 6. ***I'm visiting** various cities next month to speak to …*
>
> **Decisions made at the time of speaking**
> 7. *So, I think **I'll begin** …*
> 8. ***I'll give** you the references to his work at the end of my lecture.*
>
> For more information and practice, see page 160.

5 Work in pairs. Look at the grammar box. Answer these questions.

1. Which of the predictions 1–3 seems to be the most definite? And the least definite?
2. Which future form do we often use to predict something happening very soon?
3. Which prediction is based on some present evidence?
4. Which sentence describes an intention or plan? And which describes an arrangement made with other people?
5. Which sentence is an offer? Which is a decision made at the moment of speaking?

6 Work in pairs. Discuss which future form is used in each sentence (1–7) and why.

1. I'm going to go to Lima tomorrow.
2. I don't think they'll win the election.
3. The weather is about to get much worse.
4. Don't worry. I'll pick you up from the airport.

5. I'm afraid I might be home late tonight.
6. We're meeting at 6:00 p.m. outside the theater.
7. Oh, that's my phone. I'll take the call in the other room.

7 Circle the correct future forms to complete the text.

> I'm just [1] *going to wait / waiting* a few moments for everyone to arrive … OK, I'm aware of the time, so [2] *I'm beginning / I'll begin* now. Hello everyone and thank you for coming today. I'm [3] *about to / going to* speak for about thirty minutes, and then I hope there [4] *will be / might be* time for questions at the end. And my colleague, Liesel Babel, is [5] *about to give / giving* a talk tomorrow in the green seminar room about appropriate technology. I think [6] *you'll / you're about to* find her session very useful. OK, I'm [7] *going to show / showing* you a short film now, so could someone at the back please turn the lights down?

8 ▶ 25 Work in pairs. Act out these conversations, putting the verbs in parentheses in an appropriate future form. Then listen and compare your answers.

1
A: What (you / do) this weekend?
B: I'm not sure, but we (go) to the beach if the weather stays nice.
A: Sounds good. I (just / stay) at home and relax.

2
A: I (buy) a wedding dress on Saturday. Jen and I (travel) up to Seattle to choose one.
B: How exciting! (you / show) it to anyone else before the wedding?
A: I (let) you see it, if you want.

3
A: (you / help) me move this table? It (not / take) long.
B: Sure. I (just / finish) writing this email first.

4
A: Have you started your new job yet?
B: No, but I (start). Next Monday is my first day.
A: Good luck. I'm sure you (be) fine.

Speaking *my*Life

9 Work in pairs. Have conversations like the ones in Exercise 8, using future forms. Talk about:

- your plans for the weekend.
- something you intend to buy.
- a favor you want to ask.
- a change in your life coming very soon.

3b Just press "print"

Vocabulary materials

1 Look at the words in the box. Choose one or two materials from the box that you would expect each of the items (a–f) to be made of. Then compare your ideas with a partner.

brick	cardboard -	concrete	cotton
glass	leather	metal	nylon
plastic	rubber	wood	

a a chair   c a shirt   e a pair of shoes
b a wall   d a box   f a screen

Listening

2 Work in pairs. Answer the questions.

1   Do you know what 3D printing is and what it is used for?
2   Have you ever seen or used a 3D printer? If so, give details.

3 ▶ 26 Listen to an interview from a radio program. Work in pairs and answer the questions.

1   What is a 3D printer?
2   How is it similar to an ink-jet printer?
3   How do the layers of printed objects stick together in 3D printing?
4   What are its advantages over traditional construction?
5   What's the most amazing thing a 3D printer can print?
6   What are its disadvantages?
7   Where will 3D printing be fifteen years from now?

4 ▶ 26 What 3D-printed objects are mentioned in the interview? Listen again and make a list.

Design for a 3D-printed
canal house, Amsterdam

Wordbuilding compound nouns

> ▶ **WORDBUILDING compound nouns (noun + noun)**
>
> We can combine two nouns together to form a compound noun with a new meaning.
> *light switch, phone charger*

For more practice, see Workbook page 27.

5 Work in pairs. Combine a noun from box A with a noun from box B to make compound nouns to describe useful objects.

A	
can	coat
coffee	credit
cup	printer

B	
card	cartridge
cup	holder
hook	opener

6 What other compound nouns can you make using a noun from box B (e.g., *bottle opener*)? Discuss with your partner.

Grammar future continuous and future perfect

> ▶ **FUTURE CONTINUOUS and FUTURE PERFECT**
>
> **Future continuous**
> *A Dutch architect is currently printing a house in Amsterdam. He thinks that in the future, his firm **will be building** a lot of houses this way.*
>
> **Future perfect**
> *3D printers are expensive. But in ten years' time, the cost **will have come** down a lot.*

For more information and practice, see page 160.

7 Look at the grammar box. Circle the correct options to complete these statements.

1 The future continuous is used to describe *a completed action* / *an action in progress* at or around a certain time in the future.

2 The future perfect is used to describe an action completed *before* / *after* a certain time in the future.

8 Complete these sentences from the interview using the future continuous or the future perfect form of the verbs in parentheses.

1 Some printed body parts—like new 3D-printed ears—already exist, but I expect twenty years from now scientists _will be making_ (make) all kinds of body parts.

2 A lot of people _will have already bought_ (already / buy) their own 3D printers by then.

3 In time, we _will all have forgotten_ (all / forget) what life was like before 3D printers existed.

9 Complete these predictions about 3D printing. Use the future continuous or the future perfect form of the verbs in parentheses.

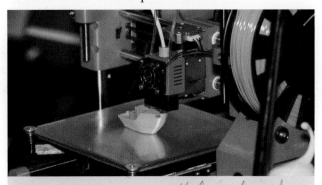

Before long, every child [1] _will have learned_ (learn) how to use a 3D printer by the time they leave school. Many students [2] _will be wearing_ (wear) clothes they have designed and printed themselves. People also expect there to be huge growth in 3D food printing, allowing us to create new, healthier foods. In the future, we [3] _will be eating_ (eat) things like insects without realizing it, because food manufacturers [4] _will have found_ (find) ways to make them look like something else. Some people think 3D printing will improve our standard of living. They say that because the cost of a 3D printer [5] _will have come_ (come) down so much, people [6] _will be making_ (make) all kinds of things for themselves that they couldn't afford to buy before. But other people are worried. They think 3D printing will need to be regulated. Otherwise, very soon, people [7] _will have tried_ (try) to print things like guns using instructions from the internet.

10 Check your answers to Exercise 9 with a partner. Do both of you agree with the predictions?

Speaking *my* Life

11 Work in pairs. Using the prompts below, ask your partner questions about their future. Use the future continuous or the future perfect. Take turns asking and answering the questions.

1 How many more years do you think you / study / English?
   How many more years do you think you'll be studying English?

2 What things do you hope you / achieve / by the end of this year?

3 What do you think you / do / in five years' time?

4 Ten years from now, which of your friends or colleagues do you think / enjoy / the most success in their careers?

3c Appropriate technology

Reading

1 Work in pairs. What's your favorite device or piece of technology? How is it useful to you?

2 Work in pairs. Look at these devices from the article. Then read the article and answer the questions.

> a solar-powered lamp   a central heating system
> a water purifier   a machine for shelling corn

1 In what country or situation is each device used?
2 What do the devices have in common?

3 Read the article again. What characteristics make technology "appropriate"? Check (✓) the correct ideas.

- [✓] It provides a long-term solution.
- [ ] It is easy for the user to understand.
- [✗] It is only used in developing countries.
- [✗] It is a new form of technology.
- [✓] It does not upset people's way of life.

4 Delete TWO words in each of these sentences to make them true.

1 Gandhi wanted technology that would improve the lives of rich and poor people.
2 The Swedish company Jernhuset found a way to cut the station's heating costs by using people's body heat.
3 The engineers in Guatemala were successful in trying to make the village women's work quicker and easier.

Critical thinking supporting examples

5 Match the types of technology (1–3) with the supporting examples (a–c) from the article.

1 cheap and eco-friendly—for developing countries
2 cheap and eco-friendly—for developed countries
3 time-saving, but not suitable with the local social practices

a a machine for shelling corn ____
b a solar-powered lamp ____
c a central heating system ____

6 Which example of appropriate technology in the article appealed to you most? Why? Discuss with a partner.

Vocabulary describing technology

7 Complete the sentences (1–6) with these adjectives to show the meaning of the expressions in **bold**.

easy	efficient	long-term
old	recycled	useful

1 It's a **time-consuming process**. We need to find a solution that's more _efficient_ .
2 We don't just want a **quick fix**; we want a(n) _long-term_ solution.
3 It's a **handy gadget**, much more _useful_ than an average penknife.
4 It's not **cutting-edge technology**, but often the _old_ ways are the best.
5 It's essentially a **labor-saving device**; it makes cutting up wood very _easy_ .
6 It's an **environmentally friendly product** because it's made from _recycled_ materials.

Speaking _my_Life

8 Work in groups. Look at the products below (1–4).

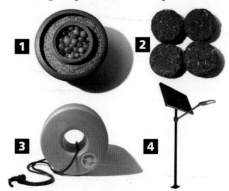

- Read the description of the product assigned to your group. Products 1 and 2 are on page 154, product 3 is on page 155, and product 4 is on page 153.
- In your group, prepare a brief presentation of the product: what it is, how it works, what it is appropriate for, and why it is special. Do some research if necessary.
- As a group, give your presentation. Think about the questions you may be asked.
- Take turns giving and listening to the presentations, asking and answering questions as you go.
- Take a class vote on which invention you think is the best "appropriate technology" product.

Appropriate technology

▶ 27

Even if the term "appropriate technology" is relatively new, the concept certainly isn't. In the 1930s, Mahatma Gandhi claimed that the advanced technology used by Western
5 industrialized nations did not represent the right route to progress for his homeland, India. He wanted affordable technology that would lead to greater social equality: technology that could empower the poor
10 villagers of India and help them become self-reliant.[1] His favorite machines were the sewing machine—a device invented "out of love," he said—and the bicycle, a means of transportation that he used all his life.

15 The term "appropriate technology" was first used by E.F. Schumacher in his 1970s book *Small is Beautiful*, which promoted his own philosophy of technological progress. Do not start with technology and see what it can
20 do for people, he argued. Instead, "find out what people are doing, and then help them to do it better." According to Schumacher, it did not matter whether the technological solutions were simple or sophisticated. What
25 was important was that they were long-term, practical, and in the hands of the people who used them.

So, "appropriate technology" suits the needs and abilities of the user, and also takes into
30 account environmental and cost considerations. For this reason, it is often found in rural communities in developing countries. Examples include solar-powered lamps that bring light to areas with no electricity, and water purifiers
35 that work by simply sucking through a straw. But the principle of appropriate technology does not only apply to developing countries. It also has its place in the developed world. For example, a Swedish state-owned company,
40 Jernhuset, has found a way to use the energy produced each day by the 250,000 bodies rushing through Stockholm's central train station. Their body heat is absorbed by the building's ventilation system, and then used
45 to warm up water that is pumped through pipes to heat a new office building nearby. It's old technology—a system of pipes, water, and pumps—but used in a new way. And it is expected to bring down central heating costs
50 in the office building by up to twenty percent.

Finally, appropriate technology needs to be culturally appropriate. In other words, it needs to fit in with people's customs and social practices. This cannot always be guaranteed,
55 as in the case of a device for shelling corn developed to help women in a Guatemalan village. Some engineers who were visiting the village observed how labor-intensive and slow it was for women to shell corn by hand. So
60 they designed a simple mechanical device to do the job more quickly. The new device certainly saved time, but after a few weeks, the women returned to the old manual method. Why? Because they enjoyed the time they spent hand
65 shelling: It gave them an opportunity to chat and exchange news with each other. It is exactly this kind of sensitivity to what is appropriate that Gandhi and Schumacher, in their different ways, were trying to highlight.

[1] **self-reliant** (adj) /self rɪˈlaɪənt/ able to manage without the help of other people

A woman and child shell corn in Todos Santos Cuchumatán, Guatemala.

3d I can't get the TV to work

Real life dealing with problems

1 Work in pairs. What things can cause difficulties or problems for people when staying in a hotel room?

2 Match the two halves of each sentence to make seven common problems in hotel rooms.

1 I can't connect to ○	○ the air conditioning.
2 There's no hot ○	○ for the TV doesn't work.
3 The sink ○	○ is flickering on and off.
4 I can't seem to adjust ○	○ the internet in my room.
5 The remote control ○	○ to open with this key.
6 The main light ○	○ is clogged.
7 I can't get the door ○	○ water in my room.

3 ▶ 28 Listen to three conversations in a hotel between guests and a receptionist. Complete the chart.

Conversation	Problem	Resolved? Yes / No / Partly
1		
2		
3		

4 ▶ 28 Work in pairs. Look at the expressions for dealing with problems. Then listen to the conversations again and circle the expressions you hear. Who said each expression: guest 1, guest 2, guest 3, or the receptionist?

> **▶ DEALING WITH PROBLEMS**
>
> **Asking for help**
> Do you have any idea how I can turn off the ...?
> Can you tell me how to ...?
>
> **Explaining problems**
> I can't seem to open / turn on / connect (to) the ...
> I can't get the ... to work / open / turn on.
> The ... won't close / open / work.
> The ... is broken / blocked / stuck / faulty.
> There's no ... in the room / bathroom.
> There's a lot of noise / a bad smell coming from ...
>
> **Responding to a problem**
> Have you tried turning / putting ...?
> I'll send someone to look at it.
> I'm afraid there's not much I can do about it.

5 Pronunciation stress in two-syllable words

a ▶ 29 Listen to these two-syllable verbs and nouns. Underline the stressed syllable in each word.

Verbs

adjust	believe	connect
open	repair	suggest

Nouns

basin	bathroom	control
mirror	signal	window

b ▶ 30 Work in pairs. Look at these other verbs and nouns. Where do you think the stress falls in each word? Listen and check. Underline the stressed syllable in these two-syllable words.

carpet	curtain	entrance	intend
prefer	provide	replace	undo
pleasure	wallet	wardrobe	manage

6 Work in pairs. Choose one of the problems in Exercise 2. Act out a conversation between a guest at a hotel and a hotel receptionist.

Receptionist: Hello. Is everything OK with your room?
Guest: Actually, no, it isn't. ...

3e Technical help

Writing short email requests

1 Match the emails below (1–4) with the replies (A–D). Write the correct name in each reply.

2 **Writing skill** being polite

a Underline the four phrases used to make requests in emails 1–4, and underline the five phrases used to apologize in emails A–D.

b Work in pairs. Answer the questions.

1 What is the relationship between each pair of correspondents?
2 Which are big requests, and which are small requests?
3 Which phrases for requests and apologies are only used formally? And informally?

3 **Word focus** *out of*

a Work in pairs. Look at the expressions with *out of* in **bold** in emails 1, 3, and 4. Discuss what you think they mean.

1
Hello,

I wonder if you can help me. I have an X3000 digital camera that I bought from a shop in Chicago that has since **gone out of business.** The camera is great, but I have lost the user manual. Could you please tell me where I can find one? I've looked on the internet, but without success. Thank you. Kate Winslow

2
Dear Sir/Madam,

I bought a KJ450 printer from your online store three months ago, but it is very slow. I would like to return it and get a refund. Please can you advise me how to go about this? Yours sincerely, Kevin Lyons

3
Hi Jim,

Thanks a lot for the advice about the car. I changed the air filter, and it's running much better now. Just **out of interest**, do you know what kind of oil is best to use with an old car? If so, can you drop me a line and let me know? Cheers, Nathan

4
Chris,

Would you mind stopping over to take a look at the air conditioning in my apartment? It's making a strange noise. I'd be really grateful. Please **don't go out of your way**, though. Anytime in the next week or so is fine. All the best, Sophie

b Complete these other expressions with *out of* using the words in the box.

date	order	practice	time

1 I'd love to play tennis with you some time, but I'm really out of _____ .
2 I'm afraid that printer is out of _____ . You'll have to use the one in the next office.
3 This information is out-of- _____ . It's got last year's figures on it, not this year's.
4 I'm sorry. We are out of _____ . Let's continue the discussion tomorrow.

4 Look at the following situation and write a short email requesting help.

You bought two ink cartridges for your printer online, but when they arrive, you notice that the expiration date on them has already passed. Write and ask for replacements to be sent.

5 Exchange emails with a partner. Use these questions to check your partner's email. Then write a reply to their email.

- Is the situation and the action demanded clear?
- Is the email in the correct register (formal or informal) and polite in its request?

A
Sorry, _____ , I'd normally help, but I'm going on vacation tomorrow for three weeks. Why not call a technician from Jacob's Air Conditioning? They're very good and not too expensive.

B
Dear _____ ,

I am sorry, but we only give refunds in case of mechanical failure. I am, however, attaching some tips for you on how to make your printer run faster. I hope this helps. My apologies again. Davina Miles

C
Hi again, _____ ,

I'm afraid I've no idea. Try looking at the discussion boards for your particular car model on the internet. I'm sure someone'll know. Good luck.

D
Dear _____ ,

I regret to say that we only supply user manuals with the equipment at the time of purchase. However, you can download one by following the link below. Kind regards, Justine Bagnall

3D-printed prosthetic limbs

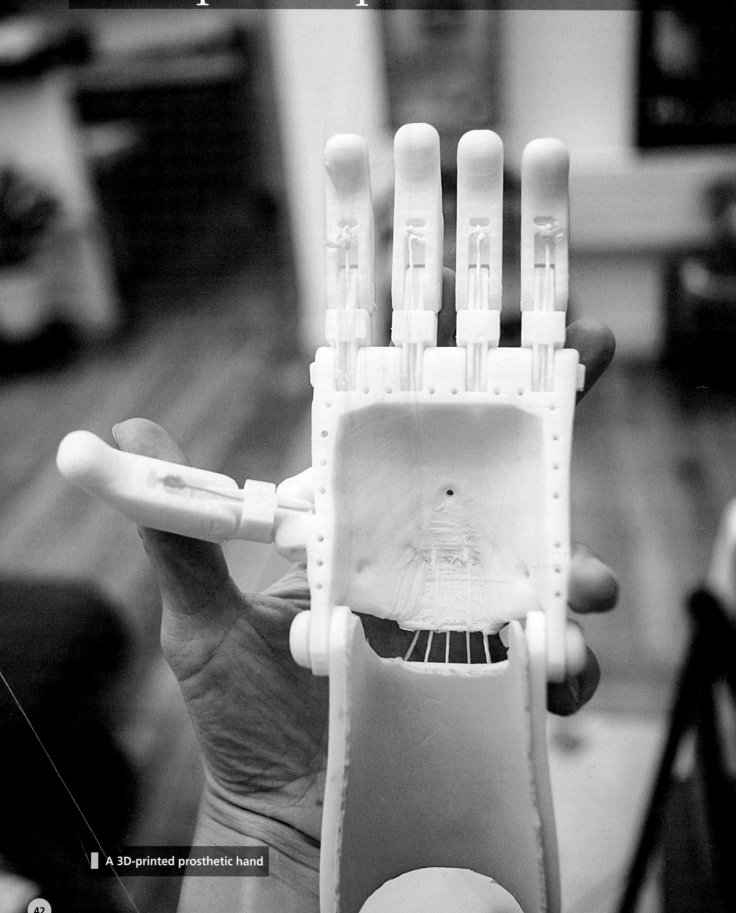

A 3D-printed prosthetic hand

Before you watch

1 Work in pairs. What kinds of things did you most enjoy doing when you were five years old?

2 Look at the photo on page 42 and the caption. What is a prosthetic hand? What do you think this hand can do? Discuss with a partner.

While you watch

3 ▶ **3.1, 3.2** Watch Parts 1–2 of the video. Work in pairs and answer the questions.

1 What adjectives would you use to describe the little girl, Charlotte?
2 What are the advantages of the 3D-printed prosthetic limbs for Charlotte and her family?

4 ▶ **3.1** Watch Part 1 of the video again. Then answer the questions with a partner.

1 According to Charlotte's mother, what surprises people about Charlotte?
2 What does Charlotte say about needing help?
3 How does the presenter describe the prosthetic limbs Charlotte has used up to now?
4 How does Charlotte operate the hook on her prosthetic arm?
5 How often does Charlotte need a new prosthetic arm? Why?

5 ▶ **3.2** Watch Part 2 of the video again. Circle the correct options to complete these sentences about a 3D-printed prosthetic hand.

1 "At a target price of *£200 / £1,200*, it's within range of *normal / wealthy* families."
2 "If I flex my *hands / muscles*, the hand in response will open and close all of the fingers."
3 "First, a 3D scan is made using a *scanner / tablet computer*. Then a 3D printer constructs it, *bit by bit / minute by minute*."
4 "At the moment, children are a bit under-served by the *robotics / prosthetics* industry."
5 "It's still at the prototype stage, but … for Charlotte, a *moving / working* hand is not far off in the future."

After you watch

6 Vocabulary in context

a ▶ **3.3** Watch the clips from the video. Choose the correct meaning of the words and phrases.

b Complete these sentences in your own words. Then share your sentences with a partner.

1 I'd say that my *hands* skills are _on a par_ with …
2 I recommend buying a … They don't cost the earth, and they … *are very cheap*.
3 It would be great if someone could custom-build a … for me. Then I could …

7 Work in pairs. Summarize the video about Charlotte and the new 3D-printed prosthetic limbs in your own words. Begin like this:

Charlotte is a young girl who had an illness that affected her limbs when she was younger. In spite of this, she …

8 Work in pairs. Look at the photo below and the description of virtual voice assistants. Then discuss these questions.

1 What are the benefits of this kind of program, and who could it be most useful for?
2 What other things do you think this program could do to help people in their homes?
3 Are there any disadvantages to using this program? If so, what?

Virtual voice assistants are programs that can both understand what you say, and speak to you. They are usually installed in your tablet or smartphone, and they answer commands and questions like "Tell me the news headlines" or "Call a taxi to come in ten minutes." They can also be linked to devices in the home—like the oven, the front door lock, or the central heating system—so that you can control these devices with a simple voice command.

9 Work with a new partner. Do you use any similar voice assistant technology on your phone or tablet? When do you find it most useful?

UNIT 3 REVIEW AND MEMORY BOOSTER

Grammar

1 Circle the most appropriate verb forms to complete the text.

One of the biggest problems we [1] *will face / are facing* in the next fifty years is global warming. Scientists predict that by the end of this century, temperatures [2] *will be rising / will have risen* by 4 degrees Celsius. The invention of a super battery [3] *will be solving / might solve* this problem. We currently have ways to produce electricity— like wind and solar power—that don't emit carbon dioxide, but we have no control over when they are available. But if there was a super battery that could store the energy for later use, it would be different. Elon Musk, CEO of Tesla, is confident that his company [4] *might / is going to* produce such a battery in the near future. In fact, he believes the energy storage market [5] *is about to boom / will be booming*. In 2014, Tesla started building a huge battery factory outside Reno, Nevada. The facility is scheduled for completion in 2020.

2 Work in pairs. What problem does the author think a super battery can solve, and how can it do this?

3 >> MB Work in pairs. Answer the questions about the future forms in the text above.

1 Can you find a future form that describes a completed action at a certain point in the future?
2 Can you find a future form that predicts something happening very soon?

I CAN	
use different future forms	
use the future continuous and future perfect	

Vocabulary

4 Complete the sentences. The first letter of each missing word is provided.

1 It's not c_____-edge technology; it's a bit out-of-d_____ , really.
2 I see that this car r_____ on electricity, not gas. But just out of i_____ , where do you recharge it?
3 It's a portable phone charger. It's a really h_____ gadget, and it's very e_____ to carry around with you.
4 This water container can h_____ almost 60 liters.

5 >> MB Correct the errors in 1–7. Write the material each object is commonly made of. Then compare your answers with a partner.

1 a ~~glass~~ sheet _____*cotton*_____
2 a plastic wallet _____
3 a rubber floor _____
4 a brick window _____
5 a cardboard wall _____
6 a leather bottle _____
7 a concrete box _____

I CAN	
talk about objects and materials	

Real life

6 >> MB Put these words in the correct order to make sentences. Then write *P* next to the sentences that are said by the person with a problem.

1 get / can't / the shower / to / I / work / . ____
2 you / have / turning / the thermostat / tried / up / ? ____
3 to / connect / I / to / seem / the internet / can't / . ____
4 idea / I / the / any / how / have / heating / can / you / turn off / do / ? ____
5 send / 'll / at / someone / I / to / look / it / . ____
6 much / do / afraid / about / I'm / not / can / I / it / there's / . ____
7 a / coming / bad / the bathroom / from / there's / smell / . ____

7 >> MB Work in pairs. Using the problems in Exercise 6, act out conversations asking for and giving help.

I CAN	
ask for and give help with problems	

Unit 4 Art and creativity

A woman sits arranging flowers—
a performance artwork, Lima, Peru.

FEATURES

1 Work in pairs. Look at the photo and the caption. What is unusual about this artwork? Can you describe any other performance art you have seen?

2 Work in pairs. Look at these words about artists and performances. Put them into three categories: who, what, and where. Then form four sentences describing who does what, and where.

an actor	an artist	a band
a street performer	a circus performer	a classical concert
a comedian	a concert hall	a dancer
an exhibition	a gallery	a live music venue
a musical	a (night)club	an orchestra
a performance	a play	a show
the street	a theater	a singer

Who	What	Where
a dancer	*a performance*	*a theater*

You can see dancers give a performance in a theater.

3 ▶ 31 Listen to a conversation about two people who are creative in their free time. Work in pairs and answer the questions.

1 What does each person do as their normal job?
2 What creative thing does each person do, and where do they do it?

4 Do you (or does anyone in your family) do anything creative? What is it? When and where do you/they do it? Tell your partner.

4a Reverse graffiti

Reading

1 Work in pairs. What do you think about graffiti in cities? Do you think it improves or damages the appearance of a place?

2 Look at the photo and title of the article. What do you think *reverse graffiti* is? Read the article and check your ideas.

3 Use the information in the article to complete these sentences (1–5). Use one word in each blank.

1 Most city authorities say that graffiti is wrong because it is done without _____ .
2 Reverse graffiti works by cleaning away the _____ on walls.
3 The aim of reverse graffiti artists is to highlight the problem of _____ in cities.
4 In removing soot from the car tunnel, Alexandre Orion wasn't actually guilty of a _____ .
5 The only solution the São Paulo authorities could think of was to clean every _____ in the city.

4 Work in pairs. Cover the article.

Student A: Retell the story from Alexandre Orion's point of view.

Student B: Retell the story from the city authority's point of view.

R E V E R S E   G R A F F I T I

▶ 32

Graffiti involves finding a blank wall and spray-painting an image on it that expresses a particular idea. Some graffiti artists use pictures, some use words, some both. But because the images are usually painted on walls that
5 the artist has no permission to paint on, the policy of most city authorities is to remove graffiti where they find it.

The principle of "reverse graffiti"—a growing movement in the last fifteen years—is different. Reverse graffiti artists take a dirty wall and make images by removing
10 the dirt. Each artist has their own style, but they all share a common aim: to draw attention to the pollution in our cities. Brazilian artist Alexandre Orion turned one of São Paulo's many car tunnels into a rather scary mural by scraping away the dirt caused by pollution from cars.
15 Made up of white skulls, the artwork reminds drivers of the effect that their pollution is having on the planet.

"Every motorist sits in the comfort of their car, but they don't give any consideration to the cost that has for the environment, and ultimately for them too," says Orion.
20 The city authorities in São Paulo were annoyed. Since Orion hadn't committed any crime, they had only two choices: to remove the graffiti or to leave it. Both options seemed unsatisfactory, but in the end, they decided that any graffiti was wrong and that they
25 should remove Orion's work. In other words, they chose to clean all parts of the tunnel that Orion had already "cleaned." Encouraged by this, Orion continued making reverse graffiti on both sides of the tunnel. The city officials then decided to take drastic action. They
30 not only cleaned the whole tunnel, but also every other car tunnel in São Paulo.

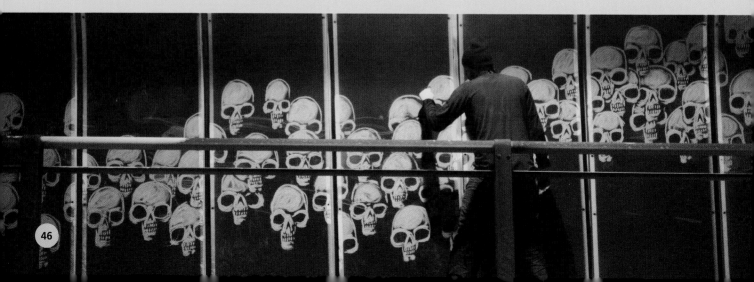

Vocabulary art

▶ WORDBUILDING word families

When you learn a new word, try to learn other words from the same family at the same time, e.g., *artistic*, *artwork*.

For more practice, see Workbook page 35.

5 Complete the sentences (1–4) using these words and phrases related to art.

exhibition	gallery	artists	artistic
artwork	fine arts	street art	performing arts

1 We went to see an art _____ over the weekend in the new _____ in town. It was by a group of local _____ .
2 If you walk around the city, you will see lots of examples of _____ . For example, the station wall is covered with _____ by local graffiti artists.
3 "_____" is the term for painting, drawing, and sculpture, whereas the expression "_____" describes creative fields like acting, music, and dance.
4 I enjoy going to see art, but I don't really have any _____ talent myself.

Grammar determiners

▶ DETERMINERS

+ singular noun: *each, every, the whole, either, neither*
Each artist has their own style, but they all share a common aim.
They cleaned the whole tunnel.

+ plural noun: *all, both, most*
The policy of most city authorities is to remove graffiti where they find it.
Both options seemed unsatisfactory.

+ singular noun, plural noun, or uncountable noun: *any, no*
The artist has no permission to paint on the walls.

+ plural noun or uncountable noun: *all, certain, some*
Some graffiti artists use pictures, some use words.

For more information and practice, see page 162.

6 Look at the grammar box. Then underline examples of determiners in the article. What type of noun is used with each determiner? Discuss with a partner.

7 Rewrite these sentences using the determiners in parentheses.

1 Every motorist sits in the comfort of their car. (each)
2 Orion hadn't committed any crime. (no)
3 Both options seemed unsatisfactory. (neither)
4 They decided that any graffiti was wrong. (all)
5 They chose to clean all parts of the tunnel. (the whole)

8 Circle the correct determiners to complete this text about another "reverse graffiti" artist.

> The UK's Paul Curtis (known as "Moose"), who works in Leeds and London, has had some trouble with the authorities. He had been paid by ¹ *any / certain* companies to make reverse graffiti advertisements for their products in ² *either / both* cities. However, the Leeds City Council said, "We view ³ *all / each* advertising of this kind as environmental damage and will take strong action against ⁴ *some / any* company carrying out such campaigns." In fact, ⁵ *no / any* action was taken against the companies, but Moose himself was ordered to clean up the graffiti. But how was he supposed to do this? By making ⁶ *all the / the whole* buildings he had cleaned with his reverse graffiti dirty again? ⁷ *Most / Every* people agree that this would be a ridiculous solution.

9 ▶ 33 Work in pairs. Read the sentences (1–5) about art and predict which of these determiners will go in each blank. Then listen to an interview with an artist and complete the statements with the determiners you hear.

all	certain	either	no	some

1 _____ art should contain something pleasing for the viewer.
2 Art should involve _____ hard work on the part of the artist.
3 To be an artist, you need to possess _____ technical skills.
4 Art should make a social or a political point; without _____ , it's not true art.
5 There is _____ such thing as bad art.

10 Work in groups. Discuss which of the statements in Exercise 9 you agree with.

Speaking *my*Life

11 Complete these sentences about art or music in your own words. Then share and discuss your sentences with a partner.

1 I like certain …
2 Some … is/are really difficult to understand.
3 Both … are musicians.
4 All … should have free admission.
5 Some people say that all … is/are the same, but I think that each …

4b All about Melbourne

Listening

1 Work in pairs. Ask and answer these questions.

1 What cultural or arts events are there in your country?
2 Is there an exhibition or performance that you've enjoyed recently?
3 What type of cultural activities do you think Australia offers tourists?

2 ▶ **34** Listen to a feature about Melbourne on a weekly radio program. Work in pairs. Answer the questions.

1 What is the main difference between Melbourne and Sydney?
2 What does Melbourne offer visitors?
3 What events do local people particularly enjoy?

3 ▶ **34** Listen to the radio program again. According to the speaker, are these sentences about Melbourne true (T) or false (F)?

1	Melbourne always has sunny weather and has many places of natural beauty.	T	F
2	It is known as the cultural capital of Australia.	T	F
3	It has a thriving arts scene.	T	F
4	Festivals in Melbourne only take place in the summer.	T	F
5	Melbourne's Formula 1 Grand Prix and tennis tournament are world famous.	T	F
6	Not many visitors know about the local sports in Melbourne.	T	F

4 Would you like to visit Melbourne after hearing this radio program? What would you like to do there? Discuss with a partner.

Grammar expressions of quantity

> **► EXPRESSIONS OF QUANTITY**
>
> **+ plural countable noun:** *(not) many, (a) few, a (small/large) number of, several*
> *Several festivals take place during the winter months.*
>
> **+ uncountable noun:** *(not) much, (a) little, a bit of, a (large/huge/small) amount of*
> *Cricket enjoys a huge amount of support.*
>
> **+ plural countable noun or uncountable noun:** *a lot of, lots of, plenty of, loads of, (a/no) lack of, (almost) no, (not/hardly) any, some, enough, the majority of*
> *A lack of natural attractions has meant that Melbourne …*

For more information and practice, see page 162.

5 Work in pairs. Look at the grammar box. Which words or expressions of quantity indicate:

a a large number/amount?
b a small number/amount?
c neither a large nor a small number/amount?

6 Look at track 34 of the audioscript on page 183. Find and underline as many expressions of quantity as you can that mean:

1 *many* or *much*
2 *not many* or *not much*
3 *some*

7 Work in pairs. Choose an expression of quantity to replace the **bold** words and phrases in the sentences below.

a She has **many** friends. *a lot of*
b There is **a lot of** pollution. *amount of*
c I don't have **much** time. *any*
d There aren't **many** good stores.
e I have **some** ideas. *several / a lot of*
f Do you want **some** help?

any

8 Circle the correct options to complete the sentences.

1 A visit to the opera can cost *much* / *a lot of* money.
2 A reasonable *number* / *amount* of winter festivals are free.
3 There is almost *no* / *any* rain in Melbourne at Christmas time.
4 There are *few* / *a few* tickets for the tennis tournament available on the day—if you get there early.
5 We saw *several* / *some* interesting street art at the Sweet Streets festival.
6 *Almost* / *Hardly* anyone attended the afternoon performance.
7 Most visitors show *a little* / *little* interest in Australian rules football—and why should they?
8 There aren't as *many* / *much* differences between Melbourne and Sydney as people say.

9 Pronunciation weak form *of*

a ▶ **35** Listen to these phrases. Notice how *of* is unstressed.

1 a bit of relaxation time
2 a lot of information
3 a huge amount of support
4 lots of people
5 a huge number of galleries
6 a lack of natural attractions

b Work in pairs. Practice saying these phrases using the weak form of *of*.

- as a matter of fact
- just the two of us
- first of all
- most of the time
- in spite of that
- of course
- instead of me
- that's kind of you

Speaking *my*Life

10 Work in pairs. Look at the infographic below showing Australians' participation in the arts. Then complete these sentences with expressions of quantity. Use one word in each blank.

1 Overall, quite a ____lot____ of Australians take an interest in the arts, and a small _____ of them also participate creatively.
2 ____Lots____ of Australians read literature, and a _____ of them also write creatively.
3 There is certainly no _____ of interest in the visual arts, with almost a quarter of the population being involved in some way.
4 The main reason for not participating in music is having too _____ time. But the _____ of money it costs to be involved is also an important factor.

11 Work in groups. Research how much your classmates participate in the arts, and then report your findings. Follow these steps:

- Each group should choose ONE of the following: visual arts and crafts; theater and dance; literature; music.
- Make questions about students' participation (both creative and receptive).
- Circulate around the class asking and answering questions (and get reasons for non-participation).
- Work in your group again. Put your results together and make conclusions, using expressions of quantity.
- Present your findings to the class.

A lot of students read novels, but very few do any creative writing.

Australians' participation in the arts

Participation by art form

- Creative participation only (making and doing) %
- Receptive participation only (watching, reading, etc.) %
- Both receptive and creative participation

Visual arts & crafts
16%
23%
14%

Theater & dance
3%
33%
5%

Literature
0%
71%
16%

Music
7%
44%
13%

Participation in music: Reasons for non-participation

- It's difficult to find the time.
- I'm not really interested.
- It costs too much.
- There aren't enough opportunities close to where I live.

28%
54%
43%
41%

4c Why do we need music?

Reading

1 Write down the names of two of your favorite songs or pieces of music. Then work in pairs and answer these questions.

1 What kind of music is each one: pop, traditional/folk, classical, rock, R&B/soul, hip-hop, etc.?
2 Where and when do you usually listen to this piece of music?
3 Why do you particularly like this piece of music?

2 Look at the title of the article. Why do you think we need music? Discuss with your partner. Then read the article and compare your ideas.

3 Cover the article. How many of these details can you remember in three minutes? Compare your answers with a partner and see who remembered more details correctly.

1 how much time we spend listening to music
2 what "motherese" is
3 why we listen to sad songs when we feel sad
4 what rap music around the world is about
5 how music is like language

4 The words in **bold** below are from the article. Circle the correct meaning (a, b, or c) of each word. Look at the article again to help you.

1 music has the power to excite or **soothe** us (line 12)
   a calm   b inspire   c please
2 can give you **goosebumps** (line 15)
   a a feeling of worry   b a feeling of excitement
   c a feeling of sadness
3 sad music seems to help us **regulate** negative feelings (line 25)
   a prevent   b get rid of   c control
4 we've made a kind of intellectual **conquest** (line 54)
   a victory   b progress   c solution

Critical thinking identifying opinions

5 Read the article again and look at these opinions (1–5). Whose are they? Write A for the author, S for Valorie Salimpoor, or U for unknown source.

1 Music stimulates us emotionally and intellectually. ____
2 We listen to sad songs because it helps us feel like someone is sharing our sadness. ____
3 Music can make a verbal message more powerful. ____
4 Music stimulates us intellectually because we use our brains to predict the direction of a piece of music. ____
5 Music satisfies key human needs. ____

6 Work in pairs. Which of the opinions in Exercise 5 do you think:

a are supported by clear evidence in the article?
b need more evidence to be convincing?
c are convincing because they reflect your own experience?
d summarize the main argument of the article?

Word focus *spend*

7 We use *spend* with expressions of money or time, as in "We spend a fifth of our waking lives listening to music." Complete these sentences with the correct word (*money* or *time*).

1 It was great to spend _____ together and catch up on all your news.
2 He spends _____ like there's no tomorrow.
3 How do you like to spend your free _____ ?
4 We all need to spend _____ alone sometimes.

8 Complete these sentences in your own words. Then share your sentences with a partner.

1 I spent hours trying to …
2 I've spent a fortune on …
3 Once, I spent a night in …
4 I don't spend a lot on …

Speaking myLife

9 Imagine you are making a playlist for the following situations. Think of one song or piece of music for each situation. Then compare your playlist with two other students. Say why you think each piece of music fits the situation.

- exercising at the gym
- driving
- for a friend who is feeling sad
- eating at a restaurant
- doing housework

WHY DO WE NEED MUSIC?

▶ 36

1 Humans, on average, spend a fifth of their waking lives listening to music. Music is deeply rooted in all cultures across the world and yet, unlike food or shelter, it is not something we actually
5 need in order to survive. Why is it so important to us? Valorie Salimpoor, a neuroscientist at Montreal's McGill University, has researched the effects of music on the brain. She believes that the answer lies in music's ability to stimulate us both
10 emotionally and intellectually.

2 On an emotional level, music has the power to excite or soothe us, and it can do this more effectively than any other way humans have come up with so far. Think how a rousing national anthem at the Olympic Games
15 can give you goosebumps; or how a calming lullaby can stop tears or help babies to sleep. The musical way of speaking to babies, known as "motherese," is a feature of every culture around the world.

3 Music produces emotions that we immediately feel
20 and understand, but that we find difficult to explain. Why, for example, do we like listening to sad songs when we have experienced loss or are feeling down? You would imagine they would make us feel even more unhappy. But actually, sad music seems to help
25 us regulate negative feelings and even lift us out of them. Some people say the reason for this is a sense that someone else is sharing our loss; others say we are comforted by knowing that someone is suffering more than we are. But no one really knows the
30 answer.

4 Music's emotional power also comes from the fact that it can make a verbal message stronger. Rap and hip-hop began in America as songs with a social message— they described life for people who lacked the same
35 opportunities as the rich. These days, some commercial hip-hop artists in America rap about the things that fame and money have brought them, but in other parts of the world, rap music is a powerful tool for expressing the injustice that people in poor communities feel.

5 On an intellectual level, Salimpoor says that music
40 challenges our brains to understand and recognize certain systems and patterns. Just as with languages, music has patterns that are culturally specific. Western pop music, for instance, follows very different patterns to traditional Chinese music. But when we figure out how a new system
45 works—in other words, when we "understand" the music and are able to predict the direction it will take—we find this intellectually rewarding. We experience exactly the same satisfaction when we begin to understand a new language and its patterns. Interestingly, says
50 Salimpoor, we enjoy new music most when it moves in an unpredictable, but still understandable, direction. In that situation, she says, "We've made a kind of intellectual conquest."

6 Humans have various needs—physical, emotional, and
55 psychological—and while music may not fulfill the first, it clearly plays an important role in satisfying the others. You probably didn't think of this when you first heard your favorite song, but perhaps it explains why you have
60 listened to it so often since.

4d Personal tastes

Real life describing likes and dislikes

1 Do you like musicals? Why or why not? Which ones have you seen? Did you see them live or in movies? Tell a partner.

2 ▶ **37** Listen to a conversation in which Tom and his friend Jake talk about the musical *The Lion King*. Complete the chart below with information about Tom's likes and dislikes.

	Like (✓)	Dislike (✓)
musicals in general		
visual effects of *The Lion King*		
Disney comic characters		
this production of *The Lion King*		
the music of *The Lion King*		
Elton John		
cost of tickets for most musicals		

3 ▶ **37** Look at the expressions for describing likes and dislikes. Listen again and circle the expressions Tom and Jake use to express each like and dislike.

> ### ▶ DESCRIBING LIKES AND DISLIKES
>
> **Do you like ...?**
>
> | **Positive** | **Negative** |
> |---|---|
> | Yes, a lot. / Yes, very much. | Not really. / Not particularly. / |
> | Yes, ... is great/amazing. | Not especially. |
> | I love ... | No, it's not my kind of thing. |
> | I really like ... | I'm not (really) a fan of ... |
> | I'm a big fan of ... | I'm not so into ... |
> | I'm really into ... | ... doesn't really do anything |
> | I have a lot of respect for ... | for me. |
> | I could watch / listen to ... | I can't stand ... |
> | all day. | ... get(s) on my nerves. |
> | | I get kind of tired of ... |

4 Pronunciation disappearing sounds

a ▶ **38** Listen to these words from the conversation. Cross out the disappearing sound—the part or letter of the word that is not pronounced.

generally   everyone   different

b ▶ **39** Work in pairs. Cross out the disappearing sound in each of these words and practice saying them. Then listen and check if you were right.

beautifully   chocolate   basically
interesting   vegetable   broccoli

5 Read the sentences. Cross out the option that does NOT fit in each sentence.

1 I'm not *kind of / especially / so* into romantic comedies.
2 I'm *kind of / really into / very* tired of reality TV shows.
3 I'm not *really / very / especially* a fan of musicals.
4 Jazz music doesn't *so / really / particularly* do anything for me.

6 What musicals, plays, movies, concerts, TV shows, or exhibitions have you enjoyed recently? Choose one. Then work in groups. Describe your choice to the group, and discuss your likes and dislikes.

4e You have to see this

Writing an online review

1 Work in pairs. Read the online review of an exhibition by a visitor to New York. Would you follow their recommendation? Why or why not?

2 Work in pairs and answer the questions.

1 How are the following themes organized in the review? Number them in the order they appear (1–5).
____ the author's recommendation
____ an introduction
____ the content of the exhibition
____ the occasion of the visit
____ the details of where and when the exhibition is on

2 What information about the exhibition does the author include?

3 Is the tone of the review personal or impersonal?

3 Writing skill personalizing your writing

Work in pairs. Look at the features of personal and impersonal writing. Find examples of personal language in the online review.

Personal tone
- use active verbs
- use contractions
- use phrasal verbs
- add personal details
- use conversational linking phrases (e.g., *besides*)
- share your feelings

Impersonal tone
- use passive verbs
- avoid contractions
- use formal verbs
- avoid personal information
- use formal linking phrases (e.g., *furthermore*)
- be objective in your judgments

TravelReviews
http://www.travelreviews.com

I find that it's always worth checking out the parks when you visit a foreign city. Besides providing a welcome break, they can hold some very interesting surprises. Last week, absolutely exhausted from visiting two museums and too tired to even think about shopping anymore, my boyfriend and I took a walk in Central Park. I'm so glad we did, because otherwise we'd have missed *The Gates*, an installation by Christo and Jeanne-Claude.

The artists put up 7,503 "gates" made from saffron-colored fabric panels along the walkways of the park. The giant art project of rectangular flags reflects the grid pattern of the surrounding city blocks. The gates can be seen from far away through the leafless branches of the trees, dressing the park in orange. What I liked best about them was the way they brightened up the bleak winter landscape. It was so funny to see children running through the lines of gates with their arms stretched out.

The secret of this exhibition's success is that it makes you appreciate what is already a wonderful park even more. It will be on until February 27th. If you are in New York, I'd definitely recommend taking the time to go and see it for yourself. And by the way, it's free!

4 Write a personalized online review of a visual or performance art event you have seen and enjoyed. Write 150–180 words.

5 Exchange reviews with a partner. Compare what you have written. Use these questions to check your partner's review.

- Does the review include all the themes listed in Exercise 2?
- Does it feel like a friendly and personal recommendation?
- What features has the writer used to give this impression?
- After reading the review, would you want to go and see this event?

4f Making plants into art

Pearl Fryar in his topiary garden

Before you watch

1 Work in pairs. Look at the photo and the caption. Then read the definition of topiary below. Explain to your partner in your own words what Pearl Fryar does.

> **Topiary** is the practice of clipping shrubs or trees into ornamental or decorative shapes. It is said to have originated in ancient Rome about two thousand years ago. As an art form, it is a type of living sculpture.

2 Key vocabulary

a Work in pairs. Read the sentences (1–7). The words and phrases in **bold** are used in the video. Guess the meaning of the words and phrases.

1 We get our flowers from a local **nursery**.
2 The gardener **trimmed** the hedges to remove the dead wood.
3 She had to **invest** a lot of time in remodeling the house.
4 By working together, they **accomplished** their goal.
5 After living in New York City for a while, he became **accustomed to** using the subway.
6 They **landscaped** their property with flowering plants and shrubs.
7 I enjoyed the exhibition of **abstract** art, but it was a bit difficult to understand what some artists were trying to communicate.

b Write the words and phrases in **bold** in Exercise 2a next to their definitions (a–g).

a achieved or completed successfully
  _____

b (of art) expressing ideas and emotions, rather than showing people or things _____

c made an area of land more attractive by planting trees, flowers, and other plants
  _____

d made something neat by clipping, smoothing, or pruning _____

e put money, time, or effort into something to make a profit or get an advantage _____

f used to or familiar with something
  _____

g a place where plants are grown and sold
  _____

While you watch

3 ▭◀ **4.1** Watch the video about Pearl Fryar with the sound OFF. Answer these questions on your own. Then compare answers with a partner.

1 What adjectives would you use to describe the plants you see in Pearl's garden? Make a list.
2 What message is spelled out using plants in the garden? Complete this phrase: "Love, _____, and _____"

4 ▭◀ **4.1** Watch the video with the sound ON. Work in pairs and answer these questions.

1 Where is Pearl Fryar's topiary garden located?
2 Where do many of the plants in his garden come from?
3 According to Jean Grosser, what is astounding about the way Pearl works?
4 How long does it take Pearl to complete a piece?
5 How has Pearl's lack of formal training helped him?
6 How has Pearl's garden affected tourism in the region?
7 According to Pearl, what is the theme of his garden? Complete this sentence: "My garden is about _____."
8 How many visitors come to Pearl's garden every year?

After you watch

5 Vocabulary in context

a ▭◀ **4.2** Watch the clips from the video. Choose the correct meaning of the words.

b Complete these sentences in your own words. Then share your sentences with a partner.

1 I think … is astounding.
2 When I …, I instantly …
3 It's important to maintain …

6 Work in small groups. Your town or city would like to commission an artwork that would a) improve the appearance of an area in the town or city; b) be fun; and c) attract visitors.

• Discuss what kind of artwork you would like to have.
• Decide who you would like to make the artwork.

7 As a group, present your ideas to the class. Then vote on the best idea.

UNIT 4 REVIEW AND MEMORY BOOSTER

Grammar

1 Complete the text about the Edinburgh Festival Fringe using the words and phrases in the box.

a few	lots	both	every	lack
no	many	much	number	whole

The Edinburgh Festival Fringe is the world's largest arts festival. It takes place ¹_____ year in August. For the ²_____ month, the city is taken over by actors, street performers, comedians, artists, musicians, etc. There is certainly no ³_____ of variety. The festival attracts a huge ⁴_____ of visitors from all over the world, and two million tickets are sold for over 2,000 different shows. The tickets don't cost ⁵_____—£10 or £15 typically—but if you go to ⁶_____ of shows, then the costs can add up.

⁷_____ artists just come to perform for the fun of it, but ⁸_____ are young performers hoping that this will be their chance to be noticed by critics and producers. The festival has launched the careers of several famous actors and comedians, but there is ⁹_____ guarantee of success. ¹⁰_____ the famous and the unknown can succeed or fail.

2 Read the text above again. Are these statements true (T) or false (F)?

1 It's cheap to visit the festival even if you see a lot of performances. T F

2 The Edinburgh Festival Fringe has a mixture of amateur and professional artists. T F

I CAN	
use determiners	
use expressions of quantity	

Vocabulary

3 Match each person or group (1–3) with the correct place.

1 an artist ○ ○ a comedy club
2 an orchestra ○ ○ a gallery
3 a comedian ○ ○ a concert hall

4 **» MB** Work in pairs. Describe the type of art or artist that you see in each photo below. Add any details that you can remember (what, where, who, etc.).

5 **» MB** Write down as many words or two-word phrases as you can from the root word *art*. Then compare your list with a partner. Whose list is longer?

I CAN	
talk about art and artists	

Real life

6 Complete these exchanges. Use one word in each blank.

A: Do you like watching live comedy?
B: No, ¹_____ really.

C: I'm not so ²_____ this music. Can I change the station?
D: Sure. It's not really my ³_____ of thing, either.

E: I'm a big ⁴_____ of Kurosawa's movies.
F: Me, too. I have a lot of ⁵_____ for Kurosawa. I think he's an amazing director.

G: Don't you ⁶_____ tired of watching musicals?
H: No, I could watch them ⁷_____ day.

7 **» MB** Work in pairs. Use the first four words of each exchange in Exercise 6 to begin a conversation about TV shows that you like and dislike.

I CAN	
describe likes and dislikes	

Unit 5 Development

The Belo Monte hydroelectric dam complex, Pará, Brazil

1 Work in pairs. Look at the photo and the caption. How do you think this dam will benefit people? How will it affect the landscape and the lives of people living in the area?

2 ▶ 40 Listen to someone talking about the Belo Monte dam. Compare what he says with your answers in Exercise 1.

3 Look at these verbs (1–5). Match the verbs with their meanings on the right.

1 benefit ○	○	add to and improve
2 enhance ○	○	do well
3 expand ○	○	be good for
4 boost ○	○	get bigger
5 thrive ○	○	help to increase

4 Work in pairs. Think about your own personal development and the development of the place you live in. Describe something that:

• has boosted your confidence at work or in your studies or hobbies.
• has benefited the local economy.
• has enhanced the quality of life in your country.

5a From reality to fantasy

Vocabulary urban features

1 Work in pairs. Match words in box A with words in box B to make as many urban features as you can. Then check your answers on page 153.

A apartment   bus   business   parking   city
green   high-rise   sports   luxury   office
pedestrian   railway   residential   shopping

B area   apartments   building   center   hall
mall   space   station   lot   zone

high-rise
= skyscraper
– tower
– building

2 Which urban features in Exercise 1 does your town or city have? In your opinion, which does it have too many of? And not enough of? Discuss with a partner.

Reading

3 Work in pairs. Look at the photo of Dubai. Discuss these questions.

1 Where was the photo taken from?
2 What can you see in the photo?
3 What do you know about Dubai?

FROM REALITY TO FANTASY

▶ 41

There once was a sheikh with big dreams. His land was a sleepy village occupied by pearl divers, fishermen, and traders. A small river ran through the village to the sea, and it was here that Sheikh Rashid bin Saeed al
5 Maktoum imagined building a gateway to the world. But he could not afford to make his dream a reality. So in 1959, he asked a neighbor to lend him a few million dollars. He made the river wider and built roads, schools, and homes. He built it, and the people came.
10 Then it was his son's turn to carry on developing this vision. Sheikh Mohammed bin Rashid al Maktoum transformed Dubai into an air-conditioned fantasy world of nearly three million people. No project

seemed to be too ambitious for him. He built the
15 world's tallest high-rise building (the 828-meter Burj Khalifa), the world's biggest shopping mall, and the world's largest highway intersection. He helped little Dubai become the shopping capital of the Middle East.
20 Dubai attracts more than three million tourists a year, some of whom have second homes there. Its most famous landmark—the Palm Jumeirah, an artificial island built in the shape of a palm tree—provides vacation villas for the rich and famous. The financial
25 crisis of 2008 made people feel nervous about investing because they risked losing money. So, for a few years, Dubai failed to sell many of its new luxury apartments. But more recently, property in Dubai has been increasing in value again, and it has been easier to get
30 people to invest.

The rest of the world watches with a mixture of wonder and suspicion. Is this a model that people want to copy? Or do they feel that Dubai has chosen to reject its heritage and instead become the Las Vegas of the
35 Middle East?

Dubai, United Arab Emirates

4 Work in pairs. Read the article on page 58 and answer these questions.

1 What was Dubai like about sixty years ago, and how has it changed?
2 What world records does Dubai hold?
3 How did the 2008 financial crisis affect Dubai?
4 Would you like to visit Dubai? Why or why not?

Grammar verb + infinitive or *-ing*

> ▶ **VERB + INFINITIVE or *-ING***

verb + infinitive
*He could not **afford to make** his dream a reality.*

verb + object + infinitive
*He **asked a neighbor to lend** him a few million dollars.*

verb + object + base form of the verb
*The financial crisis of 2008 **made people feel** nervous about investing.*

verb + *-ing*
*Sheikh Rashid **imagined building** a gateway to the world.*

For more information and practice, see page 164.

5 Look at the grammar box. Read the article again and underline more examples of the patterns from the grammar box. Find:

1 four more verbs + infinitive.
2 one more verb + object + infinitive.
3 one more verb + object + base form of the verb.
4 two more verbs + *-ing*.

6 Complete these facts about Dubai. Use the correct form of the verbs in parentheses.

1 The population of Dubai grew from half a million in 1990 to 1.5 million in 2008, and has kept on _growing_ (grow) to this day.
2 Sheikh al Maktoum decided _to make_ (make) Dubai the region's most important financial center.
3 Attracting foreign banks and companies involved _reducing_ (reduce) taxes for companies and individuals.
4 The expansion of Dubai International Airport has allowed _it to become_ (it / become) the third busiest international airport in the world.
5 By planting 10,000 trees a year, the city planners have managed _to create_ (create) many green spaces.
6 The Dubai authorities let _its police drive_ (its police / drive) cars like Lamborghinis and Ferraris so that they can stop other supercars that are speeding.

7 Circle the correct options to complete these sentences.

1 I don't mind *to work / working* late during the week, but I hate having to work on weekends.
2 She offered *to help / helping* me, but I told her that I could manage.
3 I failed *to get / getting* the job I wanted, but I'm going to keep *to look / looking*.

8 Complete these sentences in your own words, using appropriate verb patterns. Then compare your sentences with a partner.

1 I like … because it helps me …
2 I've decided … because I don't want to risk …
3 Were you allowed … when you were young? My parents didn't let me …

9 Complete the description of a redevelopment of a city center using the verbs in the box.

afford	avoided	decided
involved	needed	seemed

There used to be a beautiful residential area in the city center, but in the 1960s, the local authority ¹ _____ to redevelop it as a shopping district. This ² _____ knocking down all the houses and building huge parking lots to create space for shoppers from out of town. The residents ³ _____ to accept that the area ⁴ _____ to be modernized, so no one opposed the idea. The result was that people shopped there during the day, but at night, everyone ⁵ _____ going to that area because of drug dealing and crime. Now, fifty years later, the local authority is building houses there again, but rents are so high that ordinary people can't ⁶ _____ to live there.

Speaking *my* **Life**

10 Write a description (similar to the one in Exercise 9) of an area in your town or city that has changed in your lifetime. Use at least four of these verbs.

afford	allow	avoid	consider	decide
fail	involve	make	manage	propose
seem	suggest	want		

11 Work in pairs. Tell your partner how this area has changed, and if you think the change has been positive or negative.

*A few years ago, the city council **decided to redevelop** the area around the canal. That **involved building** new paths and bridges and …*

5b The Kerala model

Listening

1 Work in pairs. Look at the two photos above taken in the Indian state of Kerala. Which of these adjectives could you use to describe the places shown in each photo? What other adjectives could you use?

exotic	tranquil	hectic
lush	remarkable	wealthy

2 ▶ 42 Listen to an interview with a journalist who has recently been to Kerala. Check (✓) the different aspects of Kerala's development that the journalist mentions.

- ☐ income
- ☐ education
- ☐ housing
- ☐ politics
- ☐ transportation
- ☐ mix of people

3 ▶ 42 Listen to the interview again. Are these sentences true (T) or false (F)?

1	The journalist went to Kerala to write an article.	T	F
2	The state of Kerala has a lot of people in a small area.	T	F
3	Many people in Kerala have a high level of education.	T	F
4	Kerala has a high rate of infant mortality.	T	F
5	One reason for Kerala's success is the attitude of Keralites to people who are different.	T	F

4 Work in pairs. What surprised you most about Keralan society? Give reasons for your answer.

Wordbuilding adverb + adjective

> **WORDBUILDING adverb + adjective**
>
> Adverbs and adjectives can be combined to describe people and things.
> *highly literate, well-organized*
>
> For more practice, see Workbook page 43.

5 Work in pairs. Find the adverb + adjective phrases in **bold** in track 42 of the audioscript on page 184. Then match the phrases with these meanings.

1 with a good level of education
   well-educated
2 willing to accept differences in other people
3 very involved in politics
4 able to read and write very well
5 with a satisfactory standard of living
6 very knowledgeable about current affairs

6 Complete the phrases (1–4) with these adverbs.

badly	extremely	reasonably	well

1 a(n) _____ damaged car
2 a(n) _____ priced meal
3 a(n) _____-written book
4 a(n) _____ talented singer

7 Pronunciation rhyming words

a ▶ 43 Work in pairs. Match the words from the interview (1–8) with the words that rhyme in the right column. Then listen and check. Practice saying the rhyming pairs.

1 state	○	○ faced
2 low	○	○ plane
3 head	○	○ opt
4 course	○	○ though
5 main	○	○ weight
6 stopped	○	○ force
7 none	○	○ fun
8 waste	○	○ said

b Work in pairs. Look at the words in the box. Can you think of a word that rhymes with each one but has a different spelling pattern?

| break | foot | height | signed | walk | word |

Grammar verbs with both -ing and the infinitive

▶ **VERBS WITH BOTH -ING and THE INFINITIVE**

Verbs with two meanings
go on, mean, regret, remember, stop, try
I **remember sending** you a copy last week.
Remember to send me a copy when it's published.

Verbs with no change in meaning
continue, hate, like, love, prefer, start
I was so interested that I **started to write** an article about it.
I was so interested that I **started writing** an article about it.

For more information and practice, see page 164.

8 Look at the grammar box. Work in pairs. Discuss the different meanings of the verbs in **bold** in the pairs of sentences below.

1 a I **remember going** to Kerala in the 1990s.
 b Please **remember to send** me a copy.
2 a Have you **tried taking** aspirin?
 b I'm **trying to learn** to write Chinese script.
3 a After spending a few days in Paris, we **went on to visit** my aunt in Bordeaux.
 b The students **went on protesting** for four days.
4 a It was **meant to be** a vacation.
 b Usually, a low income would **mean** people **having** a poor quality of life.
5 a I don't **regret changing** my plans.
 b No land is wasted, which I **regret to say** isn't always the case in some developing countries.
6 a I **stopped to visit** an Indian journalist.
 b Keralites never **stop debating**.

9 Complete the text with the correct form of the verbs in parentheses. Sometimes more than one answer is possible.

I remember ¹ _reading_ (read) an article about Kerala fifteen years ago, and I've been meaning ² _to visit_ (visit) ever since. The government has tried ³ _to improve_ (improve) people's quality of life through various measures, such as land reform. In the 1960s, it stopped ⁴ _allowing_ (allow) landlords to charge rent to farmers. This meant ⁵ _giving_ (give) the land back to the people who worked on it. At the same time, the government started ⁶ _to invest (both)_ (invest) in education. So poor people in Kerala have benefited financially and are now better educated. But no system is perfect, I regret ⁷ _to say_ (say). The problem in Kerala is that the economy is still based on agriculture. Most students who graduate with a degree won't want to work in the fields. So although they may prefer ⁸ _to live (both)_ (live) in Kerala, a lot of young people are trying ⁹ _to move_ (move) to more developed parts of India to find decent jobs.

10 Complete these sentences in your own words. Then share your sentences with a partner.

1 **Education:** I regret (not) … when I was at school.
2 **Plans:** I've been meaning … for some time.
3 **Free time:** Recently, I've started …
4 **Eating:** I prefer …

Speaking myLife

11 Look at the questionnaire below. Take turns asking and answering the questions with a partner. Then compare your answers with another pair.

Are people in your community generally happy?

1 How satisfied do people seem with the amount of money they have?
*Not very satisfied. People are always **trying to earn** more money so they can buy more and more material things.*

2 Do people have a good work/life balance?
3 How happy are people with the education they get?
4 What kind of food do people eat? Is it healthy?
5 Are people active in politics and cultural activities?
6 Are people tolerant of the different groups in society?

5c The teenage mind

Reading

1 Look at these stages of human development. Work in pairs and answer the questions.

infancy → childhood → adolescence → adulthood

1 What ages do these stages represent?
2 What ages would you say these people are: a teenager, a baby, a middle-aged man, a young woman, a toddler?

2 Work in pairs. Think of three typical characteristics of teenage behavior. Then read the first paragraph of the article and compare your ideas with the characteristics mentioned there.

3 Read the rest of the article. Work in pairs and answer these questions.

1 What types of behavior do all teenagers share?
2 Does the writer think these are positive or negative qualities? Why?

4 Read the article again. Circle the correct options to complete these sentences.

1 After age fifteen, our search for exciting or unusual experiences *becomes more difficult / decreases.*
2 Doing things at the moment we think of them is a characteristic of *young children / teenagers.*
3 According to the article, teenagers *don't understand / are fully aware of* the risks they take.
4 The author thinks teenagers *overreact / react appropriately* when they have problems with friends their own age.
5 Wherever you go in the world, teenagers show the same *characteristics / respect for adults.*

5 Find the words and expressions in **bold** below in the article. What do they mean? Circle the correct definition (a or b).

1 **on the spur of the moment** (line 15)
   a with no planning   b all the time
2 **thrills** (line 19)
   a exciting experiences   b physical actions
3 **ultimately** (line 25)
   a especially   b in the end
4 **novelty** (line 37)
   a something friendly   b something new
5 **vital** (line 43)
   a essential   b useful

Critical thinking ways of arguing

6 Look at these ways to argue a point in a less absolute or less direct way. Then underline the words and phrases in sentences 1–3 that have the same effect.

She is, underline{perhaps}, the greatest writer of our generation. This, underline{for me at any rate}, is no longer true.

1 But rather than being critical of specific behavior like this, it is probably more useful to think about what lies behind it.
2 Such behavior might seem dangerous, but sensation seeking can also be a positive thing, …
3 But actually, we should celebrate them, because—in scientific terms, at least—they make teenagers quite possibly the most adaptable human beings around.

7 Work in pairs. Do you think being less direct helps to persuade the reader?

Word focus *fall*

8 Work in pairs. Look at the phrases in **bold** with the word *fall*. Discuss what each phrase means.

1 Teenagers usually react badly when they **fall out with** a friend.
2 I was sick for four days, and I've **fallen behind** with my work.
3 I've worn these shoes every day for a year, and now they're **falling apart**.
4 Our plan to go camping this weekend **fell through** because I couldn't find my old tent!

9 Work in pairs. Use the phrases with *fall* in Exercise 8 to describe four similar situations from your own experience.

Speaking my Life

10 Look at these stages of life. Work in groups and answer the questions.

| childhood | adolescence | young adulthood |
| middle age | old age | |

1 What are the positive and negative aspects of each stage of life?
2 Do you think people's attitudes change at different stages of life (e.g., toward friendships, money, health)?
3 Which do you think is the best stage of life?

The teenage mind

▶ 44

1 We tend to think of adolescence as a difficult stage in human development. Mention the word "teenager" and certain stereotypical behavior comes to mind: not wanting to communicate with adults, 5 doing silly or dangerous things like skateboarding down a stair rail, or constantly chatting to friends on social media. But rather than being critical of specific behavior like this, it is probably more useful to think about what lies behind it.

2 10 We all like new and exciting things, and never more so than when we are adolescents. At around age fifteen, we peak in what scientists call "sensation seeking"—the hunt for unusual or unexpected experiences. Sensation seeking doesn't mean being 15 impulsive—acting on the spur of the moment to satisfy your wishes. That is more a characteristic of toddlers and young children, and from the age of about ten, it begins to decrease. Teens, like adults, actually plan their thrills (a bungee jump, driving a 20 fast car) quite deliberately.

3 Such behavior might seem dangerous, but sensation seeking can also be a positive thing, because trying out new things can expand your world. The desire to meet new people, for example, can lead to a wider circle of 25 friends and, ultimately, a happier life. The difference with adult behavior is not that teens ignore risks; in fact, they recognize them just as adults do. Teens take more risks because they value the reward of getting something they want more highly. Researchers 30 believe this willingness to take risks is linked to the need to adapt to new surroundings when you are young. As you start to grow up, you have to move out of your home and into a new, less secure environment. And that is risky.

4 35 Another characteristic of adolescents is that they prefer the company of people their own age. This is partly because they feel that their peers offer more novelty than their own family. But there is another, more powerful reason: Teenagers need to invest in the future. 40 We enter a world made by our parents. But we will live most of our lives in a world managed and remade by our peers, so understanding and building relationships with them is vital. The importance of peer influence can be seen clearly in how strongly teenagers react 45 when they fall out with a friend or are excluded from a social peer group. They react as if their future depended upon these friendships! And, in many ways, it does.

5 Excitement, novelty, risk, the company of peers. We think of these elements as characteristics of 50 the modern Western adolescent—but they define adolescence in almost all human cultures, modern and ancient. As adults, we often complain about these characteristics. But actually, we should celebrate them, because—in scientific terms, at least—they make 55 teenagers quite possibly the most adaptable human beings around.

5d A controversial issue

Real life debating issues

1 ▶ **45** Work in pairs. Listen to the opening words at a public meeting. Why is the skate park the subject of the meeting?

2 Work in pairs. Imagine this skate park was near *your* home. What would be the benefits? What could be the disadvantages? Make a list.

3 ▶ **46** Listen to people at the meeting debating what should happen to the skate park. Write the views of each of the local people who speak.

Person	His/Her View
First woman	
First man	
Second man	
Second woman	

4 ▶ **46** Work in pairs. Look at the expressions for debating issues. Discuss what the missing words could be. Then listen to the debate again and complete the expressions with the words you hear.

> ▶ **DEBATING ISSUES**
>
> **Making points**
> First, … and secondly, …
> More importantly, …
> The ¹ _thin_ /point/fact is that …
> I think … / I don't think …
> I think we're forgetting that …
> ² _For_ me, … is just one factor.
>
> **Responding to a point**
> Well, that depends.
> I understand/appreciate that …, but …
> Actually, I'm not too ³ _bothen_ by/about …
> I'm more ⁴ _concern_ that/about …
> Sorry, but I (don't) think that's …
>
> That's a very ⁵ _good_ point.
> Yes, you're right.
> Absolutely.
> I agree ⁶ _completely_ .
>
> I don't think most of you have really ⁷ _thought_ about / considered …
> … doesn't make any ⁸ _sense_ to me.

A skate park in a residential area

5 Pronunciation sentence stress

a Work in pairs. Look at these sentences. Underline the word you think is most stressed in each sentence.

1 Quite honestly, that's a good thing.
2 For me, that's not the point.
3 Sorry, but I think that's an exaggeration.
4 It just doesn't make any sense to me.

b ▶ **47** Listen to the sentences in Exercise 5a and check your answers. Then practice saying the sentences with the correct stress.

6 Look at the development proposal. Imagine you are a resident of this town. Make notes on how you feel about this proposed development. What are its advantages and disadvantages?

> **Development proposal**
> Conversion of a public library and public swimming pool into a new shopping mall and private gym. The main argument for closure of the library and swimming pool is that they do not get used very often.

7 Work in groups. One group should support the development proposal, and the other group should oppose it. Have a debate, using expressions for debating issues where appropriate.

5e Big cities, big problems

Writing an opinion essay

1 Work in pairs. Answer the questions.

1 Why do you think people want to live in big cities? Give reasons.
2 What problems do big cities create?

2 Look at the title of the opinion essay below and read the response. What is the opinion of the writer?

> **Our cities have become too big. The problems they create outweigh the benefits. Discuss.**
>
> In 1800, only two percent of the world's population lived in cities. But since then, more and more people have moved to cities looking for work and a better life. As a result, more than half the world's population now live in cities, and that number is expected to grow. Cities are evidence of the amazing organizational abilities of human beings. However, in some cases, they also bring many social, economic, and environmental problems. The question is: Do the problems they create outweigh their benefits?
>
> Cities exist because they are more convenient places to live. Jobs, schools, and hospitals are all close to people's homes. There is a wide range of people to socialize with, and there are good opportunities for entertainment and leisure.
>
> On the other hand, there also seems to be more crime, more poverty, and more pollution, and often these problems are all found in a particular area of a city. But this is not so surprising, if you think about it. The same problems exist in the countryside and in smaller towns, but they are not so concentrated. Because of this, they are noticed less.
>
> As long as the population of cities does not grow more quickly than the services available for it, cities can solve a lot of our problems. In addition, they can provide jobs and a more interesting life. The problem with cities is not how big they are, but how well-managed they are.

3 Work in pairs. Does the opinion essay in Exercise 2 follow this structure?

> Introduction → Arguments for → Arguments against → Conclusion

4 The introduction in an opinion essay can take different forms. Which of these (a, b, or c) does the writer in Exercise 2 use?

a giving a dramatic example of the problem
b telling a story about the problem from the writer's own experience
c giving some statistics that illustrate the seriousness of the problem

5 Writing skill linking words

a Look at the linking phrases in the chart below. Then write the highlighted phrases from the opinion essay in the correct places in this chart.

Adding an argument	Introducing a contrasting fact	Explaining the consequences
Furthermore, As well as	Then again,	Consequently,

b Complete these sentences with an appropriate linking phrase from Exercise 5a. There is sometimes more than one possible answer.

1 Certain cities in the world have become especially large. _____ , we have seen the emergence of what are called megacities: cities with over ten million inhabitants.
2 A lot of people have found a better standard of living in big cities. _____ , big cities also contain some of the poorest people.
3 _____ being convenient for the residents, cities also make life easier for businesses.

6 Read the statement below. Write an opinion essay. Use the correct structure and linking phrases.

> In our busy urban lifestyles, we have lost our sense of community. We need to return to a way of life that involves more caring and interaction between people. Discuss.

7 Exchange essays with a partner. Use these questions to check your partner's essay.

- Is it organized in clear sections/paragraphs?
- Does it follow the structure suggested in Exercise 3?
- Does it use one of the introduction techniques suggested in Exercise 4?
- Do you find the arguments convincing?

The Øresund Bridge, between Denmark and Sweden

Before you watch

1 Work in pairs. Look at the photo of the Øresund Bridge. Answer the questions.

1 What's the bridge like?
2 What other ways can people use to get across a stretch of water that separates two pieces of land?

2 Key vocabulary

a Work in pairs. Read the sentences (1–5). The words in **bold** are used in the video. Guess the meaning of the words.

1 Tokyo is a lively **metropolis** where millions work and live.
2 The **Strait** of Dover between France and England is the busiest shipping channel in the world.
3 The Burj Khalifa, currently the tallest building in the world, **soars** over Dubai.
4 The new apartment building completely **obstructs** our view of the park.
5 The nuclear power plant will be built by an international **consortium**.

b Write the words in **bold** in Exercise 2a next to their definitions (a–e).

a a group of companies that join together to work on a project _____
b rises or flies very high _____
c a narrow strip of water between two pieces of land _____
d a large, busy city _____
e gets in the way of; blocks _____

While you watch

3 ▶️ 5.1 Look at the chart below. Then watch Part 1 of the video and complete the facts.

1	The width of the Øresund Strait: _____
2	What Copenhagen needs: _____
3	What Malmö needs: _____
4	What type of transportation the bridge is for: _____
5	Height above the sea: _____
6	Height of each support tower: _____

4 ▶️ 5.2 Watch Part 2 of the video. Work in pairs and answer the questions.

1 What did the computer simulation show?
2 Why did the engineers not build a lower bridge?
3 What does the project director say about the tunnel solution?
4 What solution did the engineers eventually come up with?
5 Why did they need to build an island for their solution?

5 Complete the summary. Use one word in each blank. The first letter of each missing word is provided.

> The Øresund Bridge was built to connect Denmark and Sweden over the Øresund [1] S_____ in the Baltic Sea. The idea was to connect Malmö and Copenhagen to create one large [2] m_____ with economic benefits for all. The two countries signed an agreement in 1991, and a [3] c_____ of companies was formed to do the work. But the project faced a lot of technical difficulties because of [4] a_____ and sea traffic. A tunnel would have been the ideal solution, but it was too [5] e_____ . So in the end, the engineers decided to build part [6] t_____ and part [7] b_____ . The result is one of the [8] l_____ bridges in Europe.

After you watch

6 Vocabulary in context

a ▶️ 5.3 Watch the clips from the video. Choose the correct meaning of the words and phrases.

b Complete these sentences in your own words. Then share your sentences with a partner.

1 The weather in … is always lousy.
2 The most frustrating thing about my job/studies is …
3 The project suffered a big setback when …

7 Work in groups. Think of a town you know well. Make a new transportation plan for the town that would do the following things. Then present your plan to another group.

- make access to the town easier
- reduce the number of cars on the streets
- be environmentally friendly
- be inexpensive
- make the town more attractive for visitors

UNIT 5 REVIEW AND MEMORY BOOSTER

Grammar

1 Complete the conversation between an interviewer (I) and an official (O). Use the correct form of the verbs in parentheses: *-ing*, the infinitive, or the base form of the verb. Sometimes more than one answer is possible.

I: The Nam Theun 2 hydroelectric power plant in Laos became operational in 2010. Did Laos start ¹ _____ (see) benefits immediately?

O: Yes, very quickly. The plant has helped Laos ² _____ (be) energy independent. We also sell electricity to Thailand. We agreed with the World Bank ³ _____ (invest) this money in health and social programs for our people.

I: And what about the environmental impact? I know the project involved ⁴ _____ (move) people from their homes, and also the destruction of natural forests.

O: You can't avoid ⁵ _____ (affect) some people's lives with something this size. But we have tried ⁶ _____ (minimize) the impact. It's true that the dam made some fishermen ⁷ _____ (give up) their old way of life, but actually, 85% of resettled people say their lives are now better. As for the forest, the government has suggested ⁸ _____ (use) profits from the plant to fund conservation in other parts of Laos.

2 What have been the two main benefits and problems of the Nam Theun 2 project?

3 **≫ MB** Work in pairs. Which of these pairs of phrases mean the same thing? If they mean something different, explain the difference.

1 stop to talk / stop talking
2 begin to rain / begin raining
3 don't like to wait / don't like waiting
4 remember to mail / remember mailing

I CAN
use verbs which are followed by the gerund or the infinitive ☐

Vocabulary

4 Circle the correct options to complete this paragraph.

Life in the city was so ¹*exotic / hectic* that we decided to move. In any case, we needed a bigger house for our two ²*adolescents / toddlers*, who were just beginning to walk. We found a nice house in a small village, but the move fell ³*through / down* at the last moment because the owner decided to stay. Luckily, we found another ⁴*extremely / reasonably* priced house in the same area.

5 **≫ MB** Complete these urban features using a word that rhymes with the word in parentheses.

1 sports _____ (enter)
2 pedestrian _____ (own)
3 shopping _____ (crawl)
4 green _____ (chase)

6 **≫ MB** Work in pairs. Describe the features of a city you know, and what you like or dislike about it.

Our capital city is very nice to walk around in. Traffic is not permitted in the city center, and there are lots of green spaces.

I CAN
talk about the different features of a city ☐

Real life

7 Use the words in the box to complete the responses (1–4) to the question below.

understand	considered	concerned	depend

What do you think of the idea to build a new sports complex downtown?

1 Well, that will _____ on what it looks like.
2 I _____ that we need some new facilities. But I just don't think we have the money.
3 I'm more _____ about the lack of green space downtown, actually.
4 I don't think the planners have really _____ where people are going to park their cars.

8 **≫ MB** Work in small groups. Respond to this question using phrases from Exercise 7.

What do you think of the idea of closing the downtown area to all traffic?

I CAN
debate issues and respond to points other people make ☐

Unit 6 Alternative travel

A mountainside guesthouse in the Swiss canton of Appenzell

FEATURES

1 Work in pairs. Look at the photo and the caption. What do you think there is to do in and around this hotel? Would you like to stay here? Why or why not?

2 ▶ 48 Listen to someone describing her stay in this place. What did she like about her stay? What didn't she like? Tell your partner.

3 Work in pairs. Circle the correct options to complete these questions. Then take turns asking and answering the questions.

1. When you book a hotel, do you usually ask for a room with a *sight / view*?
2. Do you generally take a lot of *suitcase / luggage* when you travel, or do you prefer to travel light?
3. What is your favorite kind of *scenery / countryside*: the coast, forests, mountains, or deserts?
4. Which *airplane / airline* do you prefer to fly with?
5. When you last went on vacation, how long did it *take / last* to get to your destination?

6a Staycations

Vocabulary vacation activities

1 Work in pairs. Are you familiar with all of these vacation activities? Discuss which you have done and where you did them. Then think of three more vacation activities and discuss where people do them.

buying souvenirs	camping
going on safari	hiking
photographing wildlife	rafting
sightseeing	snorkeling
sunbathing	taking guided tours
visiting museums	visiting a theme park

2 Work in pairs. Which are your favorite vacation activities? Where have you done these?

One of my favorite things to do on vacation is to climb to a high point, whether it's in a city or in the countryside, to get a view of the area …

Reading

3 Work in pairs. How well do you know your country's capital city? Ask and answer these questions.

1 Can you name five important tourist attractions in your country's capital city?
2 How many of these have you visited?
3 Have you ever been on a bus tour or walking tour of your country's capital city?
4 Do you know the name of a good, reasonably priced hotel in your country's capital city?

4 Read the blog post about staycations. Are these sentences true (T) or false (F)?

1 Staycationers go out and do different activities during their staycations.　T　F
2 Staycations have all the stresses of normal travel.　T　F
3 Staycations often imitate traditional vacations.　T　F

STAYCATIONS

▶ 49

You probably don't like the term "staycation." Me neither. But don't be put off. As a concept, it's quite attractive. Staycations are vacations at home. But they don't just mean staying in and doing things around the house. They involve things that you might do on vacations—like sightseeing, eating out,
5 going swimming, etc.—but instead, you do them in your local area. You could even camp in your yard or at a local campsite. Anything goes really— you just can't go to work!

Staycations became popular around 2007–2010, when people were looking for a cheaper kind of vacation during the global financial crisis. Wouldn't it
10 be nice, people thought, to take a vacation without all the costs? But let's not ignore the other benefits here: You get none of the problems associated with travel—no packing, long drives, or delays at the airport; and also, you bring money to the local economy.

Some staycationers like to follow a set of rules: They fix a definite start
15 and end date; they plan activities in advance; and they avoid their normal routine. You don't have to do these things, but they help to create the feel of a traditional vacation. Others, aware that a barbecue and a visit to the local zoo probably won't match the thrill of foreign travel, take it a step further. Karen Ash, whose story I read in the *Wall Street Journal*, was one.
20 Karen, who lives in New York, decided not to go to Japan as originally planned, but instead took a week-long Japanese vacation in her own city. She bought postcards and souvenirs at a Japanese market, admired bonsai plants, ate ramen—she even spoke Japanese when ordering—all without leaving New York. Her itinerary also included participating in a traditional
25 Japanese tea ceremony, attending a taiko drumming concert, and watching Japanese soap operas. I don't think everyone would take that much trouble over their staycation, but it gives you an idea of the possibilities!

5 Work in pairs. Use the information in the blog post to complete these sentences.

1 People first started having staycations because …
2 Staycations are good for the local economy because …
3 Some people think that visiting local attractions isn't as exciting as …

Grammar negative forms

> ▶ **NEGATIVE FORMS**
>
> **Negative statements with *think, believe, suppose, imagine***
> 1 *I **don't think** everyone would take that much trouble.*
>
> **Negative form of *have to* and *can***
> 2 *You **don't have to** do these things.*
> 3 *He **can't** afford to fly first-class.*
>
> **Negative short answers with *hope, expect, believe, guess, suppose, be afraid***
> 4 *I **hope not**.*
>
> **Negative infinitive**
> 5 *Karen Ash decided **not to go** to Japan.*
>
> **Negative suggestions**
> 6 ***Let's not** ignore the other benefits.*
>
> **Negative words: *neither, none, no***
> 7 *You get **none** of the problems associated with travel.*
> 8 *There was **no** delay at the airport.*
> 9 *You probably don't like the term "staycation." Me **neither**.*
>
> **Negative imperative**
> 10 ***Don't be** put off.*

For more information and practice, see page 166.

6 Write the affirmative version of sentences 2–9 from the grammar box using one (or two) word(s) in each blank below.

2 You _____ do these things.
3 He _____ afford to fly first-class.
4 I hope _____ .
5 Karen Ash decided _____ to Japan.
6 _____ ignore the other benefits.
7 You get _____ of the problems associated with travel.
8 There was _____ delay at the airport.
9 You probably _____ the term "staycation." Me _____ .

7 Circle the correct options to complete the text.

Let's ¹ *don't forget / not forget* that the main reason for choosing a staycation is to save money. Would you be staying at home if you could afford to go away? I ² *don't guess so / guess not*. So try ³ *not to / to not* spend the same amount as you would do on a foreign vacation. For example, ⁴ *don't / doesn't* eat out all the time in restaurants. If you go on a day trip, take a picnic with you.

You can still be adventurous while saving money. Take a tent and set out on a walk with ⁵ *no / none* of your usual luxuries (smartphone, GPS, etc.) and ⁶ *no / none* fixed idea of where you are going (but don't forget a good map!). After all, the fun of any vacation is discovering new places. Why should a staycation be any different?

8 Rewrite these sentences using the negative form of the underlined ideas, so that they have the opposite meaning.

1 <u>Let's spend</u> a lot of money on a foreign vacation.

_____

2 <u>All of the hotels</u> had rooms available.

_____

3 I told them <u>to wait</u> until the last moment before booking their vacation.

_____

4 <u>Take</u> a bathing suit—<u>there's a</u> swimming pool at the hotel.

_____

5 I <u>like</u> foreign travel, and <u>Sarah does too</u>.

_____
_____

9 Work in pairs. Complete these sentences giving advice about traveling abroad in your own words.

1 You don't have to … to have a good vacation.
2 In remote places, there is often no … , so …
3 Don't be put off by …
4 I don't think using a travel guidebook …

Speaking my Life

10 Work in small groups. Plan a five-day staycation in the area you live in. Try to give the staycation a theme as in the blog post (e.g., a sports theme or a foreign theme). Prepare a short itinerary with at least five activities.

A: *What about a food theme, like eating out in a different restaurant every day?*
B: *I **don't think** that would work—it **wouldn't** be a very cheap staycation.*
A: *No, I **suppose not**.*

11 As a group, share your itinerary with the class. Listen to the other groups as they share their itineraries.

12 Have a class vote on which staycation sounds the most fun and easiest to carry out.

6b Voluntourism

Vocabulary travel

1 The to-do list below contains things to do before going on a foreign trip. Complete the list using these words.

boarding	information	guidebook	insurance
spray	money	vaccinations	valid

To-do list

Buy ¹ _____ about local area

Print ² _____ passes

Buy sunscreen and bug ³ _____

Check passport is ⁴ _____ (minimum six months)

Book doctor's appointment to get
⁵ _____

Change ⁶ _____

Check travel ⁷ _____ plan is up-to-date

Write list of addresses and contact
⁸ _____ to leave with friends

Listening

2 ▶ 50 Work in pairs. Look at the photo below. What kind of volunteering do you think people do here? Listen to the interview and check your ideas.

3 Which of the statements (a–c) best summarizes Katie Samuel's definition of what a good volunteer vacation should offer?

a a working vacation where you learn practical and useful skills (e.g., building, teaching)

b a cultural experience where both the visitor and the host benefit

c an enjoyable way to help other people less fortunate than yourself

4 ▶ 50 Listen to the interview again and complete these sentences with the words you hear. Then work in pairs and discuss what each expression in **bold** means.

1 Don't most people just want to _____ **off to** the beach and relax?
2 This should be **a rewarding travel experience**, not just **a work** _____ .
3 In return, the locals take the volunteers for _____ **walks**.
4 They have to pay for their own airfares and _____ **expenses**.
5 The CRTP restores **cultural** _____ **sites** around the world.

5 Work in groups and discuss these questions. Then tell your ideas to the class.

1 What do you think of this type of vacation?
2 Is it right that people have to pay to volunteer?
3 What other ways can you think of to get close to the local way of life on a vacation?

Grammar question forms

▶ **QUESTION FORMS**

Direct questions
1 *Have you ever **thought** about doing some building work?*

Direct negative questions
2 ***Don't** most people just **want** to head off to the beach?*

Indirect questions
3 ***Is it possible that** people **could come** back with a new skill?*
4 ***Do you know where** listeners **can find** upcoming volunteer vacation possibilities?*
5 ***Surely** they **don't want** people without experience just turning up?*

Tag questions
6 *It's not really a vacation as we know it, **is it?***
7 *But the volunteers pay for the trip, **don't they?***

For more information and practice, see page 166.

6 ▶ 51 Work in pairs. Look at the grammar box on page 72 and listen to the different question forms (1–7). Then answer questions 1–5 below.

1 In which three questions is the questioner saying something they expect the listener to agree with?
2 In which four questions is the questioner asking a more open-ended question?
3 How do you make the indirect questions (3 and 4) into direct questions?
4 How do we form tag questions?
5 In which tag question does the intonation rise at the end? In which does it fall?

7 Rewrite these ideas (1–5) using question forms. You may need to make other changes to the sentences.

1 I can't believe he intends to give up his well-paid job in order to travel.
  Surely _____
  _____ ?
2 Which travel company did you use?
  Can you tell me _____
  _____ ?
3 I bet it rained a lot when you were in England.
  Didn't _____
  _____ ?
4 I'm pretty sure that you've been to America.
  You've _____ ,
  _____ ?
5 Does this bus go downtown?
  Do you know _____
  _____ ?

8 Pronunciation intonation in question forms

a ▶ 52 Work in pairs. Practice saying the rewritten question forms in Exercise 7 with the most appropriate intonation. Then listen and check.

b ▶ 53 Work in pairs. Do the tag questions in these sentences rise or fall? Listen and check.

1 It's a nice day, isn't it?
2 You haven't seen my phone anywhere, have you?
3 He doesn't look well, does he?
4 It wasn't my fault, was it?

9 Read this telephone conversation between Mike (M), a volunteer, and Jeff (J), an employer. Complete the questions in **bold** with appropriate tag forms.

M: Hi, I'm interested in helping to repair trails on the Continental Divide Trail this summer. [1] **I can work for just a few days, _____** ?

J: Absolutely. You can work anywhere from two days to two months.

M: That's great. I have about a week in June. [2] **Volunteers usually pay something to take part, _____** ?

J: No, actually. It's free.

M: Sorry—free? [3] **Surely I have to pay for my accommodation, _____** ?

J: No, it's completely free. You just have to register by filling out a form and sending it to us.

M: I couldn't find a form online. [4] **It's not on your website, _____** ?

J: You have to collect the form from our office, or I can email it to you.

M: Great. And where on the trail can I work?

J: New Mexico, Montana, Wyoming, …

M: [5] **You don't have something in Colorado, _____** ?

J: Yes, we do. We have spaces in Winfield, Colorado, and a few in Mount Elbert.

M: And can you tell me how long the training is?

J: There's no training beforehand. We train you as you work. But we are looking for a chef at the moment. [6] **You don't have any cooking experience, _____** ?

M: No, I'm afraid not. I really just want to work for a few days helping to build trails.

10 ▶ 54 Listen to the conversation in Exercise 9 and check your answers. Notice the intonation in question forms. Then work in pairs and act out the conversation.

Speaking *myLife*

11 Work in pairs. Take turns inquiring about a volunteer vacation you'd like to go on.

1 helping to repair a school building in Mali (Saharan Africa)
2 recording types of plants in a tropical rain forest in Borneo (Indonesia)

Student A: Turn to page 153 to prepare a list of questions about program 1.

Student B: Look at the information on page 155 about program 1.

In pairs, ask for and give information about program 1. Then change roles and repeat for program 2 (Student B should look at the information on page 154 about program 2).

6c Unusual places to stay

Reading

1 Work in pairs. Make a list of all the different types of accommodations that people stay in on vacation (e.g., hotel, tent). Give one advantage and one disadvantage of each. Then compare your ideas with another pair.

2 Read the excerpt from a travel magazine's guide to unusual places. Work in pairs and answer these questions.

   1 Which seem like comfortable places to stay?
   2 Which place seems to have the most disadvantages?

3 Read the travel guide again. Circle the correct option (a or b) to complete each sentence.

   1 Karosta's description of its hotel is ___ .
     a not pleasant
     b not truthful
   2 The writer thinks the cost of a night in the Karosta naval jail is ___ .
     a too high
     b about right
   3 For a long time after the gold rush, Virginia City was ___ .
     a uninhabited
     b a rich town
   4 The cabins at the Nevada City Hotel and Cabins are ___ .
     a old and uncomfortable
     b comfortable inside
   5 The caves of Sassi di Matera ___ .
     a are unchanged since the Bronze Age
     b were changed a little during the Renaissance
   6 The owners of Le Grotte Della Civita want their guests to ___ .
     a have a good TV viewing experience
     b enjoy the original atmosphere of the caves

4 Work in pairs. Which of these words or phrases are parts of a building? Which are pieces of furniture? Explain the meaning of each term to your partner. Draw a picture if it helps.

bed	bench	hallway	chest of drawers
fridge	porch	shutters	vaulted ceiling

5 Which of the places in the travel guide would you prefer to stay in? What are your reasons? Tell your partner.

Critical thinking analyzing tone

6 The tone of a piece of writing affects how the reader interprets the information in it. Which of these (a–c) best describes the tone of this travel guide?

   a serious and factual
   b light and conversational
   c critical and negative

7 Work in pairs. Find examples of this tone in the guide. Does the tone make you more or less likely to want to stay in these places?

Word focus *mind*

8 Work in pairs. Look at the two highlighted expressions with the word *mind* in the guide. Discuss what each one means. Then guess what these other expressions with *mind* mean.

   1 I **am of two minds** about whether to stay at a hotel or drive back home tonight.
   2 If you **change your mind** about coming with me, let me know before Friday.
   3 Sorry I haven't gotten back to you about the weekend. I've **had** a lot **on my mind** lately.
   4 Sorry, I know I've heard his name before, but my **mind's gone blank**.

9 Work in pairs. Act out short conversations using the phrases with *mind* (1–4) from Exercise 8. Take turns beginning each conversation with a sentence from Exercise 8.

   A: *I **am of two minds** about whether to stay at a hotel or drive back home tonight.*
   B: *I would stay the night if I were you. You don't want to drive when you are tired.*

Speaking and writing   **myLife**

10 Work in small groups. Create your own idea for an unusual place to stay. Discuss:

   • where the hotel is and what it's called.
   • how your hotel is different.
   • whether your hotel should be luxurious or basic.
   • what facilities you can offer that fit with the theme.

11 As a group, write a short review of your hotel for a travel website. Use an appropriate tone. Then present your idea and read the review to the class. Vote for which hotel sounds the most interesting.

Unusual places to stay

▶ 55

PRISON HOTELS

Built in 1905, the Karosta naval jail in Latvia originally
housed badly behaved Russian sailors. Now a hotel, it
offers guests "an opportunity to stay overnight on real
5 prisoners' benches and mattresses." The hotel's website
proudly describes Karosta as "unfriendly, unheated, and
uncomfortable." They are not lying. This is more a reality
jail experience than a hotel. "Reception" is a dark hallway
where a former prison guard explains the rules to you (no
10 luggage except a toothbrush, no attempts to escape), and
then fires his gun in the air to show you he is serious. After
a meal of bread and sweet Russian tea, "guests" are given
five minutes to wash up before making their own bed from
a wooden bench and thin mattress. Sound unpleasant? It is.
15 But for $12 per night, what do you expect?

PERIOD HOTELS

Would you be interested in stepping back in time to
America's Wild West? Virginia City in Montana, a former
gold-rush town of the 1860s, was a ghost town until it began
20 to be restored for tourists in the 1950s. Owned largely by the
state government, the town now operates as a large open-air
museum. Nearby is the Nevada City Hotel and Cabins, where
you can sit on the porch and enjoy life as a cowboy. The
rooms feature period furniture, and downstairs there's a real
25 Wild West saloon. The cabins look extremely basic from the
outside, but inside they have large double beds and private
bathrooms. Keep in mind that if you stay there on weekdays,
you might be disappointed. The city only really comes to life
on weekends, when actors walk around dressed as sheriffs,
30 cowboys, and gold prospectors.

CAVE HOTELS

If you have even more primitive accommodation in mind,
why not try a cave hotel? Cold, damp, dark? It doesn't
have to be. The caves of Sassi di Matera in Italy are Bronze
35 Age homes that were given a makeover during the
Renaissance, with vaulted ceilings, doors, and shutters.
More recently, until the 1950s, they were the homes of
local peasants who lived there with their animals. But
now, the caves have been renovated to provide hospitality
40 in a historical setting. Although visitors to Le Grotte Della
Civita must do without television or fridges, the rooms are
comfortably furnished with antique furniture—the suite
has a beautiful oak chest of drawers. The hotel owners
wanted the caves to still feel authentic, so they kept as
45 many original features as possible, like the iron rings
where peasants used to tie up their animals. Prices start at
a less peasant-friendly $300 per night.

6d Couch surfing

Real life getting around

1 Work in pairs. Read the description of couch surfing below. Is it something you would do? Why or why not?

2 You are going to listen to a conversation between a couch surfer and a host. Look at the expressions to talk about getting around. Who do you think says each one: the couch surfer or the host? Discuss with a partner.

> ► **GETTING AROUND**
>
> I'm coming in by ¹ _____ sometime in the afternoon.
> That's kind of you, but I can ² _____ .
> How do I get to ³ _____ from the center of town?
> You can hop on ⁴ _____ to Stoney Creek.
> It's only a twenty-minute ⁵ _____ .
> The ⁶ _____ thing is to give me a call, and I'll come out and meet you.

3 ► **56** Listen to the conversation. Check your answers from Exercise 2 and complete the expressions for getting around with the words you hear.

4 Pronunciation intonation in sentences with two clauses

a ► **57** Listen to these two sentences with the word *but*. Notice how the speaker's intonation rises at the end of the first clause, indicating that they have not finished speaking.

1 I wanted to pick you up, but my car will be at the garage that day.
2 You could just get a taxi, but it's about eleven kilometers from the center of town.

b Work in pairs. Practice saying these sentences using the same intonation as in Exercise 4a.

1 I'll try to get home by six, but I can't promise I will.
2 Normally it's a ten-minute drive, but the road construction has made it longer.
3 I can't make it today, but I'll stop by tomorrow.
4 It's kind of you to offer, but we can make our own way.

5 Work in pairs. Take turns playing the roles of couch surfer and host. Call your host and ask about the best way to get to their home from another city.

Couch surfing originated with a New Hampshire student who was looking for somewhere cheap to stay in Iceland. He emailed 1,500 students at the University of Iceland asking if he could sleep the night on their couches. Couch surfing is now an established worldwide practice. This is how it works:

When you have made your travel plans, you contact people on the couch surfing network to find out if they can offer you a bed for the night in the places you are going to visit. There's no fee. The only obligation on your part is to be able to offer a place to stay at your home when someone asks in the future. Apart from being free, the benefit is that you meet people with local knowledge. If you're lucky, some might even become long-term friends.

6e A disappointed guest

Writing a letter/email of complaint

1 Work in pairs. Have you ever had a bad experience on vacation that you complained about? What happened and what was the outcome?

2 Read the letter of complaint from a guest about a stay at a hotel. Work in pairs and answer the questions.

1 Why is the guest unhappy?
2 What does she want the hotel to do about it?
3 Does her complaint seem justified?

---

44 Cherry Tree Lane
Boston, MA 02108
USA

Sweet Hotel Group
54 Erwin Street
Los Angeles, CA 90018
USA

Dear Sir/Madam,

I am writing to express my dissatisfaction with my stay at the Star Hotel on April 12th. I made a reservation through another website that was offering one night for two people—with an evening meal and breakfast—for $200. However, when we arrived at 5:30 p.m., we were informed that there was no table available in the restaurant, and that we could either dine at 6:00 p.m. or find another restaurant in town.

We had the strong impression that, because of the discounted offer, we did not receive the same level of hospitality as regular, full-paying guests. The situation was embarrassing and inconvenient. After some discussion with the staff, we opted to dine in the restaurant, but much later than we wished—at 9:30 p.m. No one apologized for this.

Compensation is not actually my principal concern. I would just like you to investigate the matter and ensure that this situation does not arise in the future with other guests.

Yours faithfully,

A S

Anne Smith

---

3 Work in pairs. Formal letters follow certain conventions. Answer these questions.

1 What is the correct position for each address?
2 Where is the reason for writing mentioned?
3 Where is the request to the recipient of the letter for action?
4 How would the format be different if this was an email?

4 Writing skill formal language

a Work in pairs. Underline the formal words or phrases in the letter that mean the following:

1 say I was unhappy
2 they told us
3 a cheap deal
4 after we talked to
5 chose to eat
6 what I'm most interested in
7 look into
8 make sure

b Rewrite the sentences below replacing the expressions in **bold** with more formal language.

1 We **want** to **tell you how unhappy we were** with the standard of the food on the cruise ship *Royal Dawn*.
   We wish to express our dissatisfaction with the standard of the food on the cruise ship Royal Dawn.
2 I **told** the receptionist that I had **booked the room** for two nights, not one.
3 After **I'd talked to** the manager, she **said she was sorry** and promised to **look into** the problem with the shower. **But** no action was taken.
4 I would have expected that the safety of the guests was **what the staff was most interested in**.
5 Given the **trouble** this caused us, we expected to **get some money back**.

5 Read this situation. Then write a letter or email of complaint to the hotel.

> You recently stayed at a small hotel in the Hamptons in New York. During the night, you were woken up by some noisy people trying to climb a wall into the hotel courtyard. You went down to reception to tell a member of the hotel staff, but no one was there. You are angry and upset that no staff members were on duty that night.

6 Work in pairs. Exchange letters with your partner and compare what you have written. Use these questions to check your letters.

- Does the letter begin with the reason for writing?
- Does the letter end with what action is expected?

6f The unexpected beauty of traveling solo

A lone traveler crosses a bridge, Lithuania.

Before you watch

1 Work in pairs. Look at the title of the video. Make a list of the benefits of traveling alone and the benefits of traveling with someone else.

Traveling alone	Traveling with someone else

2 Compare your list with another pair. Which way of traveling do you think is better for you?

While you watch

3 ◼ 6.1 Watch the video. Work in pairs and answer the questions.

1 What kind of places does the man visit?
2 Why do you think he is traveling alone?

4 ◼ 6.1 Read these statements. Then watch the video again, listening carefully to the voicemail messages. Are the sentences true (T) or false (F)?

1	The woman really wanted to go with the man on the trip.	T	F
2	The man really wanted to make the trip alone.	T	F
3	The woman blames the man for what happened.	T	F
4	The woman doesn't know if the man is angry or just too busy to call back.	T	F
5	The man is an avid photographer.	T	F
6	The man finally calls her back.	T	F

5 Complete the chart with the things you saw in the video. Write as many things as you can in four minutes. Then compare your list with a partner.

Types of transportation	Activities
plane	*picking flowers*

6 ◼ 6.1 Watch the video again and see how many more types of transportation or activities you notice. Do you think the video makes a good case for traveling alone? Why or why not? Discuss with a partner.

After you watch

7 Vocabulary in context

a ◼ 6.2 Watch the clips from the video. Choose the correct meaning of the words and phrases.

b Complete these sentences in your own words. Then share your sentences with a partner.

1 I find it really weird when …
2 It's very tough to …
3 I can't figure out why …

8 You are going to leave phone messages for a friend while you are on a trip. Follow these steps:

1 Plan a solo trip. Think of three or four places you will visit and what activities you will do there.
2 Work with a partner. Turn your chairs back-to-back so you cannot see your partner's face.
3 Take turns "calling" each other. Leave voicemail messages about where you are, what you are doing, and how you are feeling.
4 When you are finished, change partners and tell each other about the messages you received from your first partner (i.e., Where did they go? Did they have a good experience? etc.).

A: Your call cannot be taken at the moment, so please leave your message after the tone. [Beep]
B: Hey, it's me, Daniela. I tried to catch you before I got on the plane, but I missed you. I'm in Scotland now …

UNIT 6 REVIEW AND MEMORY BOOSTER

Grammar

1 ▶▶ **MB** Work in pairs. Look at the photo below. Form questions about it by completing the sentences (1–3).

1 Do you know where …?
2 It looks … , …?
3 Have you ever …?

2 Circle the correct options to complete the conversation between Marianna (M) and Paulina (P).

M: You're planning to go to Mexico for your vacation, ¹ *are you / aren't you*?

P: Well, that was the plan, but I've decided ² *not to go / not going* now. I always travel to exotic places, so I thought, why ³ *I don't find / don't I find* out more about my own city for a change?

M: That's called a staycation, ⁴ *is it / isn't it*? It'll certainly be a lot cheaper, ⁵ *do you think / don't you think*?

P: Well, yes, but that's not the point. I ⁶ *let's not / don't want to* stay at home. I'm going to stay in the new hotel downtown—the one that's been getting great reviews. I'm planning to visit a few museums and check out some local restaurants that I've always wanted to go to. I just hope it ⁷ *doesn't rain / no rain* all the time.

M: Well, I think it's a great idea. You ⁸ *not to / don't have to* worry about getting visas or changing money. There'll be ⁹ *none / not* of that stress.

3 Work in pairs. Answer the questions.

1 How is Paulina going to spend her vacation? What reason does she give?
2 What are the benefits of her plan?

I CAN	
use negative forms correctly with a range of verbs	
form indirect, negative, and tag questions	

Vocabulary

4 ▶▶ **MB** Work in pairs. Discuss what you remember about the places in the photos below. Where are they, and why are they unusual? What kinds of things can you do or not do in each one?

5 Complete these questions with one word in each blank. Then work in pairs and take turns asking and answering the questions.

1 Where do you _____ in mind for your next vacation?
2 What is the longest time it's _____ you to travel somewhere?
3 Have you ever forgotten to check that your passport is _____ before traveling?
4 Have you ever had to get _____ against diseases before traveling?
5 What should a person vacationing in your country _____ in mind?

I CAN	
talk about vacations and travel	
use expressions with *mind*	

Real life

6 Match the sentence beginnings (1–6) with their endings on the right.

1 I'll pick you up ○   ○ my own way.
2 Are you coming in ○   ○ ride.
3 Look out for the post office ○   ○ to your house?
4 I can easily make ○   ○ by train?
5 It's only a ten-minute ○   ○ on your right.
6 How do I get ○   ○ from the station.

7 Choose a well-known place or meeting point in your town or city. Then work in pairs and take turns telling your partner how to get there using public transportation. Use at least one of the phrases from Exercise 6.

I CAN	
ask for and give directions and vacation advice	

Unit 7 Customs and behavior

A crowded Tokyo subway train during evening rush hour

FEATURES

1 Work in pairs. Look at the photo and the caption. What rules or customs do people follow in this situation? Make a list of polite/ thoughtful behavior and a list of rude/inconsiderate behavior.

2 ▶ 58 Listen to someone describing customs on the Tokyo subway. Work in pairs and answer the questions.

1 Did the speaker mention any of your ideas from Exercise 1?
2 Which customs or behaviors are unique to the Tokyo subway?

3 Look at the rules of behavior (1–4) for students attending college lectures. Complete the sentences with these words.

chew	interrupt	raise	show	stare

1 Don't _____ the lecturer. _____ your hand first if you have a question.
2 Be attentive. By all means take notes, but don't just sit and _____ at your laptop screen.
3 Don't eat food or _____ gum during a lecture or seminar.
4 Be polite, respectful, and _____ consideration to other students.

4 Work in pairs. Do you agree with the rules of behavior in Exercise 3? Are there any more rules you would add?

7a Cruel to be kind

Reading

1 Work in pairs. Which of these things (1–6) do you think should be:
- controlled strongly by parents;
- controlled a little by parents; or
- left to the child to decide? Give reasons.

1 watching TV
2 practicing a musical instrument
3 going out to play with friends
4 doing homework
5 choosing which subjects to study in school
6 choosing activities outside school (e.g., sports, hobbies)

2 Read the article. Work in pairs and answer the questions (1–3).

1 What is a "tiger mother"?
2 What are a tiger mother's attitudes to the first four things in Exercise 1?
3 What are the results of Amy Chua's "tiger mother" parenting?

Vocabulary raising children: verbs

3 Work in pairs. Look at the pairs of verbs in **bold**. The first verb in each pair is from the article. Discuss the differences in meaning between the verbs in each pair. Use a dictionary if necessary.

1 **bring up** and **educate** children
2 **praise** and **reward** good behavior
3 **give in to** and **spoil** your children
4 **encourage** and **force** your children to do something
5 **punish** and **shame** someone
6 **rebel against** and **disobey** your parents

C R U E L   T O   B E   K I N D

▶ 59

Is there a right way to bring up children? Some parents read books to find an answer, some follow their instincts. Whatever they do, a doubt always remains: "When my children have grown
5 up, will I have any regrets about my parenting?"

But "doubt" is not in the vocabulary of Amy Chua, a successful lawyer, professor, and author of *Battle Hymn of the Tiger Mother*, a guide to bringing up children. According to Chua, most
10 mothers are too soft on their children. They praise them for every effort, even if the result is coming last in a race or playing a piano piece badly. Often, when their children ask to go out and play rather than do their homework, the
15 parents just give in to them.

The tiger mother's approach—described by Chua as "the Chinese way"—is very different. Tiger mothers accept nothing less than "A" grades in every subject; if the child fails
20 to achieve this, it simply shows they have not worked hard enough. Tiger mothers encourage their children not with praise, but with punishment. "Unless you learn this piano piece," Chua told her daughter, "I will donate
25 your doll house to charity." She even rejected her daughter's homemade birthday card because it had been drawn in a hurry.

But Chua says that this is a more honest and direct approach. If her child has been lazy, she says, she will punish them—that is the tiger
30 mother's way. In the same situation, other parents usually tell their children not to worry: If they keep trying, they will do better next time.

A strict routine of work before play, no TV or video games, plus constant nagging—it doesn't seem much fun for the children. But perhaps it works. Chua's daughters have not rebelled against her.
35 They attend Ivy League colleges now, and are proficient at violin and piano. Chua is convinced that as long as she continues to push them, they will have successful careers.

Amy Chua (middle)
with her two daughters

Grammar zero and first conditionals

4 Look at the grammar box above. Work in pairs and answer these questions.

1 Which tenses or verb forms are used in zero and first conditional sentences?
2 Which type of conditional do we use to talk about:
   a a fact or something that is generally true?
   b a particular possible future situation?
3 In which sentences can you use either *if* or *when* with a similar meaning?
4 How are the words *as long as* and *unless* different in meaning from *if*?

5 Circle the correct options to complete these zero and first conditional sentences.

1 If Charlie *continues / will continue* drinking soda all the time, it *will ruin / ruins* his teeth.
2 Some children *become / will become* very confused if they *won't / don't* have an established routine.
3 If a child *will be / is* misbehaving, it *will be / is* important to understand why.
4 When parents *will be / are* too strict, it *is / will be* natural for some children to rebel against them.
5 When I *will have / have* children, I *will try / try* to be the kind of parent that praises, not punishes.

Grammar time linkers

6 Look at the grammar box about time linkers. Circle the correct option to complete the rule below.

In a sentence about the future where two clauses are connected by a time linking word, we use a *present / future* verb form after the time linking word.

7 Look at the prompts. Write complete sentences about the future using appropriate verb forms.

1 I / go and get / some milk / before / the store / close.
2 She / stay / in her current job / until / she / find / a better one.
3 She / meet / us / after / she / finish / work.
4 As soon as / everyone / board / the plane, / we / be / able to leave.
5 I / have / to take the bus to work next week / while / the car / be / repaired.
6 Dinner / be / ready for you / when / you / get / home.

8 Circle the best options to complete the sentences.

1 I'll continue to live at home *as long as / until* I find a reasonably priced apartment to rent.
2 My dad says he'll teach me how to drive *while / as long as* I pass all my exams.
3 *Unless / If* you do as you're told, we won't be going to the festival on Saturday.
4 I'm sure you'll be able to watch the game *while / until* you're waiting at the airport.
5 I think he'll change his mind about going to college *until / after* he has had time to think about it.
6 Los Angeles is a great place to live *before / if* you have a car and plenty of money.

9 Below are expressions commonly said by adults either to or about children. Complete them in your own words. Then compare your sentences with a partner.

1 "If you don't finish your dinner, …"
2 "Children only appreciate how difficult it is to be a parent when …"
3 "If you do well in your exams, …"
4 "It's fine for children to live at home until …"

Speaking my Life

10 Work in small groups. Think of four traditional rules of behavior that parents have given to children. Then discuss which are still good rules, and which you think are old-fashioned or no longer appropriate.

*"Don't speak until you are spoken to." I think this rule is old-fashioned and wrong because if you **tell** your children not to speak, they **won't develop** good communication skills.*

7b A matter of taste

Listening

1 Work in pairs. What is the strangest thing you have ever eaten? Why did you eat it? What did it taste like?

2 ▶ 60 Listen to an excerpt from a radio program about the diet of the indigenous people of northern Alaska. Work in pairs and answer the questions.

1 What kind of food forms their traditional diet?
2 What is surprising about their diet?

3 ▶ 60 Listen to the excerpt again. Circle the correct option (a, b, or c) to complete each sentence.

1 In less _____ countries, people don't eat so much meat.
   a well-off
   b cold
   c populous
2 In northern Alaska, there aren't many _____ available to eat.
   a dairy products
   b small animals
   c plants
3 The speaker has been told that whale skin is very _____ .
   a nutritious
   b delicious
   c tough
4 Harold Draper says that what is important is eating the right _____ .
   a nutrients
   b foods
   c vitamins
5 Since Alaska Natives have started eating more processed foods, they have had more _____ problems.
   a health
   b financial
   c social

4 Work in pairs. Are you surprised by the Alaska Native diet? Why or why not? Do you think we should eat less processed food? What would you miss most if this were the case?

Grammar *usually, used to, would, be used to,* and *get used to*

▶ **USUALLY, USED TO, WOULD, BE USED TO, and GET USED TO**

usually + simple present
1 We **usually eat** fruit to get more vitamin C. ____

used to + base form of the verb
2 Heart conditions among Alaska Natives **used to be** about half the number in the wider population of North America. ____
3 They **didn't use to have** a so-called balanced diet. ____

would + base form of the verb
4 They **would cook** the meat in seal oil. ____

be used to + noun or *-ing*
5 On the whole, we **are used to eating** a range of foods. ____

get used to + noun or *-ing*
6 We **have gotten used to eating** certain foods in order to get each nutrient. ____

For more information and practice, see page 168.

5 Look at the sentences in the grammar box. Match the phrases in **bold** (1–6) with the descriptions below (a–e).

a a repeated past action, habit, or situation that no longer happens (two phrases)
b a repeated action or habit (<u>not</u> a state or situation) in the past
c a habit or action that happens regularly or is generally true
d something that seems or seemed normal (not strange or difficult)
e a new thing that people adapt to or that becomes normal

6 Circle the correct options to complete the paragraphs about eating habits.

A Fifty years ago, people in the US ¹*used to sit / got used to sitting* down for meals with their families each evening. Families nowadays ²*get used to eating / usually eat* together no more than three times a week, because busy lives, work, and TV get in the way. But it is believed that if more families could ³*be used to dining / get used to dining* together again, it would strengthen family relationships.

B When I was young, I ⁴*was used to eating / used to eat* a lot of candy. Every Saturday, my sister and I ⁵*would go / got used to going* to the store and spend our allowance on chocolate, gum, and all kinds of things that were bad for our teeth.

7 Complete these sentences with *usually, used to, would, get used to,* or *be used to*. Where there is a verb in parentheses, put it in the correct form.

1 We _____*used to eat*_____ (eat) out a lot, but restaurants are so expensive these days that we don't anymore.
2 I go to that café a lot. I _____ (order) the salmon when I go there.
3 I _____ (take) sugar in my coffee, but now I drink it without sugar. It took a little while to _____ the taste, but now it feels normal.
4 When I was little, if I didn't like some food on my plate, I _____ (hide) it in my napkin when no one was looking and put it in my pocket.
5 When I was staying with my grandparents, we _____ (have) dinner at six o'clock every evening. It was strange, because I _____ (eat) dinner much later.

8 Are any of the sentences in Exercise 7 true for you? How is your experience different? Discuss with a partner.

9 Pronunciation /juː/ and /uː/

a ▶ 61 Look at the words in **bold** below. The letter *u* (underlined) is pronounced /juː/. Listen to the sentences and repeat.

1 I **u**sually eat a big breakfast.
2 Did you **u**se to eat a big breakfast?
3 I'm not **u**sed to eating a lot of meat.

b Work in pairs. Practice saying these words with the /juː/ sound (underlined).

reg<u>u</u>lar	c<u>u</u>cumber	f<u>u</u>ture	h<u>u</u>man
c<u>u</u>te	rep<u>u</u>tation	h<u>u</u>ge	val<u>u</u>e

c ▶ 62 In these words, there is no /j/ sound before the /uː/ sound. Practice saying the words. Then listen and check. Which sounds come before /uː/?

fruit	juice	June	junior	rule	true

Vocabulary and speaking food and eating habits *my*Life

10 ▶ 63 Work in pairs. Look at these food items. Put each food item in the correct category in the chart. Then listen and check your answers. Think of two more food items for each category.

mustard	cucumber	beef	lettuce
apple	ketchup	lamb	muesli
raspberries	cheese	tuna	butter

1 Fruit and vegetables	
2 Dairy products	
3 Breakfast cereals	
4 Sauces	
5 Meat and seafood	

11 Find out about your classmates' eating habits. Ask three classmates questions about these areas and take notes.

- **Meals:** times, who they eat with, what they eat
- **Fast food:** how often and what
- **Fruit and vegetables:** which and how much
- **Candy:** which, when, and how often
- **Eating habits in general:** have they changed?

12 Work in pairs. Compare your notes from Exercise 11 and make conclusions using *usually, used to,* and *get used to*.

*Most people don't **usually** eat a big breakfast.*
*Mary **used to** eat dinner with her family every night, but now she **usually** buys fast food.*
*Scott is trying to **get used to** cooking for himself.*

7c Cultural conventions

Reading

1 Work in pairs. Imagine you are at a job interview. Discuss what you would do.

1 **Clothes:** dress professionally or casually?
2 **Posture:** sit forward or lean back?
3 **Distance:** be close to the interviewer or not?
4 **Voice:** speak loudly, softly, or confidently?
5 **Eye contact:** keep strong eye contact or not?
6 **Body language:** fold arms or keep hands down?

2 Read the first paragraph of the blog. What do the terms "personal space" and "turn-taking" mean?

3 Read the rest of the blog. Which of these statements (a–c) best summarizes the author's findings about personal space and turn-taking?

a There are cultural differences in these areas, but they are not significant.
b More scientific evidence is needed to support claims of cultural differences.
c The differences in these areas are small, but need to be resolved to improve communication between different cultures.

4 Work in pairs. Answer these questions.

1 What do you think is meant by "contact" and "non-contact" cultures?
2 What does Edward Hall think we risk if we fail to understand differences in personal space?
3 According to the author, what is missing from the research done so far into personal space?
4 What do the two stories about turn-taking in Nordic countries tell us?
5 What is the average time that people anywhere in the world take to respond in conversation?

5 Work in pairs. Underline words or phrases in the blog that mean the following:

1 made bigger than it really is (paragraph 1)
2 proof based on personal stories/accounts (paragraph 3)
3 a line on which we measure things (paragraph 4)
4 the usual way (paragraph 6)

Critical thinking questions and answers

6 Work in pairs. What question does the author ask at the start of the blog? What is his answer?

7 Work in pairs. Look at these other questions that the blog raises. Is there an answer to them in the blog? What are the answers?

1 Why do anthropologists seem to exaggerate cultural differences?
2 Why do we need to be careful about making cultural comparisons?

Word focus *same* and *different*

8 The expression with *difference* below is from the blog. Complete the sentences (1–6) with the words *same*, *different*, or *difference*. Then compare answers with a partner. Which two **bold** phrases mean the same thing? Which two are complete opposites?

*In other words, the **difference** is minimal.*

1 We didn't fight! We just **had a _____ of opinion**.
2 I don't mind where we eat tonight. **It's all the _____ to me**.
3 Being able to speak a language is one thing; being able to teach it is **a completely _____ matter**.
4 You say money's not important, but if you were poor, you'd be **singing a _____ tune**.
5 Really, **it makes no _____ to me** where we stay. A youth hostel is fine.
6 A jail and a prison are **one and the _____ thing**.

Speaking my Life

9 Work in pairs. Discuss the customs in your own culture regarding personal space and turn-taking.

10 Look at this list of the most common first words in turn-taking in English conversation. Which of these words do *you* most use in conversation? Tell your partner.

| Yeah | Umm | I | And | Oh | So |
| No | Yes | Well | But | You | Right |

11 Work in pairs. Have short conversations using these opening questions and statements (a–c). Use words in Exercise 10 to give you time to respond.

a Do all cultures smile to show they're happy?
b Do you use gestures a lot when you speak?
c You can tell a lot about people from their body language.

CULTURAL CONVENTIONS

▶ 64

1 Whenever I read about cultural differences in communication, I always find myself asking if these are real differences or something imagined or exaggerated. So recently, I decided I would
5 investigate. I chose two areas—personal space and turn-taking—to try to find out the truth. Personal space means how close we stand or sit next to other people. Turn-taking refers to the rules of conversation—how long you speak for and how long
10 the other person waits before responding.

2 The idea that different cultures perceive space differently was first investigated by an American anthropologist, Edward Hall. He put the range for "personal distance" (family or close friends) at 45 cm to 1.2 m, and for
15 "social distance" (colleagues, neighbors, etc.) at 1.2 m to 3.5 m. Hall claimed that in "non-contact" cultures (the USA, northern Europe, parts of Asia), the distance is greater; in "contact" cultures (Latin America, the Middle East, southern Europe), it is smaller. He warned
20 that not respecting the correct distance between people could lead to misunderstanding or, worse, offense. He gave an example of an American at an airport who finds a seat in an empty seating area. The man feels uncomfortable when a Mediterranean-looking
25 man comes and sits right next to him.

3 There is a lot of anecdotal evidence to support claims of cultural differences, but little scientific evidence. While the ranges for the amount of space we need seem accurate, the actual amount depends on many more factors than
30 just cultural background: the age of the people, gender, where they live, social position, and personality.

4 Anthropologists also give examples of big cultural differences in turn-taking. Nordic cultures (Denmark, Sweden, Norway, Finland) are reported to have
35 long delays between one turn and the next. One anthropologist describes offering coffee to a Swedish guest in his house. After a minute's silence, the offer was accepted. Another gives an account of two men in Häme, Finland, walking to work one morning. The
40 first man says, "I lost my knife here yesterday." As they return home from work that evening, the other man asks, "What kind of knife was it?" Cultures at the other end of the scale include Japanese, Korean, and Dutch. In Antigua, for example, studies have
45 observed that speakers usually talk over one another, with no delay at all between turns.

5 However, scientific data shows that there is little cultural difference in the actual time delays in turn-taking. The typical pause across cultures
50 is about 0.2 seconds. The maximum gap is 0.47 seconds (Danish), and the minimum only 0.07 seconds (Japanese). In other words, the difference is minimal.

6 How, then, do stories of exaggerated differences
55 come about? One reason could be that when it comes to personal space and waiting for a response, we are sensitive to any variation from the norm. But I suspect the main reason is that we find contrasts entertaining. There is nothing wrong
60 with that, but we must be cautious when we make comparisons and keep in mind that our similarities are, in fact, much greater than our differences.

7d Wedding customs

Vocabulary weddings

1 Look at these words and phrases related to weddings. Match them with their definitions (1–6).

bride	groom	bachelorette party
reception	veil	bachelor party

1 a pre-wedding party for the man
  _____

2 a pre-wedding party for the woman
  _____

3 a party after the wedding
  _____

4 a woman on her wedding day
  _____

5 a man on his wedding day
  _____

6 a piece of thin cloth that covers the woman's face _____

Real life describing traditions

2 ▶ 65 Work in pairs. Listen to the first part of a description of a traditional pre-wedding "henna night" in eastern Turkey. Who attends the event, and how is it celebrated?

3 ▶ 66 Listen to the second part of the description. Number the stages of the ceremony in the correct order (1–5).

____ A child presents the hennaed coin to the groom.

____ The bride's head is covered with a red veil.

____ The bride's hands and feet are decorated with henna.

____ A gold coin is put into the remaining henna, and the guests sing separation songs.

____ The henna is prepared by the daughter of another couple.

4 ▶ 67 Work in pairs. Retell the stages of the ceremony (from Exercise 3) using the expressions for describing traditions. Then listen to the complete description again and compare your version.

5 Pronunciation the letter *s*

a ▶ 68 Work in pairs. Listen to these words. How is the underlined *s* pronounced in each word: /s/, /z/, or /ʒ/?

cu<u>s</u>tom	dre<u>ss</u>	friend<u>s</u>	mu<u>s</u>ic	occa<u>s</u>ion
plea<u>s</u>ure	suppo<u>s</u>e	spend<u>s</u>	wedding<u>s</u>	

b ▶ 69 Work in pairs. How do you think the underlined *s* is pronounced in these words? Listen and check.

deci<u>s</u>ion	ea<u>s</u>tern	lo<u>s</u>e	plan<u>s</u>
ring<u>s</u>	<u>s</u>ingle	surpri<u>s</u>e	u<u>s</u>ual

6 What special events or customs take place before, during, or after a wedding in your country? Choose one tradition and prepare a description. Think about:

• the timing of the event and its significance.
• the sequence of the events.

7 Work in small groups. Describe the event or custom you chose to your group members.

7e Fireworks festival

Writing a description

1 Work in pairs. Read the description below of a festival. What does the description say about each of these things?

a the name and date of the festival
b the reason for the festival
c the main attraction at the festival
d other activities that take place
e the high point of the festival

2 Read the description again. Underline all the adjectives used to describe the festival. What overall impression do you think the writer wants to give? Discuss with a partner.

Las Fallas—or the "Festival of fire"—in Valencia, Spain, is one of the most unusual and exciting festivals in the world: a joyful mixture of parades, music, food, and fireworks. It takes place every year between March 15th and 19th, and marks the beginning of spring—a time when everything bad is burned to welcome in the new season.

The focus of the festival is extraordinary statues called *ninots*—many as tall as houses—made of cardboard, wood, and plaster. The *ninots* often poke fun at people from real life, like politicians and celebrities, and are placed at different points all around the city. Each *ninot* is judged for its creative design, and prizes are given to the winners.

During the festival, people celebrate in the streets, drinking, eating paella (the traditional local dish), and watching fireworks. Late in the evening on March 18th, young men cut holes in the *ninots* and stuff them with fireworks. Then at exactly midnight comes the climax of the festival, when all the *ninots* across the city are set on fire in one spectacular burning ceremony. It is a unique, and very noisy, display.

3 Writing skill adding detail

a When you write a description, it is important to add interesting details. Work in pairs and answer these questions.

1 What details does the writer add about these things?

the beginning of spring	the *ninot* statues
the people from real life	the celebrations

2 How are the details added: with adjectives, with an explanation, with a list, or with examples?

b Work in pairs. Add details to the description of a music festival, using the guide in parentheses.

1 In the middle of the park, there is a … stage. (adjectives to describe the stage)
2 People then make their way to the main square, … (list of activities while making their way, e.g., singing)
3 There are all kinds of foods to eat, such as … (examples)
4 The festival takes place in mid-July, a time when … (explanation)

4 Write a description of a festival you know well. Start with the basic facts (use the ideas in Exercise 1) and then add more interesting details.

5 Exchange descriptions with a partner. Use these questions to check your partner's description.

- Does the description include the date of the festival, its significance, its high point, and the activities people do?
- Does the description give you a strong overall impression of the festival?
- Does it include interesting details?
- After reading the description, would you like to go to the festival?

7f Eating insects

Unusual food for sale
at a street market

Before you watch

1 Match the names of the insects with the photos (A–F). What do you know about each insect?

> caterpillar _____ cockroach _____ cricket _____
> mealworm _____ mosquito _____ fly _____

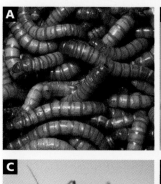

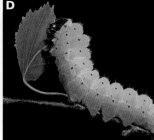

2 Key vocabulary

a Work in pairs. Read the sentences (1–4). The words in **bold** are used in the video. Guess the meaning of the words.

1 The chef Jamie Oliver is an **advocate** for healthy eating for kids.
2 She served the fish with a simple **garnish** of herbs.
3 There is a **niche** market for sugar-free chocolate.
4 Avocado ice cream? That sounds **revolting**.

b Write the words in **bold** in Exercise 2a next to their definitions (a–d).

a serving a small group _____
b someone who speaks in favor of something

  _____
c disgusting _____
d a small amount of food used for decoration

  _____

3 You are going to watch a video about eating insects. Work in pairs. Discuss the answers to these questions before you watch.

1 Which regions or continents include insects in their diets?
2 Is eating insects a new trend?
3 Why is producing insects better for the environment than producing meat?
4 Are insects nutritious?

While you watch

4 ▢◀ **7.1** Watch the video and check your answers from Exercise 3.

5 Work in pairs. Try to remember the insects that you saw in these foods.

1 apples covered with _____
2 a lollipop with a _____ in it
3 a cocktail made with _____ , not shrimps
4 a banana and cream dessert with a

  _____ on top

6 ▢◀ **7.1** Look at these questions. Then watch the video again and take notes. Check your answers with a partner.

1 How long has Larry been trying to get Americans to eat insects?
2 According to Larry, why do most Americans not like eating insects?
3 How many species of insects are eaten around the world?
4 What does one of Larry's dinner guests want to know about the cockroach on his plate?

After you watch

7 Vocabulary in context

a ▢◀ **7.2** Watch the clips from the video. Choose the correct meaning of the words and phrases.

b Complete these sentences in your own words. Then share your sentences with a partner.

1 … is anything but new.
2 I can't stomach …
3 My friend disagreed with me about … , but I was able to win him/her over by saying …

8 Would you eat the meals shown in the video? Why or why not? Discuss with your partner.

UNIT 7 REVIEW AND MEMORY BOOSTER

Grammar

1 Circle the correct options to complete the description.

If you ¹ *used to eat / are used to eating* lunch in the middle of the day and dinner around 7:30 p.m., then you ² *get / will get* a shock if you go to Argentina. Lunch ³ *usually takes / is used to taking* place at around 2 p.m., and dinner after 9 p.m.

But it's not just eating times that are different. At home in England, I ⁴ *used to eat / didn't use to eat* a big breakfast, very little lunch, and then I ⁵ *will / would* have a reasonably big supper when I got home from work. Here, breakfast is just coffee and a piece of toast, and lunch is a big deal. And the meat! I don't think I'll ever ⁶ *be used to / get used to* eating so much meat. As you know, when you eat a big lunch, you generally ⁷ *feel / feels* pretty sleepy afterward. The answer to that is to take a short nap or "siesta" in the afternoon. Actually, in Buenos Aires, the traditional siesta is not as common as it ⁸ *was used to being / used to be*, but you still find people in the provinces taking them.

2 What are four things that the writer finds strange about eating habits in Argentina? Tell a partner.

3 Complete this sentence with the verb in parentheses. Use one of the grammatical forms from the description in Exercise 1.

My parents never wasted food. Often, we _____ (eat) leftovers from the day before.

4 ▶▶ **MB** Write two similar sentences with blanks about your own past or present eating habits. Then work in pairs. Ask your partner to complete the sentences.

I CAN	
use *usually, used to, would, be used to,* and *get used to*	☐
use the zero and first conditionals and time linking words	☐

Vocabulary

5 Complete these rules of good behavior. Reorder the letters of the words in parentheses.

1 Don't _____ others. (rupterint)
2 Try not to _____ at people. (estra)
3 Don't speak when you are _____ food. (whingec)
4 Show _____ to others. (isticonaroned)
5 Be aware of other people's _____ space. (nosapler)

6 ▶▶ **MB** Work in pairs. Cross out the word or phrase that doesn't belong in each group and explain why.

1 disobey bring up look after raise
2 encourage shame praise reward
3 beef cheese goat lamb
4 tuna raspberries apple banana
5 bride guest groom veil

I CAN	
talk about parenting and behavior	☐
talk about food and eating habits	☐

Real life

7 Match the sentence beginnings (1–6) with the endings (a–f) to make sentences about a coming-of-age tradition.

1 It marks ____
2 It takes place ____
3 It's customary for ____
4 The ceremony begins ____
5 Typically, ____
6 Once the child ____

a people to give presents to the child.
b the moment when a child becomes an adult.
c the child stands up and gives a short speech.
d with the parent and child entering the hall.
e has given their speech, other people can also say a few words.
f on the child's sixteenth birthday.

8 ▶▶ **MB** Work in pairs. Take turns describing a special celebration in your country. Use the sentence beginnings (1–6) from Exercise 7.

I CAN	
describe a (traditional) celebration	☐

Unit 8 Hopes and ambitions

"Bucket list" wall: a public work of art on the wall of a local store

FEATURES

1 Look at the photo and the caption. Find two wishes you like.

2 ▶ 70 Listen to someone speaking about this wall. Work in pairs. What are some examples of things that people write?

3 Complete the sentences (1–3) with these synonyms of the words in **bold**.

ambition	goal	hope

1 Our **aim** / _____ / **target** is to raise $10,000 for charity.
2 Her _____ / **dream** is to be a professional dancer.
3 My parents' **wish** / _____ / **expectation** was that I would study medicine in college.

4 ▶ 70 What verbs did the speaker use in these phrases? Listen again and complete the phrases with the verbs you hear.

1 the dreams they'd like to _____ true
2 goals that are easy to _____
3 people wanting to _____ up to other people's expectations of them
4 some people will _____ their ambitions and some won't

5 Work in pairs. What are your hopes, goals, and ambitions? How easy do you think they will be to achieve?

8a Rise of the rocket girls

Reading

1 Look at the title of the article and the photo. Discuss these questions with a partner. Then read the article and check your answers.

1 Who do you think the rocket girls were, and what did they do?
2 What do you think their ambition was?

2 Read the article again. Work in pairs. Correct the underlined words below using words from the article to make these sentences true.

1 The men who flew to the moon were more _experienced_ than the women engineers and mathematicians who helped them get there.
2 In the 1950s, "computers" were _machines_ who did mathematical calculations.
3 As time went on, the rocket girls started programming actual _scientists_.
4 The rocket girls worked _fixed_ hours at the lab.
5 The author Nathalia Holt hopes that we will see more women _astronauts_ in the future.

Word focus *make* and *do*

3 Look at the article again. Underline three expressions with the word *make* and two expressions with the word *do*. Then circle the correct options to complete the sentences below.

1 We usually use *make / do* to describe performing a repetitive task or an obligation.
2 We usually use *make / do* to describe producing or creating something.
3 We use *make / do* + an object pronoun (e.g., *something, it, that*).

4 Circle the correct verbs to complete these sentences.

1 Can I *do / make* a suggestion? Why don't we take turns *doing / making* the housework?
2 I want to *do / make* something to help them: something that will really *do / make* a difference.
3 I've *done / made* a note of all the things we need to set up and all the shopping we need to *do / make* before the party.
4 Their business is struggling. They're *doing / making* everything they can, but they're still not *doing / making* a profit.
5 I'm taking a very interesting evening class at the college, and I've *done / made* some good friends there.

Rise of the rocket girls

Everyone knows Buzz Aldrin, the famous astronaut. But how many of us have heard of Eleanor Francis Helin, an engineer behind numerous successful NASA space missions? Helin was part of a group of female
5 mathematicians working at NASA's Jet Propulsion Lab (JPL) in the 1960s. Nathalia Holt, the author of a book about these women—known as "rocket girls"—says, "If they hadn't worked on the lunar project, 'man' would not have reached the moon."

10 The rocket girls started out at JPL in the 1950s, having answered a job advertisement saying "Computers needed." They were called computers because, before today's digital devices, you needed humans to do mathematical calculations. And
15 the calculations had to be extremely accurate. If someone had made the smallest mistake, a spacecraft bound for the moon would still be traveling somewhere in outer space today, having missed its target entirely.

20 The rocket girls went from being "computers" to becoming the lab's first computer programmers and engineers. One of the group's early leaders, Macie Roberts, made the decision to hire only women, and this policy continued for the next thirty
25 years. They brought in many women who wanted to be engineers but didn't have the necessary qualifications. If anyone tried to employ only men or only women today, they wouldn't be allowed to. But Roberts made the work environment at the lab
30 special. The women formed close relationships and worked flexible hours to help each other balance home and professional lives. At the same time, they felt they were doing something really valuable. As a result, many women stayed on working at JPL for
35 thirty or forty years.

Holt says that if there were more women engineers today, she probably wouldn't have written the book. She hopes that the rocket girls will now get the recognition they deserve, and inspire a new
40 generation of female engineers.

Grammar second, third, and mixed conditionals

> ▶ **SECOND, THIRD, and MIXED CONDITIONALS**
>
> **Second conditional**
> 1 *If anyone **tried** to employ only men or only women today, they **wouldn't be** allowed to.*
>
> **Third conditional**
> 2 *If these women **hadn't worked** on the lunar project, "man" **would not have reached** the moon.*
>
> **Mixed second + third conditional**
> 3 *If there **were** more women engineers today, she probably **wouldn't have written** the book.*
>
> **Mixed third + second conditional**
> 4 *If someone **had made** a mistake, the spacecraft **would** still **be** somewhere in outer space today.*
>
> For more information and practice, see page 170.

5 Look at the grammar box. Circle the correct options to complete these explanations.

1 Sentence 1 describes a situation in the *present or future / past*. It refers to a(n) *real possibility / imagined situation*.

2 In sentence 2, the *if*-clause describes an imaginary situation in the *present / past*. The result it describes is in the *present / past*.

3 In sentence 3, the *if*-clause describes an imaginary situation in the *present / past*. The result it describes is in the *present / past*.

4 In sentence 4, the *if*-clause describes an imaginary situation in the *present / past*. The result it describes is in the *present / past*.

6 Work in pairs. Read the sentences (1–4). What type of conditional sentences are they? Complete the descriptions of the actual situations and the results.

1 If I were on a spaceship traveling to Mars, I would be worried that I might never come back.
This is a second conditional sentence.
I am not on a spaceship traveling to Mars, so I'm not worried that I might never come back.

2 If some of the engineers had been men, there wouldn't have been such a special working environment.
None of the engineers _____ , so _____ a special working environment.

3 If I had read Nathalia Holt's book, I would know all the facts about the rocket girls.
I _____ Nathalia Holt's book, so I _____ all the facts about the rocket girls.

4 If I were better at mathematics, I would have studied physics in college.
I _____ at mathematics, so I _____ physics in college.

7 Work in pairs. Form conditional sentences using the information in these sentences (1–6). Notice the time of each action or situation and result.

1 We live a long way from the city, so we don't see our friends very often.

2 I really didn't understand the movie, so I walked out before the end.

3 I'm not used to the cold weather, so I had to put on an extra sweater.

4 Taking a vacation is expensive because we have three children.

5 She did well on her law exams. Now she's working for a top legal firm.

6 I didn't call you back because I was waiting for another call.

8 Pronunciation contracted or weak forms

a ▶ 72 Complete these conditional sentences. Then listen and check your answers. Notice how the missing words are pronounced: as contracted forms or as weak forms.

1 If the rent _____ cheaper, I _____ take the apartment.

2 What would you _____ done if you _____ me?

3 So sorry! If I _____ known you were here, I _____ asked Jo to get you a coffee.

4 If she _____ stayed in college, she _____ now be a fully qualified journalist.

b Work in pairs. Practice saying the sentences from Exercise 8a.

9 Complete these sentences in your own words. Then compare your sentences with a partner.

1 If I hadn't had a good English teacher, perhaps I …

2 If I were more ambitious, perhaps I …

3 If I had studied … instead of … , I …

4 If I hadn't met … , I wouldn't …

Speaking myLife

10 Work in pairs. Think of one friend or family member who has achieved their ambition and one who has changed their ambition. Describe what has happened to them using at least two *if*-sentences.

*If my mother **hadn't taken** evening classes when we were young, she **wouldn't be** a nurse now.*

8b I wish I could …

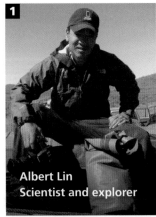

Albert Lin
Scientist and explorer

Laly Lichtenfeld
Big cat conservationist

Andrés Ruzo
Geologist

Alizé Carrère
Geographer

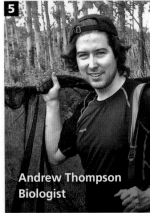

Andrew Thompson
Biologist

Catherine Workman
Conservation biologist

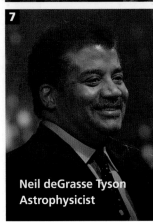

Neil deGrasse Tyson
Astrophysicist

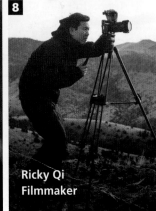

Ricky Qi
Filmmaker

Listening

1 Work in pairs. Look at the photos and captions of the National Geographic Explorers on the left. What do you think each job involves? Do any of the jobs interest you? Why or why not?

> ▶ **WORDBUILDING noun suffixes**
>
> We use certain suffixes when we talk about people who do particular jobs: *-er*, *-or*, *-ian*, *-ist*, *-ant*, e.g., *filmmaker*, *actor*, *politician*, *scientist*, *accountant*.
> Nowadays, we tend not to distinguish so much between male and female workers. For example, we say *police officer* rather than *policeman* or *policewoman*; or we use the male term for female roles, e.g., *actor* (not *actress*).
>
> For more practice, see Workbook page 67.

2 Look at the wordbuilding box. What are the job names from these verbs and nouns?

1 electricity _____
2 economics _____
3 to bake _____
4 to fight fires _____
5 law _____
6 to translate _____
7 history _____
8 reception _____
9 library _____
10 to consult about business _____

3 ▶ 73 The eight explorers in Exercise 1 were asked this question: "If you could have a superpower, what would it be?" Listen and take notes on which superpower each explorer wanted.

4 ▶ 73 Listen to the explorers again and complete these sentences (1–8).

If I had this power, …

1 I could see the world in the _____ way.
2 I could see the bigger _picture_ .
3 I could make people magically _____ me.
4 people couldn't _see_ me.
5 it would have saved me a lot of _earthmik_ .
6 I'd go and listen to what people were saying in the _conversation_ .
7 I would like to be able to turn [my power] _on / off_ .
8 that would be an _awesome_ superpower.

5 Work in pairs. What superpower would you like to have? What would you do if you had this power?

Grammar *wish* and *if only*

6 Work in pairs. Look at the grammar box. Are these statements true (T) or false (F)? If the statement is false, correct it.

1 The speakers in sentences 1 and 2 are talking about a past situation. T (F)
2 *If only* in sentence 2 has a weaker meaning than *wish*. T (F)
3 The speaker in sentence 3 is talking about a present situation. T (F)
4 The speaker in sentences 4 and 5 is talking about a present situation. (T) F
5 The speaker in sentences 4 and 5 wants someone else to act to change the situation. (T) F

7 Circle the correct verb forms to complete this person's wishes.

"I wish I ¹ *had / would have* a superhuman memory. You could say that would be a bad thing because you'd remember all the things you wish you ² *didn't do / hadn't done* or all the missed opportunities you wish ³ *you took / you'd taken*. Your life would be full of regrets. But I don't mean that I wish I ⁴ *remember / remembered* everything; I just wish I ⁵ *could remember / would remember* the things I didn't want to forget, like names, dates, and interesting facts."

8 Complete the sentences (1–6) with the correct form of the verbs in parentheses.

1 I wish I d learned _____ (learn) to play a musical instrument when I was younger.
2 Marta is very homesick. She wishes her mom would be here ____ (be) here with her.
3 I wish the weather wasn't _____ (not / be) so cold. Then we could eat outside.

4 Jerry wishes he hasn't gone _____ (not / go) out last night. He's too tired to work today.
5 I wish the builders next door would stop _____ (stop) making so much noise. I can't concentrate.
6 She has an amazing voice. If only I could sing _____ (can / sing) like that!

9 Read the notes in the box below. Then complete the sentences (1–4) using the words in parentheses as a guide.

Note that in affirmative sentences, we often use a comparative form.
I wish (something) were more …
In negative sentences, we often use *not so* + adjective.
I wish (something) weren't so …

1 Marta is very homesick. She wishes her mom _____ (not / be / far away).
2 I wish the weather _____ (be / warm).
3 I love Tokyo. I just wish it _____ (be / cheap).
4 I wish the builders next door _____ (not / be / noisy).

10 Pronunciation /ʃ/ **and** /tʃ/

a ▶ **74** Listen to six words. Circle the word you hear.

1	wish	which	4	shin	chin
2	shop	chop	5	wash	watch
3	cash	catch	6	shoes	choose

b Work in pairs. Take turns saying one word from each word pair in Exercise 10a. Your partner should decide which word they hear.

Speaking **my Life**

11 Work in pairs. Choose one of these situations or your own idea.

- a new job you have just started
- a new hobby or class you have just started

1 Make a list of all the potential problems (e.g., the boss shouts at everyone all the time, the work is boring).
2 Make at least five wishes about the situation. Use each of the forms in the grammar box at least once.

I wish my boss would stop shouting at everyone.
If only the work were more interesting.

12 Work with a new partner. Compare your wishes from Exercise 11. Were any of your ideas the same?

8c Saving Madagascar

Reading

1 Work in pairs. What do you know about the island of Madagascar: its people, its landscape, its wildlife, its industry?

2 Work in pairs. Read the article and answer the questions.

1 Which of Madagascar's natural resources is the author most worried about?
2 How is this resource collected, and where does it go from there?
3 How is Olivier Behra saving Madagascar's natural resources and making money at the same time? Give a few examples.

3 Circle the correct option (a, b, or c) to complete each sentence.

1 Most people in Madagascar are ___ .
   a very poor
   b very sad about their situation
   c becoming more politically active
2 To grow crops, Madagascans had to ___ .
   a clear the forest carefully
   b set fire to the forest
   c get government permission
3 As president, Marc Ravalomanana was particularly concerned about ___ .
   a protecting the environment
   b promoting tourism
   c improving international relations
4 A change in the law allowed people to ___ .
   a cut down hardwood trees
   b camp near hardwood trees
   c sell wood from fallen hardwood trees
5 For many Madagascans, cutting down rosewood trees is ___ .
   a easy and quick work
   b necessary to make furniture
   c against their beliefs
6 Other lighter trees are cut down to ___ .
   a build big ships
   b make medicines
   c transport the rosewood
7 The forest offers locals other ways to make money, such as ___ .
   a developing new medicines
   b taking tourists on guided walks
   c exporting flowers

Critical thinking emotive language

4 When writers feel very strongly about an issue, they often use strong or emotive language. Work in pairs. Find the emotive words or phrases that describe the following things.

1 how special a place Madagascar is (paragraph 1)
2 what a bad state the island is in (paragraphs 2 and 6)
3 how strongly ecologists feel about the situation (paragraph 3)
4 how impressive the hardwood trees are (paragraph 4)
5 how tough the work of cutting trees is (paragraph 5)
6 how badly rosewood trees are being treated (paragraph 5)

5 Do you think the writer's argument is strengthened by using this kind of language? Or would it be better to give a more objective argument? How would you rewrite the first paragraph to make it more objective? Discuss with a partner.

Vocabulary and speaking strong feelings *my*Life

6 Replace the words and phrases in **bold** below with these emotive words from the article.

| alarmed | back-breaking | bleak |
| majestic | unique | delight |

1 A lot of effort is being made to preserve this **individual** place.
2 You could see her **pleasure** when she was told she had gotten the job.
3 I was **worried** by the news that he was ill.
4 You get a beautiful view of the **tall and elegant** mountains.
5 Clearing the garden was really **physical and tiring** work.
6 With no prospect of a job, the future for many young people looks **hopeless**.

7 Think of a place that is very special and that you hope will be protected (e.g., a local green space or a traditional community). Write a short description of it (100–150 words) using emotive language. Then read your description to a partner.

1 At over 500,000 square kilometers, Madagascar is the world's fourth largest island. Although all islands have their own unique ecosystems, nature has given Madagascar incredible riches. Roughly ninety percent of
5 its animal and plant life is found nowhere else on the planet. Its carrot-shaped baobab trees and strange-looking lemurs
10 make even the most well-traveled visitor wide-eyed with amazement and delight.

Saving
Madagascar

2 But the island's beauty hides its desperate situation. The
15 average Madagascan lives on only a dollar a day, although you would not guess this from their cheerful optimism. Moreover, since the first humans arrived in Madagascar around 2,300 years ago, nearly ninety percent of the island's original forest has been lost—either cut down
20 for use as timber, or burned to create room for crops or cattle.

3 Alarmed ecologists identified Madagascar as a region in danger and demanded that the cutting and burning stop. In 2002, a new environmentally friendly president, Marc
25 Ravalomanana, was elected. But seven years later, he was replaced.

4 The new government made it legal to sell wood from hardwood[1] trees that had already been cut down or had fallen during storms. But it struggled to control the
30 loggers[2] who continue to rob the forests of wood from living trees. The main targets of this environmental crime are the rosewood tree and the ebony tree. The wood from these majestic trees is in high demand: to make expensive furniture, or as a valued material in the manufacture of
35 musical instruments.

5 The locals are caught in a trap. Poverty and the high value of rosewood—$3,000 per cubic meter—have driven them to cut down trees they traditionally believed to be sacred.[3] It is dangerous and back-breaking work. In a few
40 hours, they can bring down a tree that has stood tall for many centuries. Then they cut the trees into two-meter logs and drag them several kilometers to the nearest river. Rosewood trees are not the only victims. In order to transport
45 the heavy rosewood logs down the river, rafts[4] must be built from other wood. To make each raft, four or five lighter trees are cut down. All this disturbs the natural habitat of
50 the islands' animals and puts their survival at risk.

6 What can bring hope to this bleak landscape? One man's work may offer a possible route out of the darkness. Olivier Behra, who first came to Madagascar from France in 1987, believes that the only solution is to give local people
55 economic alternatives. He has persuaded the locals to stop cutting down trees in the Vohimana forest, and instead, to collect medicinal plants to sell to foreign companies. Meanwhile, he has trained the village lemur hunter to act as a guide for tourists who wish to photograph
60 lemurs. The same tourists also pay to visit the wild orchid conservatory that Behra has set up. Can small-scale actions like this compete with Madagascar's rosewood industry? Or will the government's promise to stop the illegal trade in rosewood come to anything? Only time
65 will tell.

[1]**hardwood** (n) /ˈhɑːrdˌwʊd/ a type of strong, hard wood from certain slow-growing trees, e.g., rosewood, ebony, and mahogany
[2]**logger** (n) /ˈlɒɡər/ a person who cuts down trees (as a job)
[3]**sacred** (adj) /ˈseɪkrɪd/ having important religious significance
[4]**raft** (n) /rɑːft/ a platform, often with no sides, used as a boat

8d Choices

Real life discussing preferences

1 Work in pairs. Which of these things are you generally choosy or picky about (careful about choosing)? Which are you easygoing about?

- the food you eat
- the movies you watch
- the clothes you wear
- the people you spend time with

2 ▶ 76 Listen to four short conversations. Complete the choices given by the first speaker in each conversation. Write which is the second speaker's preference (1 or 2) and why.

	Choice	Preference	Reason
1	1 ___drive___ 2 be driven	2	feels tired
2	1 pasta 2 _____	___	_____
3	1 walk in old town 2 _____	___	_____
4	1 Matt Damon movie 2 _____	___	more fun

3 ▶ 76 Work in pairs. Try to complete the expressions for discussing preferences. Then listen to the conversations again and check your answers.

> **▶ DISCUSSING PREFERENCES**
>
> **In general**
> I prefer driving ¹_____ being a passenger.
> I like simple food ²_____ spicy food.
>
> **On a specific occasion**
> I'd rather ³_____ to a museum.
> I'd rather you ⁴_____ , if you don't mind.
> If it ⁵_____ up to me, I' ⁶_____ say let's go to the festival.
> I think that ⁷_____ probably be more fun.
> OK. I'd prefer ⁸_____ do that, too.

4 Pronunciation *do you, would you*

▶ 77 Listen to these sentences. Notice how the pronunciation of the words in **bold** becomes merged. Practice saying the sentences in the same way.

1 **Do you** prefer coffee or tea?
2 **Would you** rather eat out tonight?
3 **Would you** rather he stayed at home?

5 Complete these questions with the correct form of the verbs in parentheses.

1 Would you prefer _____ (have) noisy neighbors or nosy neighbors?
2 Would you rather people _____ (give) you an honest opinion about your work or _____ (say) something nice about it?
3 Do you prefer _____ (give) presents or _____ (receive) them?
4 Would you rather _____ (be) talented and _____ (not / be) famous, or _____ (have) fame without being talented?
5 Would you rather your parents _____ (give) you a lot of money, or would you prefer _____ (earn) it yourself?

6 Work in pairs. Take turns asking and answering the questions in Exercise 5. Give reasons for your answers.

7 Think of choices or possibilities for the following situations. Then work in pairs and have short conversations like the ones in Exercise 2. Take turns being the first speaker.

- something to do on the weekend
- something to eat tonight
- somewhere to go on vacation

8e A wish for change

Writing an online comment

1 Work in pairs. Do you read the comments after online articles or blogs? Why or why not? Have you ever written a comment on another person's article or blog?

2 Work in pairs. Read the online comment below. Answer the questions.

1 Who wrote the comment, and what were they responding to?
2 Why did they write the comment?
3 Do you find the comment persuasive? Why or why not?

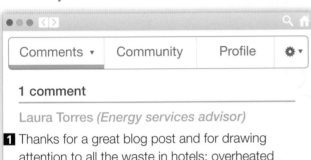

Comments ▾ | **Community** | **Profile** | ⚙▾

1 comment

Laura Torres *(Energy services advisor)*

1 Thanks for a great blog post and for drawing attention to all the waste in hotels: overheated rooms, lights that are left on all night, towels that are used once and then sent to the laundry. But why stop with hotels? It would be better to mention all the other examples of unnecessary waste in modern life.

2 Every morning, I walk down the street past stores with doors wide open, blowing hot air into the street. At night, I walk home past fully-lit office buildings, after the workers have already left; and past enormous flashing screens where advertisers try to outdo their competitors. At the supermarket, I take my frozen vegetables from a freezer that is completely open. My children leave their computers on when they go out and their phone chargers plugged in with no phone on the other end (though of course they should know better).

3 What can we do about it? Just wishing that people would act more responsibly is not enough. We would be better off if we were forced to act. Increasing the price of energy would be one idea. Another would be to make laws—just as we have traffic laws to make us drive safely—against wasting energy.

3 Work in pairs. How is the online comment organized? In which paragraph(s) (1–3) can you find the following?

a examples that illustrate the problem ____
b a recommendation or request for action ____
c a reference to the article it is commenting on ____
d a summary of the problem ____

4 Word focus *better*

Work in pairs. Underline the phrases in the online comment that use the word *better*. Match the phrases with their definitions (a–c).

a (of a person) have enough sense not to do something _____
b be in an improved situation (often financially) _____
c be more useful or desirable
_____

5 Writing skill giving vivid examples

a Work in pairs. What does the writer say about lights and towels in the first paragraph to illustrate her argument?

b Find five more examples of energy waste in the second paragraph.

6 Work in pairs. Look at this list of things that annoy some people about modern life. Complete the phrases to say what is annoying about each thing.

- magazines that …
  magazines that are full of news about celebrities
- trains that …
- cell phones that …
- TV shows about …
- supermarket food that …
- apps that …

7 Imagine you have read an article about one of the items in Exercise 6. Write a short online comment (120–150 words) on it.

8 Work in pairs. Exchange comments and compare what you have written. Use these questions to check your comments. Does your partner agree with the way you feel?

- Is the online comment well-organized?
- Does it give vivid examples?
- Is it persuasive?

What would you do if money didn't matter?

A woman meditating near a waterfall

Before you watch

1 Look at the title of the video. Write down your answer to the question on a piece of paper. Don't show it to anyone else yet.

2 Key vocabulary

a Work in pairs. Read the sentences (1–5). The words and phrases in **bold** are used in the video. Guess the meaning of the words and phrases.

1 I didn't really know what I wanted to do when I left school, so I used the **vocational guidance** service.
2 How do directors of companies **justify** having salaries of a million dollars or more?
3 There is no better surfer in the world—she's a **master** of her sport.
4 Anyone can achieve their ambition—they just have to focus on it and **desire** it enough.
5 He hates his job. He feels completely **miserable** going to the office every day.

b Write the words and phrases in **bold** in Exercise 2a next to their definitions (a–e).

a someone who does something very well _____
b service to help someone to find the right career _____
c very unhappy _____
d show or prove to be right or reasonable _____
e want something a lot _____

While you watch

3 ▣ **8.1, 8.2** Watch Parts 1–2 of the video. Work in pairs and answer the questions.

1 What is the key question the narrator mentions at the beginning and end of the video that we must all ask ourselves?
2 If we don't ask this question, how does the narrator say we will spend our lives?

4 ▣ **8.1** Read the summary below. Then watch Part 1 of the video again. Circle the correct options to complete the summary. Sometimes there is more than one answer.

The narrator often gives career advice to
¹ *his own children / interns / college students.* They say that if money wasn't important, they would be ² *painters / writers / comedians.* The narrator keeps questioning them until he has found something they ³ *are really good at / really want to do / find really fun,* and then he says do that. He says that just going after money is ⁴ *a waste of time / selfish / stupid.*

5 ▣ **8.2** Watch Part 2 of the video again. What did the narrator say about these things (1–4)? Take notes as you watch the video. Then compare notes with a partner.

1 a short life and a long life
2 what happens when you keep doing something you enjoy
3 whether other people will share your interests
4 what we are teaching our children

After you watch

6 Vocabulary in context

a ▣ **8.3** Watch the clips from the video. Choose the correct meaning of the words and phrases.

b Complete these sentences in your own words. Then share your sentences with a partner.

1 I haven't the faintest idea how to …
2 If you keep trying out different jobs, eventually …
3 I don't know how long I will go on …

7 Work in groups. Look at these comments about the video. Discuss what you think of each comment. Then write your own comment.

> **Carla P**
> It's an inspirational speech. It's saying that money doesn't bring happiness. But more important than that, it's saying you can be whatever you want to be.

> **Shinji**
> This is a nice idea, but it's not very practical. If everyone is painting and writing poetry and riding horses, who will drive the trains and work in the banks and offices?

> **Stefan**
> I like this, but I think there is a contradiction. He says money doesn't matter, but then he says if you become a master of something, you will earn money from it.

8 Work in pairs. Read aloud your answer from Exercise 1 and ask each other for more details about this. Has your idea about what you would do changed in any way since watching the video?

UNIT 8 REVIEW AND MEMORY BOOSTER

Grammar

1 Read this post on a travel website. What two things does the writer suggest taking on the trip?

It has always been my dream to visit Antarctica, and I was not disappointed when I did. I spent ten amazing days sailing on a ship from South America to Antarctica. I want to share some tips about what to take and what to leave at home. [1] **I regret not looking at this website before I left.** I would recommend packing light. [2] **I took too many clothes. I didn't know they had a good laundry service on board.** But do make sure to bring lots of waterproof and windproof clothing. I brought a thick, waterproof jacket with me, and I was glad I did. I wore it every day. [3] **It stopped me from getting cold and wet.** It can get quite rough at sea, so take seasickness tablets, too. The trip is well organized, and I'm sure you'll have a wonderful time if you go. My only complaint is that [4] **there should be more hiking at the parks,** so check with your tour guide if that's possible.

2 Work in pairs. Form conditional or *wish* sentences to express the same idea as the sentences in **bold** in the text above.

1 I wish I'd …
2 If I'd …, I …
3 I would have … if …
4 It would be better if …

3 **» MB** Work in pairs. Explain why the different grammatical forms are used in each pair of sentences below.

1 a I wish you lived closer.
   b I wish you would move back to the US.
2 a If I'd missed the plane, I would have been very upset.
   b If I'd missed the plane, I'd still be in Fiji.

I CAN	
make second, third, and mixed conditionals	
express wishes about the past and present	

Vocabulary

4 Circle the correct options to complete the sentences. Then discuss with a partner which of the sentences about the "rocket girls" are true.

1 They *did / made* tasks that computers now perform.
2 They *did / made* mathematical calculations.
3 If they *did / made* a small mistake in their calculations, it didn't usually matter.
4 They didn't *do / make* great friendships because they were focused on their work.
5 The head of NASA *did / made* the decision to hire only women.
6 They *did / made* a big difference to the NASA space program.

5 **» MB** Complete the phrases (1–4) using these emotive words. Then make a sentence with each phrase to say to your partner.

alarmed	back-breaking	delight	majestic

1 _____ work
2 the _____ on her face
3 he was _____ by the news
4 a(n) _____ animal

I CAN	
use *make* and *do* correctly	
identify and use emotive language	

Real life

6 Complete these exchanges with one word in each blank.

A: Would you [1]_____ eat out tonight or stay in?
B: I think I'd [2]_____ to stay in, if you don't [3]_____ .

C: I don't know if it [4]_____ be better [5]_____ quit my job now or wait until I've found another one.
D: I think you'd be better [6]_____ finding a new job first.

7 **» MB** Work in pairs. Talk about your own preferences. Make sentences with *I prefer* + verb/noun + *to* … Use the *-ing* form of the verb.

I prefer driving to being driven.

I prefer Japanese food to Italian food.

I CAN	
ask and talk about preferences	

Unit 9 The news

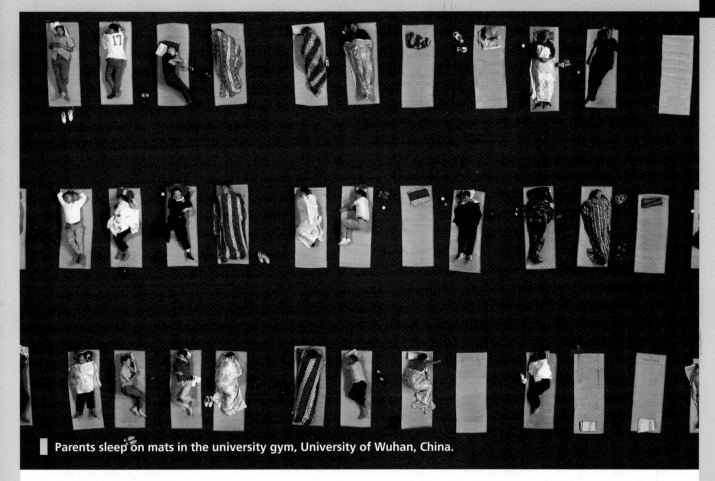

Parents sleep on mats in the university gym, University of Wuhan, China.

FEATURES

1 Work in pairs. Look at the photo and the caption. Why do you think these parents are sleeping here?

2 ▶ 78 Listen to a radio news report. Work in pairs and answer the questions.

1 Why did these parents stay overnight at the university?
2 Why did they sleep on the gym floor?
3 What do you think of the dedication of these parents?

3 Look at the pie chart below showing how US university students get their news. Discuss the questions with a partner.

1 How do most students get their news? Are you surprised?
2 Which category in the chart would you put yourself in?
3 What kind of news do you follow mostly?

- radio
- magazines
- television
- online or print newspapers
- Facebook/Twitter
- other websites
- I don't care about the news

9a A life revealed

Vocabulary reporting verbs

1 Work in pairs. Look at the sentences. Cross out ONE word that doesn't fit in each sentence. Then discuss the difference in meaning between the other two words.

1 "It was a mistake," they *denied / admitted / agreed*.
2 "Be careful," he *offered / advised / warned*.
3 "Could you please help me?" he *asked / persuaded / begged*.
4 "It's the best restaurant in town," they *claimed / complained / explained*.
5 "It's a great opportunity. Take it," he *recommended / urged / convinced*.
6 "I'll help you whatever happens," she *threatened / promised / swore*.

 79

Reading

2 Work in pairs. Look at the photo and discuss these questions. Then read the article and check your answers.

1 Have you seen either of the photos that the photographer is standing between?
2 Where are these two women from, and how old do you think they are?
3 What do you think is the relationship between these two women?

3 Work in pairs. How do you think Sharbat Gula felt when she learned how famous her photo is?

A LIFE REVEALED

She remembers the moment the photographer took her picture. The man was a stranger, but he had asked if he could, and she agreed to let him. She had never been photographed before, and until they met a second time—
5 seventeen years later—she would not be photographed again. The photographer, Steve McCurry, remembers the moment too. It was 1984, and he was reporting on the lives of Afghan refugees in a camp in Pakistan. She was living in the camp, and he admits thinking at the time that his
10 picture was nothing special. Yet the "Afghan girl" (below, left) became one of the most famous images of our time. The girl's intense expression warned us not to ignore the victims of war. In 2002, *National Geographic* persuaded McCurry to return to Pakistan to look for the girl. After
15 showing her photo around the refugee camp, he found a man who knew where to find her. The man offered to fetch her from her home in the Tora Bora mountains.

After three days, the man returned with Sharbat Gula, who was now around 29 years old. McCurry knew
20 at once that this (below, right) was her. Time and hardship had erased her youth, but her eyes still had the same intensity. Her brother explained the story of their lives. He blamed the war for forcing them and many other Afghans out of their homeland. Sharbat
25 had escaped to the mountains when she was a child, where she hid in caves and begged people to give her food and blankets. She married when she was sixteen, and now her time was occupied with bringing up her three children: cooking, cleaning, and caring for them.
30 Yet she did not complain about having had a hard life. More amazingly, she was not aware of the impact that her photo and her sea-green eyes had had on the world.

4 Work in pairs. Complete these sentences by finding the contrasting facts in the article.

1 In 1984, Sharbat Gula let McCurry take her picture, even though …
2 The picture became world famous, even though …
3 McCurry recognized 29-year-old Sharbat Gula immediately, even though …
4 Sharbat Gula did not complain about her life, even though …

Grammar verb patterns with reporting verbs

5 Find these verbs in the article. Underline them and the infinitive or *-ing* forms that follow them. How many different forms are there? Discuss with a partner.

agreed	admits	warned	persuaded
offered	blamed	begged	complain

▶ **VERB PATTERNS WITH REPORTING VERBS**

1 **verb + infinitive**
e.g., *promise, refuse, swear, threaten*
He refused to help me.

2 **verb + someone + infinitive**
e.g., *advise, ask, convince, encourage, invite, recommend, urge*
They invited us to stay.

3 **verb + -ing**
e.g., *deny, recommend, suggest*
I suggest waiting.

4 **verb + preposition + -ing**
e.g., *apologize for, confess to, insist on, object to*
He apologized for missing the meeting.

5 **verb + someone/something + preposition + -ing**
e.g., *accuse … of, criticize … for, congratulate … on, praise … for, forgive … for, thank … for*
She thanked me for supporting her.

For more information and practice, see page 172.

6 Work in pairs. Look at the grammar box. In which category (1–5) would you place each verb from Exercise 5?

7 Work in pairs. Discuss what the person actually said (or thought) at the time for each verb you underlined in Exercise 5. Then compare your answers with another pair.

She agreed to let him take her picture.
"Yes, you can take my picture."

8 Complete this text with the correct form of the verbs in parentheses. Add a preposition where necessary.

People often accuse photographers
¹ _____ (be) unethical when they take pictures without people's permission. A photographer who photographs someone in their living room with a telephoto lens cannot deny ² _____ (act) unethically—they have invaded the person's privacy. We often criticize journalists ³ _____ (do) this kind of thing. But is this the same as taking a picture of a stranger without them knowing? The person hasn't invited you ⁴ _____ (take) their picture. Perhaps they would feel uncomfortable if you asked them ⁵ _____ (pose) for a shot; they might even refuse ⁶ _____ (let) you do it. A lot of photographers insist ⁷ _____ (be) "invisible" so that the photos are more natural. They object ⁸ _____ (ask) their subjects for permission first because this would spoil the moment. However, I always advise photographers ⁹ _____ (talk) to their subjects first. In fact, I strongly recommend ¹⁰ _____ (get) to know the subjects' own stories, because then the photographs will have more meaning.

9 Work in pairs. Report these statements using the reporting verbs in parentheses. You may need to change other words (e.g., pronouns). Begin each sentence with *She*.

1 "I think you've been very brave." (praise)
She praised me for being very brave.
2 "You should consider a career in journalism." (encourage)
3 "He always puts his own interests first." (accuse)
4 "I'll look at your article when it's finished." (promise)
5 "I'm sorry I didn't introduce you to my boss." (apologize)
6 "I can lend you my camera, if you like." (offer)

Writing and speaking my Life

10 Choose one of these reporting verbs to write about something true that happened to you. Then read your brief story to a partner.

accuse	admit	apologize	complain
criticize	deny	encourage	warn
offer	thank	congratulate	

*I remember once at school, I was **accused of breaking** a window. I knew who had really done it, but I had promised not to say, so I was in a difficult situation!*

9b And finally …

Vocabulary positive adjectives

▶ **WORDBUILDING forming adjectives from verbs**

We can add -ing to many verbs to form adjectives that describe something that causes a particular feeling.
entertain ➙ *entertaining*, *move* ➙ *moving*

For more practice, see Workbook page 75.

1 Look at the wordbuilding box. News programs often like to end with a good-news story. Complete the sentences (1–4) with the correct adjective form of the verbs below.

amuse	astonish	charm
engage	inspire	

1 A(n) _____ story makes you smile or laugh.
2 A(n) _____ story shows you how much people can achieve.
3 A(n) _____ story makes you feel amazed or very surprised.
4 A(n) _____ or _____ story interests and pleases you.

2 Think of an example of a good-news story you have heard recently. Then work in pairs and tell your partner about it. Use one of the adjectives in Exercise 1.

*I saw a really **inspiring** local news story on TV about a five-year-old boy who raised money for his sick sister by …*

Listening

3 ▶ 80 Work in pairs. Look at the photo. What good-news story do you think is illustrated here? Then listen to the three news stories and make notes on each.

4 ▶ 80 Listen again and answer these questions.

Story 1 How was the Syrian man rewarded for his honesty?

Story 2 What record did the pizza makers set? Who did they give the pizza to?

Story 3 Who has Dr. Zhavoronkov been testing his drugs on, and with what results?

5 Work in groups and retell the three news stories. Which did you find the most inspiring/charming/astonishing?

Grammar passive reporting verbs

▶ **PASSIVE REPORTING VERBS**

***It* + passive reporting verb + *that* + subject**
1 *It is thought that the first Margherita pizza* was baked in Naples in 1889.

subject + passive reporting verb + infinitive
2 *The 25-year-old Syrian is believed to have been* in Germany for less than a year.
3 *Local police are* now **said to be looking** for the money's true owner.
4 *A Latvian scientist* based in the UK **is reported to be** close to finding …

For more information and practice, see page 172.

6 Work in pairs. Look at the grammar box on page 108. Do we know who is doing the thinking, believing, etc., in each sentence?

7 Look at sentences 2–4 in the grammar box. Which sentence contains:

a   a simple infinitive? ____
b   a continuous infinitive? ____
c   a perfect infinitive? ____

8 Work in pairs. Rephrase sentences 2–4 in the grammar box using *It* + passive reporting verb + *that* + subject.

2   It is believed that the 25-year-old Syrian has …
3   It is said that the …
4   It is …

9 Rewrite these sentences using passive reporting verbs.

1   People think that the man is from the Homs area of Syria.
    The man is _____ .

2   People say that the man is taking language lessons and planning further studies.
    The man is _____ .

3   The police confirmed that the man will receive a financial reward.
    It was _____ .

4   Some people claim that the Margherita pizza originated in Naples, Italy.
    It is _____ .

5   People don't generally believe that drugs can prevent aging.
    It is _____ .

10 Rewrite these sentences. Change the passive reporting verbs from one structure to the other.

1   Costa Rica is said to be the happiest country in the world.
    It _____ .

2   Frank was known to have been a gifted musician at school.
    It _____ .

3   It is known that laughing regularly increases life expectancy.
    Laughing regularly _____ .

4   It was thought that he had given up hope of ever seeing his family again.
    He _____ .

11 Complete the good-news story below using these passive reporting verbs and infinitives.

is known	it is now thought
it was demonstrated	to be
to be getting	to have stopped

And finally … Despite all the warnings about a growing hole in the world's ozone layer, ¹_____ that the hole may be shrinking. The ozone layer in the atmosphere ²_____ to protect us from the sun's radiation, since it absorbs ultraviolet rays. However, in the 1970s, ³_____ that this layer was becoming thinner and thinner, and that there was even a hole over the Antarctic. CFC gases in refrigerators and aerosol were said ⁴_____ the main reason for this. Consequently, many people urged governments to ban the use of these gases. Their efforts were successful, and the use of CFCs is believed ⁵_____ by the mid-1990s. Now, new research has shown that the ozone hole has shrunk by four million square kilometers. What's more, the ozone layer itself is thought ⁶_____ thicker again. This is good news for the planet, and for all of us who enjoy spending time in the sun.

Speaking myLife

12 Work in groups of three to prepare a good-news story. Choose one of the headlines below or your own idea. Write a good-news story, using at least one passive reporting verb. Then each person should share their story with a new group.

- Woman rescued from fire by pet
- Valuable painting found under bed
- Ten-year-old child compared to Shakespeare
- New clothing fabric invented
- Couple celebrate 80th wedding anniversary
- Dentist that people actually enjoy visiting

And finally, a woman was rescued from her burning house yesterday by her cat. **It is believed that the fire** *started shortly after midnight, on the first floor of the house. …*

9c From hero to zero

Reading

1 The headlines below are about a British Airways (BA) pilot. Look at these headlines in the order they appeared in the newspapers over several months. Then work in pairs and discuss what you think happened.

HERO BA PILOT PETER BURKILL SPEAKS: I THOUGHT WE'D DIE IN HEATHROW CRASH

"I AM NOT A HERO,"
SAYS BA CRASH PILOT CAPTAIN PETER BURKILL

REAL HERO OF BA FLIGHT 38 IS CO-PILOT JOHN COWARD

HERO PILOT "FORCED OUT OF BA"

FALLEN HERO: THAT DAY CHANGED MY LIFE FOREVER

OFFICIAL REPORT SAYS ICE FAULT CAUSED BA AIRPORT CRASH

2 Work in pairs. Read the story on page 111 quickly. Then discuss the sequence of key events with your partner. Does the story differ from your answer in Exercise 1? If so, how?

3 Read the article again. Are these statements true (T) or false (F)?

1	Some passengers were badly hurt during landing.	T	F
2	Burkill was unmarried at the time of the accident.	T	F
3	Burkill's crew read BA's internal report.	T	F
4	Burkill was praised in the AAIB report.	T	F
5	Other airlines refused to hire Burkill after he left BA.	T	F

4 Complete these sentences with appropriate words or phrases from the article.

1 Burkill went from being a hero to being a _____ (opposite of hero). (paragraph 1)
2 Perhaps Burkill's colleagues believed he wasn't _____ (good at his job). (paragraph 3)
3 The press claimed Burkill had _____ (failed) the people he was supposed to be responsible for. (paragraph 3)
4 After the official report was published, Burkill was _____ (given as a prize) a medal for his actions. (paragraph 6)

Critical thinking different perspectives

5 Work in pairs. Make notes to complete the chart about the event described on page 111. Which of these people would you have believed? Why?

People involved	Their initial view on the accident and Burkill's role in it	Motivation for taking this view
Peter Burkill	*took a risk but it worked—the rest was luck*	*did what any captain would have done*
BA staff		—
BA management		
the press		

Word focus *word*

6 Find these phrases in the article. What do you think they mean? Discuss with a partner.

1 **Word** went around (paragraph 3)
2 his **word** against that of the press (paragraph 3)
3 No **word** of it (paragraph 4)
4 had the last **word** (paragraph 7)

7 Work in pairs. What do these other expressions with *word* mean?

1 "When my husband handed me the keys to a new car for my birthday, I was **at a loss for words**."
2 "The hotel doesn't advertise at all. It just relies on **word of mouth** to get new customers."
3 "I can't believe the mayor is closing the library. He **gave his word** that he wouldn't."

Speaking *my*Life

8 Work in groups. Discuss these questions about the media in your country.

1 How respectful are journalists toward politicians?
2 How balanced is the reporting of public scandals?

FROM HERO TO ZERO

▶ 81

In January 2008, hours after saving his plane from crashing at Heathrow Airport, flight captain Peter Burkill was praised as a hero. Only days later, when reports appeared in the press accusing him of freezing at the controls, he became a villain.
5 How did this extraordinary transformation come about?

Peter Burkill was the pilot on British Airways (BA) Flight 38 from Beijing, carrying 152 people on board. But 35 seconds before landing at Heathrow, two of the plane's engines failed. With the plane losing height fast, Burkill asked his
10 co-pilot, John Coward, to take the controls while he himself adjusted the wing flaps to help the plane reach the runway. It was a risky decision, but it worked. The plane narrowly missed some houses and landed heavily on the grass just short of the runway. After a few hundred meters, the plane
15 miraculously came to a stop without turning over. The passengers escaped without serious injury. As far as Burkill was concerned, he had done what any captain would have done—the rest was luck.

However, this was not the version of events that BA's staff
20 heard in the following days. Word went around that rather than taking control of the plane, Burkill had panicked. The suggestion was that he was not competent to fly a plane. Some newspapers, seeing the chance to sell more copies, picked up the story, claiming that John Coward was the
25 real hero. They published details of Burkill's past, painting a picture of a well-paid pilot who lived the life of a playboy. But—when it had mattered most, it was suggested—he had let down his crew and passengers. Worse still for Burkill, it wasn't even his word against that of the press. Afraid of
30 bad publicity, BA banned him from speaking about the events until an independent investigation by the Air Accidents Investigation Branch (AAIB) was complete.

Overnight, Burkill's life changed. Before
35 the accident, he had had everything: a great job, a beautiful home, a loving wife, and the respect of his colleagues. Now he felt betrayed and desperate. The stress put enormous pressure on his family, and Burkill
40 became depressed. He begged the company to issue a statement to clear his name, but they refused, preferring to wait for the results of the official investigation. Even though BA's own internal report cleared
45 him of any wrongdoing, it was only read by senior management. No word of it reached Burkill's colleagues, and

rumors started going around that crew members were afraid to fly with him. He wrote to BA's chief executive
50 asking for help, but got no reply.

When the official AAIB report was finally published in February **5**
2009, it concluded that ice in the fuel system had been the cause of the problem, and that the actions of the crew had saved the lives of all on board. In particular, it praised Captain
55 Burkill's decision to change the wing flap settings.

The pilots and the air crew were awarded the British Airways **6**
Safety Medal, and the story of Peter Burkill, the hero, once again made the headlines. But the damage had been done. In August 2009, Peter Burkill left the company that he had
60 served for 25 years. He began applying for jobs with other airlines, but he was not invited to a single interview.

So did his critics win? No. Burkill himself had the last word. **7**
BA said that he was always welcome in the company, and in September 2009 they asked him to come back and fly for
65 them. Burkill accepted.

Captain Peter Burkill (right), with John Coward

9d Spreading the news

Real life reporting what you have heard

1 Work in pairs. Below are three common topics that people like to gossip about. Can you think of a recent piece of gossip that you have heard from any of these categories? Tell your partner.

- money and status
- celebrities' lives
- people's character and reputation

2 ▶ 82 Work in pairs. Listen to two conversations. Which category of gossip does each conversation fall into?

3 Work in pairs. Discuss the questions.

Conversation 1
1 What has happened to Liam, the man they are talking about?
2 Why are the speakers surprised about this news?

Conversation 2
3 What do they say has happened to Dr. Harris and why?
4 Do we know if the gossip about him is true?

4 ▶ 82 Look at the expressions for reporting what you have heard. Use the expressions to complete these sentences from the conversations. Then listen again and check your answers.

Conversation 1
1 **A:** By the way, _____ Liam?
   _____ , he's been promoted. …
   _____ Sarah, he's been given the job of area manager.
   B: Area manager? I _____ ! He's not even that good at his current job.
2 **A:** Sarah also reckons that he's going to get a huge pay raise.
   B: Well, I'd take that _____ . I don't think the company has that kind of money to throw around at the moment.

Conversation 2
3 **C:** Well, _____ that he was fired from his job yesterday.
   _____ that he's not even a real doctor.
   D: What? Who told you that?
   C: Tara.
   D: Hmm, I wouldn't take _____ of what Tara says. She _____ things.

5 Pronunciation the schwa

a ▶ 83 Unstressed syllables often produce the schwa sound /ə/. Listen to these examples and repeat. The stressed syllable (not a schwa) is underlined.

/ə/ /ə/   /ə/ /ə/
apparently   supposedly

b ▶ 84 Underline the stressed syllable in each of these words. Then listen and check. Notice how the schwa sound appears in the unstressed syllables.

according	generally	happened
information	proportion	surprisingly

c Work in pairs. Practice saying the words in Exercise 5b.

6 You are going to spread news around the class. Follow these steps:

- Work in pairs. Tell your partner two facts (one true, one false) about yourself or something you did, or two facts (one true, one false) about someone famous.
- Mingle with other students in the class and tell them the facts you heard from your partner. (Speak to at least three people.)
- Return to your partner and report the facts you heard from the other students.
- Discuss which ones you think are true. Use the expressions for reporting what you have heard.
- Tell the class what you thought and see if you were right.

> ▶ **REPORTING WHAT YOU HAVE HEARD**

Did you hear about …?
I heard/read the other day that …
Someone told me that …
According to (somebody), …
It seems that …
Apparently/Supposedly, …

Expressing belief and disbelief
That doesn't surprise me.
I can believe it.
I'd (I wouldn't) take his/her word for it.
They generally get their facts right.

I don't believe it.
He/She tends to exaggerate things.
I'd take that with a grain of salt.
I wouldn't take too much notice of what he/she says.

9e News story

Writing a news article

1 Read the newspaper article. Work in pairs and answer these questions.

1 What problem does the article describe?
2 What solution is being proposed?
3 Who might not be happy about this solution?

2 Read the newspaper article again. How is it structured? Complete the notes (1–5) using functions a–e below.

Headline: ¹_____
First short paragraph: ²_____
Second paragraph: ³_____
Third paragraph (optional):
⁴_____ or gives other relevant facts
Final paragraph:
states how the story ends, ⁵_____ , or gives an alternative side to the story

a gives the details of the story
b what is likely to happen next
c catches the reader's attention
d introduces the key information (e.g., location, the people involved)
e includes a comment or quotation about the events

3 Writing skill using quotations

a Look at the sentences (1–3). Then circle the correct options to complete the rules (a–d).

1 The head of the investigation said, "We haven't even started to write our report."
2 "Don't wait for me," she said with a smile.
3 "And what," he asked, "is the solution?"

a If the quotation is a complete sentence, always begin it with a *small* / *capital* letter.
b Always put the final punctuation of the quotation *inside* / *outside* the quotation marks.
c If the quotation is followed by a phrase like "he said" or "she asked," put a comma *before* / *after* the final quotation mark.
d If a phrase like "he said" or "she asked" comes before the quotation, put a comma *before* / *after* the opening quotation mark.

b Work in pairs. How would you rewrite these sentences with the correct punctuation?

1 Shall we eat Grandma he asked
2 I know exactly what he said she said
3 That's very kind she said but I can manage

A police officer on patrol in Bangkok

Bangkok bans illegal street racing

The military government in Thailand has issued new rules to stop street racing and to rein in teenage motorcycle racers.

Young motorcycle street racers—called *dek wan*—have drawn complaints over the years for their reckless riding in large groups. They often don't wear helmets, and many of them have been killed or involved in road accidents. Under the strict new laws, any person found guilty of possessing, selling, or modifying a motorcycle for street racing will face a six-month jail sentence and/or a US$600 fine. Their business licenses could also be revoked.

"Parents of teenage racers could face punishment as well," said the head of police. If their children violate the ban on street racing twice, the parents face three months in jail and/or a US$1,000 fine.

Authorities hope that these new laws will help control illegal street racing and lead to improved road safety in Thailand.

4 Write a short news article (150–170 words) for one of the following headlines. Use at least one quotation.

- Child's stroller given parking ticket
- Man takes wrong plane home
- Meeting to discuss shorter meetings runs out of time
- Burglar takes selfie with stolen phone

5 Exchange articles with a partner. Use these questions to check your partner's article.

- Does the article include a short first paragraph that gives the main idea or key information?
- Does the rest of the article use the structure described in Exercise 2?
- Do the quotations use the correct punctuation?

News: the weird and the wonderful

A humpback whale dives beneath the ocean, Tonga, South Pacific.

Before you watch

1 Work in pairs. You're going to watch two good-news stories. Look at the photo and the caption. What do you think the good-news story on humpback whales is about?

2 Key vocabulary

a Work in pairs. Read the sentences (1–6). The words and phrases in **bold** are used in the video. Guess the meaning of the words and phrases.

1 He has been **ruthless** in his career, pushing other people aside in his ambition to get to the top.
2 She **swiped at** the wasp with her hand.
3 Lions are not afraid to attack **prey**—like buffalo—that are larger than them.
4 I had chicken pox when I was a child, so I'm **immune to** it now.
5 I'm sorry. I dropped a spoon in my coffee and made it **splash** over the tablecloth.
6 I like to **dip** cookies in my tea and then eat them.

b Write the words and phrases in **bold** in Exercise 2a next to their definitions (a–f).

a cause a liquid to fall or hit something in a noisy or messy way _____
b made a swinging movement with the arm or hand _____
c put something in liquid for a short time _____
d not affected by something (e.g., an illness) _____
e animals that are hunted and killed by other animals for food _____
f not caring who you hurt as long as you get what you want _____

While you watch

3 ▭◀ **9.1, 9.2** Work in pairs. You are going to see two very different good-news stories. Watch and then:

1 say which story you think is "weird" and which is "wonderful."
2 write a headline for each story.

4 ▭◀ **9.1** Work in pairs. Read the questions below. Then watch the first news story again. Discuss the answers to the questions with your partner.

1 What adjectives are used to describe humpback whales?
2 What other species do they protect?
3 What adjectives are used to describe orcas?
4 How do the humpbacks fight off the orcas?
5 What benefit do humpbacks receive from protecting other species?

5 ▭◀ **9.2** Watch the second news story again. Circle the correct options to complete the statements.

1 Khan discovered his ability to handle hot oil when a *squirrel / monkey* dropped a *banana / mango* into his wok from a tree above, and the oil splashed all over his body.
2 The tourist describes Khan's ability as *inspiring / unbelievable*.
3 The tourist *thinks he knows / has no idea* how Khan can do this.
4 Khan's accident has actually helped his *sales / confidence*.

After you watch

6 Vocabulary in context

a ▭◀ **9.3** Watch the clips from the video. Choose the correct meaning of the words and phrases.

b Complete these sentences in your own words. Then share your sentences with a partner.

1 It has recently come to light that …
2 I am really put off when I see …
3 … is in a vulnerable situation because …

7 Work in groups. Discuss which news story interested you more and why. What else would you like to know about each news story?

8 ▭◀ **9.1** Work in pairs. Watch the first news story again and provide the narration for it. Follow these steps:

- Watch the video with the sound OFF. Discuss what you think the narrator was saying at each point.
- Decide how you will divide the narration between the two of you.
- Watch the video with the sound OFF again and provide the narration.

9 Work in groups of four and act out the second news story. Follow these steps:

- Decide on your roles: a) the narrator, b) Khan, c) the tourist visiting the stall, d) the director.
- Discuss what you are going to say and what the cues are for each speaker to speak.
- Try acting out the news story, with the director giving advice as necessary.
- Perform your version to another group.

UNIT 9 REVIEW AND MEMORY BOOSTER

Grammar

1 Complete this good-news story with the correct verb pattern (passive, infinitive, preposition + *-ing*, etc.) of the verbs in parentheses.

A seven-year-old boy has been found alive and well in a forest in northern Japan, five kilometers from where he is said ¹ _____ (go) missing a week ago. Yamato Tanooka had been missing since Saturday. It ² _____ (believe) that he got out of the family car on a mountain road after arguing with his parents. Soon after getting lost, Yamato found a military shelter in the forest where he stayed until he was found. Police said that he was lucky because there ³ _____ (know) ⁴ _____ (be) bears in the forest. It is not clear if Yamato had food, but the shelter had beds and safe drinking water. "He did the right thing," said a police spokesperson. Soldiers who found the boy praised him ⁵ _____ (keep) calm and ⁶ _____ (not / panic).

2 Which of these things do we know to be true (T)? Which are false (F)? Which are possibly true (PT)?

1 Yamato was missing for two days. ____
2 Yamato came across a bear in the forest. ____
3 Yamato was able to get food at the shelter. ____
4 Yamato had access to safe drinking water at the shelter. ____

3 ≫ **MB** Work in pairs. Use a reporting verb or a passive reporting verb to make two sentences about what you think Yamato did after he was found.

I CAN	
use the correct verb patterns with reporting verbs	
use passive reporting verbs	

Vocabulary

4 Circle the correct options to complete these sentences.

1 Don't just *have / take* my word for it. I *persuade / suggest* trying it out for yourself.
2 She accused him *of / for* taking her car without permission, but he *denies / refuses* it. No one else was there, so it's her word *against / over* his.
3 It's such a terrible decision that I'm almost at a loss *for / without* words. I'm going to *threaten / urge* him to reconsider. I hope I can *warn / convince* him to change his mind.

5 ≫ **MB** Work in pairs. Answer the questions about these people from the news stories in Unit 9.

1 What did Sharbat Gula agree to let Steve McCurry do?
2 What was the pilot Peter Burkill accused of?

I CAN	
use a range of reporting verbs	
use expressions with *word*	

Real life

6 Decide if the speaker is expressing belief or disbelief. Write *B* for belief or *D* for disbelief.

1 I'd take that figure with a grain of salt. ____
2 I think newspapers often tend to exaggerate these things. ____
3 Well, they generally get their facts right. ____
4 I think we can take the organizer's word for it. ____
5 I wouldn't take much notice of what the promoters say. They just want publicity. ____

7 ≫ **MB** Write down a recent claim someone has made in the news (e.g., *Apparently, …*). Then work in small groups. Take turns reading aloud each claim and responding using expressions of belief or disbelief.

I CAN	
comment on stories and rumors, express belief and disbelief	

Unit 10 Talented people

A mahout leads his elephant, Havelock Island, India.

FEATURES

1 Match these words with their definitions (a–f).

| background | experience | qualifications |
| qualities | skills | talents |

a strong natural abilities _____
b abilities developed by practice _____
c (generally positive) characteristics _____
d certificates that show you have learned something _____
e what you've done in your life _____
f your past in general (where you come from, where you studied, etc.) _____

2 Work in pairs. Look at the photo and the caption. What qualities, skills, qualifications, and experience do you think mahouts need to do their job well?

3 ▶ 85 Listen to a description of a mahout's job. Compare the description with your answers in Exercise 2.

4 Make short notes about your own background, experience, talents, etc. Then work in pairs. Take turns asking and answering questions with your partner.

What qualifications do you have?

10a An ordinary man

Listening and reading

1 ▶ 86 Work in pairs. Look at the photo. Can you answer these questions? Then listen and check.

1 What does this photo show?
2 Who do you think the person in the photo is?
3 What quotation is associated with this event?

2 Work in pairs. Read the article. What were Neil Armstrong's qualities? Give reasons for your answers.

3 Read the article again. Work in pairs and answer the questions.

1 Why do you think Neil Armstrong was called "the ultimate professional"?
2 How did he gain his experience of flying?
3 What motivated Armstrong?
4 What is meant by "the rest … is history"?
5 What did Armstrong do to avoid publicity after the Apollo 11 mission?

Vocabulary careers

> ▶ **WORDBUILDING verb (+ preposition) + noun collocations**
>
> When you learn a new noun, try to note also the verb(s) that collocate with it and any prepositions that follow the verb.
> *pursue a career*
> *graduate from high school / college*
>
> For more practice, see Workbook page 83.

4 Work in pairs. Find verbs (+ prepositions) in the article that collocate with each of these nouns, and complete phrases 1–5.

1 to _pursue_ a career
2 to _graduate_ from a school or college
3 to _take_ a course
4 to _become_ an astronaut
5 to _get_ , _apply_ , _do_ a job

▶ 87

Neil Armstrong, the most famous of the astronauts on the spacecraft Apollo 11, has been called the ultimate professional. He was hired to do a job. He did the job, and then he went home and kept quiet about it. In forty years, he
5 only gave two interviews. But how could the man who first set foot on the moon remain such a mystery?

Armstrong pursued a career that came from a passion for flying that he developed as a child in the 1930s. He learned to fly before he had graduated from high school, and then
10 took a course in aerospace engineering in the US. After that, he served for three years as a pilot in the US Navy, flying 78 missions in the war in Korea. He left the navy in 1952 and got a job with the Lewis Flight Propulsion Laboratory, where he flew experimental aircraft. He reached speeds of 6,600
15 kilometers an hour, and altitudes of over 60 kilometers.

It is not clear when Armstrong decided to become an astronaut, but it was never his ambition to be famous. His aim was simply to push the limits of flight. In 1962, news came that NASA was looking for astronauts for its Apollo program.
20 Incredibly excited, he applied for the job and was accepted. The rest, as they say, is history.

When he and the other astronauts returned from the Apollo 11 moon landing in July 1969, Armstrong was a worldwide celebrity. He could have done anything he wanted. Instead, he
25 became a teacher and also worked for an avionics[1] firm. On the weekends, he went flying to get away from all the attention.

Armstrong retired in 2002, ten years before his death. He had fulfilled his dream, but he did not feel any more special than the others who worked on the Apollo space program. He was
30 just the pilot.

An ORDINARY man

[1]**avionics** (n) /ˌeɪviˈɒnɪks/ electronic equipment used in flying

Grammar articles

▶ **ARTICLES: *A/AN*, *THE*, or ZERO ARTICLE?**

Indefinite article: *a/an* (+ singular countable noun)
*It is not clear when he decided to become **an astronaut**.*

Definite article: *the* (+ singular/plural countable noun or uncountable noun)
*He and **the other astronauts** returned from the Apollo 11 moon landing.*

Zero article (+ plural countable noun or uncountable noun)
*He learned to fly before he had graduated from **high school**.*

For more information and practice, see page 174.

5 Look at the grammar box. Complete these statements (1–3) with the correct type of article (*a/an*, *the*, or write "zero article").

1 We use ___a / an___
   • to talk about one person or thing in general.
   • to say a person or thing is one of many.
   • when we first mention something.
2 We use ___zero___
   • to talk about people or things in a general way.
   • before certain generally familiar places (school, work, hospital, college).
3 We use ___the___
   • to talk about a specific person/people or thing(s).
   • when we refer back to a person/people or thing(s) already mentioned.
   • before a superlative adjective.

6 Work in pairs. Read the first paragraph of the article again. Look at the articles and nouns (1–8) in **bold**. Which of the uses in Exercise 5 does each one match?

> Neil Armstrong, [1] **the most famous** of [2] **the astronauts** on the spacecraft Apollo 11, has been called the ultimate professional. He was hired to do [3] **a job**. He did [4] **the job**, and then he went [5] **home** and kept quiet about it. In forty years, he only gave two interviews. But how could [6] **the man** who first set foot on [7] **the moon** remain such [8] **a mystery**?

7 Find and underline an example in the article of each of the following:

1 zero article with:
   (a) a subject of study   b a country
   c a month
2 *the* with:
   (a) a period of time   b a country
   c a research lab

8 Complete the sentences. Use *the* or leave blank where no article is needed.

1 Where I live in __Ø__ New Zealand, __the__ weather is pretty nice.
2 He's thinking about joining __the__ police force after he graduates from __Ø__ college.
3 On __Ø__ weekend, I often play __Ø__ tennis or go for a run first thing in __the__ morning. Then I come back and have __Ø__ breakfast.
4 A survey showed that in __the__ US, __the__ most people go to __Ø__ bed at around 11:00 in __the__ evening and get up at __Ø__ 7:30 in __the__ morning.
5 I need to go to __the__ store and get some food before I go __Ø__ home tonight.

9 Complete the sentences. Use *a*, *an*, or *the*, or leave blank where no article is needed.

1 Armstrong could fly __a__ plane before he could drive __a__ car.
2 As __a__ boy, Armstrong played __a__ baritone horn, but he wasn't __a__ very good musician.
3 In __Ø__ Korea, one of __the__ wings on Armstrong's plane broke off and he had to eject.
4 __The__ first meal that __Ø__ they ate on __Ø__ moon was __a__ bacon and __a__ peaches.
5 Armstrong was __the__ member of __the__ team that investigated __Ø__ *Challenger* space shuttle disaster.

10 Pronunciation linking vowels

▶ 88 A /w/ or /j/ sound often links a word that ends with a vowel sound to the next word that begins with a vowel sound. Work in pairs. Listen and say which sound links the two words in 1–5 below. Then practice saying the phrases.

1 the‿ultimate professional
2 to do‿a job
3 she‿understood me perfectly
4 he‿only gave two interviews
5 a hero‿of our time

Speaking *my*Life

11 Work in pairs. Describe the path of your own career or the career of someone you know. Use these stages and try to use articles correctly.

> interests as a child → school subjects → early jobs → college or classes taken → other experiences → important events → future ambitions

As a child, I was very interested in drawing and painting. At school, I loved art and I had a fantastic art teacher.

10b The real-life Batman?

Listening

1 Work in pairs. Look at the photo and the caption. Discuss these questions.

1 What do you know about bats?
2 What is the man in the photo doing? Is it anything unusual?

2 ▶89 Listen to a description of Daniel Kish. How did he get his nickname? Discuss with a partner.

3 ▶89 Circle the correct options to complete the summary. Then listen again and check your answers.

Daniel Kish has been blind from ¹ *birth /
a young age*. He taught himself to recognize
how near objects are by clicking his ² *tongue /
fingers* and then listening for an echo. Using this
technique, he can ride a bicycle, go hiking in the
countryside, and play ³ *ball games / board games*.
He can "see" a house from a distance of about
⁴ *ten / fifty* meters. Using echolocation actively is a
skill you can learn in just ⁵ *a couple of days /
a month*. Kish ⁶ *likes / is offended by* his nickname.

4 Work in pairs. The speaker mentions an example of when echolocation could be useful for fully sighted people. What is it?

Vocabulary the senses

5 Complete the descriptions (1–4) with these five senses. Then compare your answers with a partner.

sight	hearing	touch	smell	taste

1 Eagles have an amazing sense of _____ and can spot small animals from high up. Rhinoceroses, on the other hand, are incredibly nearsighted.
2 Cats have sensitive noses, but, strangely, a poor sense of _____ . They can't recognize if something is sweet.
3 Dogs have a very keen sense of _____ . They can detect scents that would be impossible for humans to trace. They hear better than humans too, although some dogs go deaf or become hard of _____ when they are older.
4 People used to think crabs were basically numb— that they had no sense of _____ . But a recent experiment showed that crabs reacted negatively to small electric shocks.

6 Find words in Exercise 5 that mean the following:

a unable to see far _____
b unable to hear anything _____
c unable to feel anything in the body _____

7 Work in pairs. What other animals can you think of that have one very strong or weak sense?

Daniel Kish, the real-life Batman

Grammar relative clauses

▶ RELATIVE CLAUSES

Defining relative clause
1 *Kish clicks his tongue and then listens for the echo **that comes back.*** ~~Can not remove be is not is~~
2 *He can do many things **that blind people cannot** ordinarily do.*
3 *"The real-life Batman" is a description **he welcomes.***
4 *He is amused by the nickname **for which he is now famous.***

Non-defining relative clause
5 *Daniel Kish, **who has been blind since he was a year old**, taught himself to "see."*
6 *A wooden fence, **whose surface is softer than brick**, gives a "warmer" echo.*

what ...
7 *He just loves **what** he is doing.*

For more information and practice, see page 174.

8 Look at the grammar box. Work in pairs and answer these questions.

1 Which type of relative clause (defining) or non-defining) contains essential information? Extra information?
2 If you put a relative pronoun in sentence 3, what and where would it be? *that / which*
3 Can you leave out the relative pronoun in sentences 1 and 2? Why or why not?
4 Which relative pronoun means "the thing(s) that"? *what*
5 In sentence 4, we can also say … *the nickname he is now famous for.* Which version sounds more formal? *Sent. 4*
6 Which relative pronoun is used for possession? *whose*

9 Work in pairs. Look at the relative pronouns in **bold** in track 89 of the audioscript on page 188. What does each **bold** word refer to?

1 who = Daniel Kish

10 Write definitions of these people and things (1–6) using defining relative clauses. Then compare your sentences with a partner.

1 Batman is a character …
   *Batman is a character **who** first appeared in a comic.*
2 Daniel Kish is a man …
3 A blind person is someone …
4 Echolocation is a technique …
5 A click is a sound …
6 Bats are animals …

11 Circle the correct relative pronoun to complete these sentences (1–6).

1 Ancient history is not a subject *that / whose / about which* I know much about.
2 The Queen, *which / who / that* will celebrate her ninetieth birthday this year, is a much-loved figure.

3 Modern smartphones, *whose / that's / who's* screens are made of glass, are easier to break than older cell phones *what / that / who* were made of plastic. *can not remove*
4 I don't understand *that / what / which* he means.
5 The house *where / whose / that* we stayed in belonged to a local teacher.
6 She shares an apartment for *what / which / that* she paid a lot of money with her cousin.

12 Rewrite the two sentences in each item below as one sentence using a relative clause. There is sometimes more than one possible answer.

1 That's the man. Maya was talking about him the other day.
   That's the man *who Maya* ~~it was the could be removed~~ .
2 They wanted to achieve that. I think they did.
   I think they achieved *what they wanted* .
3 The study looked at how well people can use maps. It had very interesting results.
   The study, *which looked at how well people can use maps, had very important results* .
4 It's a small country. The country has had a big influence on the history of the region.
   It's a small country *that had a big influence on the history of the region* .
5 His brother is also a basketball player. His brother is six years younger than him.
   His brother *who is six years younger is also a basketball player* .

13 Work in two pairs in a group of four.

Pair A: Look at the "Down" words in the crossword on page 153.

Pair B: Look at the "Across" words in the crossword on page 155.

Write clues for these words using relative clauses. Then take turns reading your clues to the other pair to complete the crossword.

1 Down: an adjective that means "near" (can also be a verb)
2 Across: an adjective whose opposite is "quiet"

Speaking myLife

14 Work in pairs. If you could choose to have one sense (sight, hearing, etc.) with superhuman ability, which one would it be and why?

10c The king herself

Reading

1 Work in pairs. Look at the title of the article. What is strange about it?

2 Read the article. Number these events about Hatshepsut's (*Hat-shep-sut*) life in the correct chronological order (1–7).

_____ Her mummy was discovered in a less important tomb.

_____ The monuments she built were destroyed.

_____ She became queen regent.

_____ She ruled Egypt as king for 21 years.

_____ Her mummy was identified and put in the Royal Mummy Rooms.

_____ She married Thutmose II.

_____ She was born the eldest daughter of Thutmose I and Queen Ahmose.

3 Circle the correct option (a or b) to complete each sentence.

1 Hatshepsut's mummy was not identified at first because it _____ .
 a was badly damaged
 b was not in a royal tomb
2 Hatshepsut was concerned that people would _____ .
 a not know she was royalty
 b not remember her achievements
3 Thutmose III did not want people to know that Hatshepsut had been _____ .
 a king
 b related to him
4 Thutmose II's children consisted of _____ .
 a one son and one daughter
 b two sons
5 According to tradition, the queen regent was supposed to _____ .
 a do nothing
 b help the king until he was old enough to rule
6 In later statues and images, Hatshepsut appears male because of _____ .
 a the items she is holding
 b her face and attitude

Critical thinking examining the evidence

4 Find evidence in the article to support each sentence (1–5). If there is clear evidence, write *100%*. If there is no evidence, write *0%*. If the evidence is not clear, write *NC*.

1 Hatshepsut was ambitious. _____
2 If Hatshepsut had had a male heir herself, she would have allowed him to be king. _____
3 Thutmose III thought his stepmother was wrong to act as king. _____
4 Hatshepsut knew that what she had done was wrong. _____
5 Hatshepsut's wish to be remembered has come true. _____

5 Work in pairs. Compare your answers and the evidence you found. Do you think overall this story has a happy or sad ending?

Word focus *self*

6 Work in pairs. Look at the expression below from the article. Then discuss what the other expressions with *self* (1–5) mean.

… *standing in a **self-confident** manner* …

1 If you want to know how to think more positively, you should read more **self-help** books.
2 My father is a **self-made** man. He started working in a shop at 16, and had a $2 million business by the time he was 30.
3 I saw my favorite actor in the street recently, but I looked a mess and I felt too **self-conscious** to go up to her.
4 Sticking to a diet is difficult. You need a lot of **self-control**.
5 Giving so much time to the college isn't just kindness; it's also **self-interest**—he hopes to become its president one day.

7 Choose two of the **bold** expressions from Exercise 6 and write your own sentences with them. Then read the sentences to a partner without the **bold** expression and see if they can guess which one it is.

Speaking myLife

8 Work in pairs. Look at these job descriptions. Which options do you think describe the job of a leader or manager?

• working regular hours (9 a.m. to 5 p.m.), or longer?
• working with people, or things?
• making decisions, or following instructions?
• traveling, or staying in one place?
• working indoors, or outdoors?
• working full-time, or part-time?
• working independently, or as part of a team?

9 Ask your partner questions about their work preferences using the list in Exercise 8. Then discuss what their dream job might be.

THE KING *herself*

▶ 90

1 Today her body lies in the Royal Mummy[1] Rooms at the Egyptian Museum in Cairo, alongside other pharaohs. Next to her is a sign that says "Hatshepsut, the king herself (1473–1458 BC)." But in 1903, when
5 the archeologist Howard Carter found Hatshepsut's coffin[2] in the Valley of the Kings, it was empty. Had her mummy been stolen or destroyed? The truth only came out a century
10 later, when Egyptian scientists identified a mummy from a less important tomb[3] as that of Hatshepsut. None of the treasures normally found with pharaohs'
15 mummies were with it. It was not even in a coffin.

2 Hatshepsut was one of the greatest builders of ancient Egypt. She built numerous monuments and temples. At Karnak, we can still see an inscription[4] describing her
20 hopes as to how she would be remembered: "Now my heart turns this way and that, as I think what the people will say. Those who see my monuments in years to come, and who shall speak of what I have done."

3 But following her death, her successor and stepson
25 Thutmose III set about erasing her memory, ordering all images of her as the king to be removed from monuments and temples. Her statues were smashed and thrown into a pit. Yet, the images of her as queen were left undamaged. Why?

4 30 Hatshepsut was the eldest daughter of Thutmose I and Queen Ahmose. But Thutmose I also had a son by another queen, and this son, Thutmose II, became pharaoh when his father died. As was common among Egyptian royalty, Thutmose II married his sister,
35 Hatshepsut. They produced one daughter. Another wife, Isis, gave Thutmose II the male heir[5] that Hatshepsut was unable to provide.

5 When Thutmose II died from heart disease, Thutmose III was still a young boy. As was the
40 custom, Hatshepsut took control as the young pharaoh's queen regent.[6] At first, Hatshepsut respected convention and just handled political affairs while the young king was growing up. But before long, she began
45 performing kingly duties. And after a few years she no longer acted as queen regent, but fully assumed the role of king of Egypt, the supreme power in
50 the land.

6 No one really knows why Hatshepsut broke the conventional rules. Was it a key moment in Egypt's history when a strong leader was
55 needed? Did she believe she had the same right to rule as a man? Did she feel a right as a direct descendant of the pharaoh, Thutmose I? Whatever the reason, her stepson was relegated to second-in-command, and "the king herself" went on to rule for an amazing 21 years.

7 60 At first, Hatshepsut made no secret of her sex—in images her body is unmistakably a woman's—but later, she is depicted as a male king, with headdress and beard, standing in a self-confident manner with legs apart. Many inscriptions still exist that have references
65 to "my people." These suggest that she knew she had broken the rules and wanted her subjects' approval. Her stepson, Thutmose III, grew increasingly frustrated. After Hatshepsut's death, he took his revenge, doing his best to erase her memory as
70 pharaoh from history. But, ironically, in the long term, it is Hatshepsut, the King Herself, who has achieved greater fame.

---

[1]**mummy** (n) /ˈmʌmi/ a dead body wrapped in layers of cloth
[2]**coffin** (n) /ˈkɒfɪn/ a box in which a dead body is placed
[3]**tomb** (n) /tʊːm/ a structure in which a dead person is placed
[4]**inscription** (n) /inˈskrɪpʃən/ words cut into a hard surface
[5]**heir** (n) /eər/ someone who will receive a title when another person dies
[6]**regent** (n) /ˈriːdʒənt/ a person who governs a state because the real king or queen is too young or is absent

10d The right job

Real life describing skills, talents, and experience

Shelter BOX is a charity that sends boxes of essential items needed in an emergency (e.g., a tent, tools, cooking utensils, a water purification kit) to places where disasters—such as earthquakes and floods—have struck. Boxes are prepared in the US and delivered immediately by Shelterbox employees to anywhere in the world where they will help to save lives.

1 Read the description of Shelterbox. What kind of organization is it, and what service do they offer?

2 ▶ **91** Listen to someone being interviewed for a job at Shelterbox. Work in pairs and answer the questions.

1 What aspect of their work is the candidate very interested in?
2 What does the interviewer think might be a problem?

3 ▶ **91** Look at the expressions for describing skills, talents, and experience. Complete the sentences (1–10) with the correct prepositions. Then listen to the interview again and check your answers.

> ▶ **DESCRIBING SKILLS, TALENTS, and EXPERIENCE**
>
> 1 I'm familiar _____ your work
> 2 I have a friend who volunteered _____ you ...
> 3 I'm very interested _____ the idea of ...
> 4 I specialized _____ economics
> 5 I'm good at coping _____ difficult environments
> 6 I think I'd be suited _____ the work
> 7 I'm pretty good _____ computers
> 8 I'm comfortable _____ all the usual programs
> 9 I'm serious _____ wanting to help people
> 10 I need to become more knowledgeable _____ the world

4 Work in pairs. Do you think the candidate did a good job of selling himself to the interviewer?

5 Pronunciation difficult words

a ▶ **92** The spelling of a word in English does not always indicate how you should say the word. How confident are you that you can pronounce these words from the interview? For very confident, put a (✔); for quite confident, put a (**?**); and for not confident, put a (✗). Then listen and repeat.

> ☐ business   ☐ comfortable   ☐ environment
> ☐ though   ☐ world   ☐ months
> ☐ specialized ☐ suited   ☐ knowledgeable

b ▶ **93** Listen to eight more words and try to spell them. Then compare your answers with a partner.

6 Work in pairs.

Student A: Choose one of the jobs below and think about why you should get the job. Convince Student B that this would be a good job for you.

Student B: You are the interviewer. Think of some appropriate questions. Interview Student A. Then swap roles and conduct a new interview.

- a salesperson in a children's bookstore
- a tester of new video games
- a fund-raiser for your old school or college
- a volunteer firefighter (part-time)
- a trainee chocolate maker

10e First impressions

Writing a personal profile

1 Work in pairs. Which of these contexts (a–e) have you written a personal profile for before? What kind of information did you give about yourself?

a a job application
b a social networking site
c a college application
d a vacation rental website (like Airbnb)
e a voluntary organization

2 Look at these three short personal profiles. Which of the contexts in Exercise 1 was each one written for? Match the profiles (1–3) with a context (a–e) from Exercise 1.

1 ____

I'm Rachel, 28 years old, from France. My husband Jack and I just moved to Montreal and are looking to make new friends in the area. We're both very easygoing, and are passionate about traveling and discovering new places. I love cooking for people. Send me a message if you want to join us for a home-cooked French meal!

2 ____

Bright and experienced retail manager with a background in men's and ladies' fashion both in large department stores and small boutiques. A creative and adaptable professional who has a great eye for design and detail. Willing to relocate and open to international opportunities.

3 ____

I am a self-reliant and curious learner whose ambition is to pursue a career in political journalism. My experience as the editor of my high school newspaper has inspired me to learn more about world affairs, and I hope very much to deepen my knowledge by studying politics at your institution.

3 Work in pairs. Look at the three profiles above and answer these questions.

1 Which profile(s) are written in the first person? And in the third person?
2 Which profile is written in a less formal style? How can you tell?
3 Which profile do you think is the most persuasive?

4 Vocabulary personal qualities

a Find adjectives in the profiles that mean the following:

1 intelligent _____
2 wanting to know more _____
3 very enthusiastic _____
4 imaginative _____
5 with a lot of practice _____
6 independent _____
7 relaxed _____
8 can change to fit the situation _____

b Which of the adjectives above would you use to describe yourself? Tell a partner.

5 Writing skill using *with*

a Work in pairs. How would you rephrase this sentence using a relative clause?

A retail manager <u>with</u> a background in men's and ladies' fashion

b Rewrite these phrases using *with*. Where you have to change an adjective or verb to a noun, you will need to add an appropriate preposition.

1 an IT expert <u>who has</u> experience in software design
2 a young couple <u>who loves</u> travel
3 a creative individual <u>who is interested in</u> fashion
4 a bright manager <u>who is ambitious to</u> succeed
5 an easygoing musician <u>who is talented at cooking</u>

6 Write your own short profile similar to one of the profiles in Exercise 2. Choose one of the contexts from Exercise 1.

7 Exchange profiles with a partner. Check your partner's profile using these questions.

- What was the main impression the profile gave?
- Is the profile written in an appropriate style?
- Does it include adjectives to describe personal qualities?
- Does it include at least one *with* + noun expression?
- Overall, was the profile effective?

A statue of Cleopatra

Before you watch

1 Work in pairs. Look at the photo and the caption. Make notes about what you know about Cleopatra.

- who she was
- when and where she ruled
- important events in her life

2 Key vocabulary

a Work in pairs. Read the sentences (1–4). The words and phrases in **bold** are used in the video. Guess the meaning of the words and phrases.

1 As the eldest son of the Queen of England, Prince Charles is her **successor**.
2 The company is well-equipped to compete with its international **rivals**.
3 The American **Civil War** was between the Northern and Southern states of the US.
4 His comment that he doesn't believe in global warming has caused a lot of **controversy** and has **infuriated** many people.

b Write the words and phrases in **bold** in Exercise 2a next to their definitions (a–e).

a a fight for control of a country between different groups within that country
   _____
b a person who takes over a job or position from someone else _____
c made someone very angry _____
d strong disagreement about something among a large group of people _____
e people or businesses you compete against for the same goal or for superiority in the same area _____

While you watch

3 ▰ 10.1 Watch the video. Match the people in the story (1–6) with their descriptions.

People		Descriptions
1 Cleopatra	○ ○	Cleopatra's younger brother and co-ruler
2 Ptolemy 13th	○ ○	a rival to Mark Antony in Rome
3 Julius Caesar	○ ○	Cleopatra and Julius Caesar's son
4 Caesarion	○ ○	winner in Rome's civil war
5 Mark Antony	○ ○	Queen of Egypt
6 Octavian	○ ○	a potential successor to Caesar and, later, Cleopatra's husband

4 ▰ 10.1 Look at these events in Cleopatra's life. Then watch the video again and complete the sentences.

1 Cleopatra was born in _____ BC into the Ptolemaic dynasty of Egypt.
2 She became Queen at the age of _____ and ruled Egypt with her brother, but he soon forced her from power.
3 When Julius Caesar arrived in Egypt, Cleopatra managed to get to see him by hiding in a _____ .
4 Julius Caesar was charmed by Cleopatra. He defeated her _____ and helped her take back the throne.
5 Soon after that, Cleopatra had a baby that she claimed was _____ son.
6 After Caesar was murdered, Cleopatra looked for someone else in Rome to help her. She met _____ , who was also hungry for power.
7 Together, Cleopatra and Mark Antony ruled Alexandria, and eventually they _____ .
8 Mark Antony said that _____ was the true successor to Caesar. This infuriated Mark Antony's rival, Octavian.
9 Octavian defeated Antony and Cleopatra in battle in _____ BC.
10 Legend says that Cleopatra spread rumors that she was _____ , and when Mark Antony heard this, he killed himself.
11 Cleopatra tried to make peace with Octavian, but when she couldn't, she too killed herself with a _____ bite.

After you watch

5 Vocabulary in context

a ▰ 10.2 Watch the clips from the video. Choose the correct meaning of the words and phrases.

b Complete these sentences in your own words. Then share your sentences with a partner.

1 I was overjoyed when I heard that …
2 I think that … is in decline.
3 Although he is dead, Michael Jackson's … lives on.

6 What three adjectives would you use to describe Cleopatra? Discuss with a partner.

7 Work in groups and discuss these questions.

1 Who are the most famous people in the history of your country?
2 What qualities are these people known for? Are they all good qualities?

UNIT 10 REVIEW AND MEMORY BOOSTER

Grammar

1 Complete the first part of the article (1–10) with *a*, *an*, *the*, or no article (–). Then complete the second part (11–15) using relative pronouns.

Constance Adams has had ¹_____ interesting career. She studied ²_____ architecture at ³_____ Yale University before working as ⁴_____ architect in Berlin and ⁵_____ Japan. She then joined the Johnson Space Center in ⁶_____ US, where she helped design TransHab, a module for ⁷_____ International Space Station. ⁸_____ module was designed to provide ⁹_____ living accommodations for astronauts during their stay in ¹⁰_____ space.

In order to accommodate a crew of astronauts ¹¹_____ mission was to reach Mars, the designers of the TransHab module had to achieve two things. They had to design a module ¹²_____ would be only 4.3 meters in diameter when it was launched. But once it was in space, it needed to become three times that size to be big enough for the six astronauts ¹³_____ would live there. So they made a structure ¹⁴_____ could inflate and unfold in space to become a three-level "house" ¹⁵_____ astronauts could eat, sleep, and work.

2 Work in pairs. What two important design features of the TransHab module does the text describe?

3 Work in pairs. Make sentences defining two of these things. Use articles and relative pronouns in your definitions.

blind	echo	flood	heir

I CAN
use *a/an*, *the*, and zero article accurately
use relative pronouns in different relative clauses

Vocabulary

4 Complete these sentences about jobs and careers. The first letter of each missing word is provided.

1 I s_____ in the army for four years, so I understand the importance of discipline.
2 I'm very a_____ and e_____ . I can work in whatever environment you need me to.
3 I a_____ for the job because I'm good at selling and I want to p_____ a career in sales.
4 Both my parents are doctors, so it was a natural choice for me to b_____ a doctor, too.

5 **≫ MB** Work in pairs. Discuss which of these areas is being described in each sentence in Exercise 4. Then make sentences describing yourself in each of these areas.

background qualities	experience skills	qualifications talents

I CAN
describe my experience, skills, and qualifications

Real life

6 Complete these sentences with the correct prepositions.

1 I'm familiar _____ all the usual computer programs.
2 I specialized _____ mechanical engineering in college.
3 I think I'd be well-suited _____ working abroad.
4 I'm good _____ coping _____ difficult people.
5 I'm serious _____ pursuing a career _____ the fashion industry.
6 I'm very interested _____ the idea of creating new designs.

7 **≫ MB** Rewrite the sentences in Exercise 6 so that they are true for you. Make two of the sentences false. Then read all your sentences to a partner and ask your partner to guess which two are false.

I CAN
use expressions to present myself at a job interview

Unit 11 Knowledge and learning

The Children's Museum of Indianapolis, USA

1 Work in pairs. Look at the photo and the caption. Answer these
questions.

1 What kinds of things might you find in this museum?
2 What's your favorite museum? Why?

2 Look at the verbs (1–5) to do with learning. Match them with the
verbs on the right with a similar meaning.

1 acquire (e.g., a new skill)   motivate
2 be unaware of (e.g., a fact)   not know about
3 get (e.g., the meaning of something)   pick up or learn
4 inspire (e.g., a person to learn)   understand
5 take in (e.g., a lot of information)   understand and
                                         remember

3 ▶ 94 Work in pairs. Listen to someone talking about taking her
children to the Children's Museum and answer the questions.

1 What did the speaker's kids engage with? *dinosaurs*
2 Which section at the museum really inspired the speaker?

4 Work in pairs. Discuss these questions.

1 Which classes inspired you most at school? Why?
2 What knowledge or skill that you acquired at school or in
college has been most useful (to you)?

11a Innovation in learning

Vocabulary education

1 Circle the correct options to complete these sentences about education.

1 Learning *by heart / from experience* is the best way to learn your multiplication tables.
2 *Studying / Cramming* for your exams is not a good idea—trying to remember lots of information at the last moment doesn't help you remember things in the long term.
3 He *turned up for / dropped out of* high school when he was sixteen and started working full-time instead.
4 At school, I acquired a lot of *academic knowledge / practical experience*, but not many life skills.
5 I always got good *notes / grades* in English because I read a lot of English books.

▶ 95

2 Work in pairs. Discuss these questions about education in your country.

1 Does education in your country focus more on practical skills or on academic knowledge? Is there a lot of learning by heart?
2 How much emphasis is put on grades and exams? Do you think this is a good or bad thing?
3 Is there a big problem of absenteeism at school? What about people dropping out completely?

Reading

3 Read the article about the Lumiar School in Brazil. What are the main ways in which it is different from a traditional school? Discuss with a partner.

INNOVATION *in* LEARNING

It is a question that has troubled educators for centuries. How do they ensure that students don't just turn up to school to pass exams, but that they are truly engaged in their learning?

The Lumiar International School in São Paulo, Brazil, may have
5 found the answer. The founder of the school is Ricardo Semler, a businessman who developed a management style in which employees were trusted to do their jobs and make their own decisions. They were even able to set their own working hours and salaries. Semler managed to make this approach work in his own company, increasing
10 sales from $4 million to $212 million in twenty years.

Lumiar is a school unlike any other. Pupils occupy "spaces" rather than rooms, and learning takes place everywhere: in play areas, the hall, the dining room. If pupils do not feel engaged in a lesson, they can go to another one or to the library to read. Most learning is done through
15 projects that pupils design with their fellow students and teachers. Teachers are more like subject experts than traditional teachers.

On the day I visited, I attended a weekly meeting where all pupils could discuss issues affecting school life. The meeting was an opportunity for students to raise concerns, but also an occasion when they were
20 able to practice important life skills like debating and collaboration. The problem they succeeded in solving that day concerned some plates that two of the pupils had broken while running in the kitchen. Punishment was not the issue. The question was how to prevent this from happening again. Someone suggested a "No running in school"
25 rule. Then another boy spoke up: What if the school pays, but the boys themselves have to go and find the same china in the shops? I was amazed. This boy was only six years old, but he had managed to come up with an excellent solution to a difficult problem.

Ricardo Semler with some of his students at Lumiar School

4 Complete these sentences using words from the article. The first letter of each missing word is provided.

1 Ricardo Semler based the Lumiar School's approach to education on that of his own c_ompany_.

2 Pupils learn by participating in p_rojects_ with other students.

3 The weekly meetings provide an opportunity for the pupils to practice important l_ife_ s_kills_.

4 The six-year-old boy's suggestion was accepted as a very reasonable form of p_unishment_.

Grammar *could, was able to, managed to, and succeeded in*

▶ **COULD, WAS ABLE TO, MANAGED TO, and SUCCEEDED IN**

could + base form of the verb
1 *I attended a weekly meeting where all pupils **could discuss** issues affecting school life.*
2 *He was six years old, and he **could speak** confidently in front of a large group of people.*

was/were able + to + base form of the verb
3 *They **were** even **able to set** their own working hours.*

managed + to + base form of the verb
4 *Semler **managed to make** this approach work in his own company.*

succeeded in + -ing
5 *The problem they **succeeded in solving** that day concerned some plates ...*

For more information and practice, see page 176.

5 Look at the grammar box. Complete these rules (1–3) with *could, was/were able to, managed to,* or *succeeded in.*

1 We use ___could___ and ___was/were able to___ to describe a general ability to do something in the past.

2 We use ___was/were able to___ and ___managed___ to say we had a possibility or opportunity to do something in the past.

3 We use _____ , _____ , and ___was/were able to___ to describe success in a specific (difficult) task in the past.

6 Work in pairs. Look at these two sentences from the article. Which of the other forms in the grammar box could you use in each sentence?

1 The meeting was ... an occasion when they **were able to practice** important life skills.

2 ... he had **managed to come up** with an excellent solution to a difficult problem.

7 Circle the correct options to complete these sentences.

1 He had such a strong accent that I *couldn't / didn't manage* understand him.

2 He failed his exams the first time, but he *succeeded in / was able to* take them again.

3 She *could / managed to* read and write from the age of three.

4 Did she *succeed / manage* to pass her driving test last week?

5 When we got to the top of the mountain, we *could / succeeded* see for miles.

6 After trying the key for several minutes, they *managed / succeeded* in getting the door open.

8 Complete this text with the correct form of the verbs in parentheses. Add a preposition if necessary.

> Ricardo Semler's philosophy is the same in education and in business: to be democratic and to let people manage their own work. For example, if a salesperson managed ¹_____ (reach) their weekly sales target by Wednesday, they could take the rest of the week off. At Semler's weekly board meetings, two seats were open for anyone in the company—including the cleaners and lower-level staff—who could ²_____ (get) there on time. The important thing for Semler was to have people around him who were able ³_____ (think) for themselves. That's why he set up a school: to teach people to be independent. With the Lumiar School, he succeeded ⁴_____ (achieve) this.

Speaking myLife

9 Work in pairs. Describe your learning experience of TWO of the following. Use the correct forms of *could, was/were able to, managed to,* or *succeeded in* in your answers.

- riding a bike
- driving
- speaking English
- cooking
- playing a sport or musical instrument
- mastering a job or a work skill

*I remember my dad teaching me to ride a bike when I was six. At first, I **couldn't keep** my balance. Every time he let go, I **managed to ride** for about ten meters before ...*

11b Memory

Competitors memorize names and faces at the World Memory Championships, London.

HAN Zelin

HAN Zelin

Listening

1 Work in pairs. What kinds of things do you often forget? Do you find this annoying?

2 ▶ 96 Listen to the first part of a talk on memory by a psychologist. He mentions some common failures of memory. Were any of them the same as the ones you talked about in Exercise 1?

3 ▶ 97 Work in groups. Listen to the rest of the talk and answer the questions.

1 What does the woman (AJ) remember?
2 How does AJ feel about her good memory?
3 Why are people's memories now perhaps not as good as they used to be?

4 ▶ 98 Circle the correct options to complete the psychologist's statements. Then listen to the whole talk again and check your answers.

1 AJ's memory is stimulated by *events / dates* in the same way that our memories can be stimulated by certain *images / smells*.
2 Our memories are selective: We remember mostly *urgent / important* things and *good / bad* things.
3 We should be *grateful for / conscious of* all the things that our memories hide.
4 Psychologists call the technology we use to store information our "*extra / external* memory."
5 Now medical science is trying to address the problem of *poor / selective* memory.

Wordbuilding homonyms

▶ **WORDBUILDING homonyms**

Homonyms are words that are spelled and pronounced in the same way but have a different meaning.
cross (adj) = angry; *cross* (v) = to go across, e.g., a bridge or road; *cross* (n) = a symbol made of two intersecting lines

For more practice, see Workbook page 91.

5 Look at the wordbuilding box. Then read the sentences below (1–4) and look at the words in **bold** from the talk. Circle the correct meaning of these homonyms (a or b).

1 AJ's memory is stimulated in the most intense way by **dates**.
   a fruit that grows on a palm tree
   b days of the year specified by a number
2 When you **found** a pen and paper, the idea was gone.
   a established
   b located
3 I'm sure everyone recognizes these **common** failures of memory.
   a shared
   b usual, normal
4 It's a bit like it is for the **rest** of us when certain smells bring back strong memories.
   a remainder
   b period of relaxing

Grammar future in the past

▶ FUTURE IN THE PAST

was/were going to and *was/were about to* (+ base verb)
1 You **were going to write** down a great idea you had, but when you found a pen and paper, …
2 You **were about to make** a comment in a meeting, and then …

would (+ base verb) and *would have* (+ past participle)
3 You recognized someone in the street and **would have spoken** to them, but you didn't because …

was/were supposed to (+ base verb)
4 You **were supposed to send** a friend a birthday card, but then …

For more information and practice, see page 176.

6 ▶ 96 Work in pairs. Look at the grammar box. Try to remember what the speaker said in Exercises 2 and 4 to complete each sentence in the grammar box (1–4). Then listen again and check.

7 Work in pairs. Look again at sentences 1–4 in the grammar box. Do the verbs in **bold** describe actions that were completed?

8 Circle the correct verb forms to complete this description of another memory patient.

There was another interesting patient who couldn't form new memories. He could only remember events before 1960. I ¹*was going to ask* / *would ask* his doctor how someone with no memory managed to cope with daily life, but she suggested I speak to the patient directly. So I went to interview him. Our appointment ²*was supposed to be* / *would be* at 2 p.m., but the time made no difference to him since he lived only in the present. I ³*would tell* / *would have told* him my name and why I was there, but I realized there was no point: ⁴*it was supposed to mean* / *it would have meant* nothing to him. So I began by asking him about his past, and he talked about his childhood during the Second World War. But then the telephone rang. When he came back, I ⁵*was about to ask* / *would ask* him to continue, but it was clear he had completely forgotten our earlier conversation. I thought he ⁶*was about to be* / *would be* frustrated by this, but not at all. If anything, he seemed glad not to be burdened by memory.

---

9 ▶ 99 Rewrite these original plans (1–5) using future in the past forms. Then listen and check your answers.

1 I'm going to invite Sarah.
I _was going to invite_ Sarah, but I asked Kate instead.
2 Her calendar says she should be in Cairo this week.
She _was supposed to be_ in Cairo this week, but she's sick, so she couldn't go.
3 I'll send you the original, if I can find it.
He _was going to sent_ me the original, but he couldn't find it, so he sent me a copy.
4 We are supposed to arrive there by ten o'clock.
We _were about to get_ there by ten o'clock, but the train didn't get in until eleven.
5 He's about to announce his retirement.
He _was about to stay_ his retirement, but now he thinks he'll stay until next year.

10 Pronunciation contrastive sentence stress

a ▶ 99 Work in pairs. Underline the words in the rewritten sentences in Exercise 9 that give the contrasting facts. Listen again. Then practice saying each sentence using contrastive stress.

b Complete these sentences with a contrasting idea. Underline the words in the sentence that make the contrast. Then say your sentences to your partner. Your partner should say which words you stressed and why.

1 He was going to take the <u>day off</u>, but …
they needed him at work after all.
2 We were supposed to be going to Chile, but …
3 I would have driven, but …
4 They were about to buy a new TV, but …
5 I was going to order the fish, but …

Speaking **myLife**

11 Work in pairs. Look at these three situations. Think of a good excuse to explain why each one happened. Then tell your excuses to the class. At the end, vote on which excuses were best.

- You were thirty minutes late for an important business meeting and didn't call to inform them.
- You borrowed someone's car and were supposed to return it the next day, but they had to call you to find out where it was.
- It was a close friend's birthday two days ago. You didn't send a card or get them a present.

*"Sorry I'm late. My train was delayed. I **was going to call** you, but …"*

11c Who's a clever bird?

Reading

1 Work in pairs. What kinds of things can animals learn to do? Which animals seem the most intelligent?

2 Work in pairs. Read the article and say how Alex the parrot demonstrated his intelligence.

3 Read the article again. Do these statements agree with the information given in the article? Circle true (T), false (F), or not given (NG) if there is no information.

1 Pepperberg's idea was to let Alex communicate to her how he saw the world. **T** F NG
2 Pepperberg didn't want people to think she had chosen Alex for his intelligence. T **F** NG
3 Alex showed that he could distinguish between colors and shapes, but not numbers. T **F** NG
4 Pepperberg concluded that cognitive skills are necessary for survival in the wild. **T** F NG
5 Alex felt very proud of his ability to communicate in English. T F **NG**
6 Alex was capable of expressing his thoughts and emotions. **T** F NG

Critical thinking **explaining ideas**

4 When writers express an idea, they often explain it to make sure the reader understands. Read the article again and underline the sentences or phrases used to explain each idea below.

1 that a good way to find out what an animal is thinking is to teach it to speak
2 that researchers had no confidence in her idea
3 that Alex made up words for new things
4 that birds need to be able to adapt to their environment
5 that Alex showed an understanding of feelings

5 Work in pairs. Which of these ways (a–c) does the writer use to explain each idea (1–5) in Exercise 4?

a by rephrasing or saying the same thing in other words
b by giving examples
c by quoting someone who made the same point

Word focus *learn*

6 Work in pairs. Find these two expressions with the word *learn* in the article. Discuss what each expression means.

1 learn (something) by heart (lines 23–24)
2 learn (something) the hard way (line 69)

7 Work in pairs. Look at the expressions in **bold** in the sentences below. Can you figure out what these expressions mean? Which expression means the same thing as "learn the hard way"?

1 Tom's a professional photographer—ask him for advice if you're interested in **learning some tricks of the trade**.
2 Jessica wants to design the new brochure, but she's only been here a month. I told her that you have to **learn to walk before you can run**.
3 **It's never too late to learn**. My grandfather took up the piano when he was 73 years old.
4 I've **learned my lesson**. I'm never going to try to put together a piece of furniture again without reading the instructions first.
5 There's no point complaining about the changes in the organization. We're just going to have to **learn to live with it**.
6 You'd think that the company would **learn from its mistakes**, but it never does.

8 Choose two of the **bold** expressions from Exercise 7 and write your own sentences with them. Then read your sentences to a partner, omitting the **bold** expressions with *learn*. Can your partner figure out the missing expressions?

Speaking myLife

9 Take the quiz on page 154 to find out what type of learner you are. The answers are on page 155. Then work in pairs and discuss if you agree with this.

10 Work in small groups. Discuss how your learning style affects your language learning. What things can you do to learn more effectively? Look at the ideas below and add any others you can think of.

- watching English language movies with the subtitles on
- reading stories (in English newspapers, books, magazines) and retelling them
- keeping a vocabulary book and drawing illustrations of each new word

How do you find out what an animal is thinking? How do you know if it is thinking at all? One good way, thought Harvard graduate Irene Pepperberg, might be to ask it.

5 In 1977, she decided she would teach a one-year-old African grey parrot named Alex to speak English. "I thought if he learned to communicate, I could ask him questions about how he sees the world."

10 Pepperberg bought Alex in a Chicago pet store. She let the store assistant choose him because she didn't want other scientists to say that she had deliberately chosen a clever bird. Given that Alex's brain was the size of a walnut, most 15 researchers thought Pepperberg was certain to fail. "Some people actually called me crazy for trying this," she said.

But with Pepperberg's patient teaching, Alex learned how to imitate almost one hundred 20 English words, including the names of food. He could count to six and had learned the sounds for seven and eight. But the point was not just to see if Alex could learn words by heart and then repeat them. Pepperberg 25 wanted to get inside his mind and learn more about a bird's understanding of the world.

In one demonstration, Pepperberg placed Alex on a wooden perch[1] in the middle of the room. She then held up a green key and a small green 30 cup for him to look at. "What's the same?" she asked. Without hesitation, Alex's beak opened: "Co-lor." "What's different?" Pepperberg asked. "Shape," Alex said. She demonstrated that Alex could tell what a key was, whatever its size 35 or color. He also made up words for new things: he called an apple a "banerry" (a combination of banana and cherry, his favorite fruits). Many of Alex's cognitive[2] skills, such as his ability to understand 40 the concepts of same and different, are rare in the animal world. But parrots, like humans, live a long time in complex societies. And like humans, these birds must adapt to changing 45 relationships and environments.

"They need to be able to distinguish colors to know when a fruit is ripe or unripe," Pepperberg explained.

"They need to categorize things—what's 50 edible, what isn't—and to know the shapes of predators. And it helps to have a concept of numbers if you need to keep track of your flock.[3] For a long-lived bird, you can't do all of this with instinct; thinking must be involved."

55 Alex also expressed feelings and awareness of other people's feelings. If Pepperberg grew frustrated, Alex could notice this and offer an "I'm sorry" to her. "Wanna go back" he would say when he had had enough of the tests and 60 wanted to go back to his cage. "Talk clearly!" he commanded, when one of the other birds that Pepperberg was teaching mispronounced the word *green*. "He's moody," said Pepperberg, "so he interrupts the others, or he 65 gives the wrong answer just to be difficult." Through her experiments, Pepperberg certainly learned more about the mind of a parrot, but like the parent of a teenager, she learned the hard way.

---

[1]**perch** (n) /pɜːrtʃ/ a wooden bar that a bird stands on
[2]**cognitive** (adj) /ˈkɒgnətɪv/ related to thinking and thought processes
[3]**flock** (n) /flɒk/ a large group of birds

Who's a clever *bird?*

11d Keep learning

Real life getting clarification

1 Work in pairs. Look at the list of short courses offered by a local college. Which of these courses interest you and why?

ROUSHAM
ADULT EDUCATION COLLEGE

COURSE TITLE	FREQUENCY	EXAM COURSE
Basic Car Repair Apr. 5, 10 wks.	1 × 2 hrs.	✗
Introduction to Psychology Jan. 22, 18 wks.	1 × 2 hrs.	✓
Vlogging* Apr. 11, 8 wks.	1 × 1.5 hrs.	✗
First Aid Apr. 12, 4 wks.	2 × 1.5 hrs.	✓
Fitness Instruction Mar. 1, 12 wks.	1 × 2 hrs.	✓
Flower Arranging Jan. 22, 18 wks.	1 × 2 hrs.	✗
Art Appreciation Apr. 5, 10 wks.	1 × 2 hrs.	✗
Screenwriting Jan. 21, 18 wks.	1 × 2 hrs.	✗
Web Design Apr. 12, 6 wks.	1 × 1.5 hrs.	✗
Starting Your Own Business Apr. 11, 8 wks.	1 × 1.5 hrs.	✗

* A vlog (or video blog) is a blog that features mostly videos rather than text or images. Vlogging is the act of keeping a video blog.

2 ▶ **101** Listen to a telephone conversation with someone inquiring about a class. Work in pairs and answer the questions.

1 What kind of class does Ahmad initially ask about?
2 What class does Liz suggest for him instead? Why?
3 What does Ahmad decide to do?

3 Work in pairs. Look at the expressions for getting clarification that Ahmad used. Which expressions does he use to ask for repetition, and which does he use to ask for explanation?

> ### ▶ GETTING CLARIFICATION
> What do you mean by ¹ _that 8 level_ ?
> Can you speak up a little?
> Can you explain what ² _the course involve_ ?
> Sorry, I don't understand.
> Are you saying that ³ _it doesn't deal with_
> the history of art?
> Could you give me an example of
> ⁴ _the kind of thing which_ in the class?
> What was ⁵ _the class_ called again?
> Sorry, I didn't catch ⁶ _the started day_ .
> Did you say ⁷ _may fifty_ ?

4 ▶ **101** Listen to the conversation again. Complete the expressions for getting clarification in Exercise 3 with the words you hear.

5 Pronunciation linking in question forms

a ▶ **102** In certain commonly used combinations (*did you, could you, what do you*, etc.), the words are strongly linked together. Listen to these examples. Notice how the speaker links the words together.

1 Are you saying the class is full?
2 Did you say Tuesday?
3 What do you mean?
4 Could you give me an example?

b Work in pairs. Practice saying these questions.

- What are you trying to say?
- Could you repeat that?
- Did you mean September?
- What do you think?

6 Work in pairs.

Student A: You are a potential student. Choose one of the courses from the list in Exercise 1 or another class you are interested in. Tell Student B your choice. Prepare questions about the class (e.g., how long it is, what is covered exactly).

Student B: You are a college administrator. Prepare what you are going to say about Student A's chosen class (e.g., what it covers, if it offers a degree or a certificate).

Act out a conversation inquiring about the class. Then change roles and have a new conversation.

11e The wrong course

Writing an email about a misunderstanding

1 Read the email from a student to an adult education college. Answer the questions below.

Dear Sir/Madam,

I enrolled in your course Car Repair 1 in August and have attended three classes. When I originally inquired about the course, I was told that it was suitable for people with no previous knowledge of car repair. But, in fact, everyone else in the class seems to know a lot already. So despite the fact that the lessons generally start with a basic concept, they move very quickly on to more complicated ideas.

I don't blame the teacher. On the contrary, he does his best to explain concepts to me. But I feel that I am just holding everyone else back. They know how an engine works already, whereas I have no background at all in mechanics.

I was going to wait a couple of weeks before saying anything, but the last class was so difficult that I have decided to write now and ask for a refund. While I appreciate it's not really anyone's fault that this has happened, I hope you will understand how unsatisfactory the situation is for me.

I look forward to hearing from you.

Sincerely yours,

Silvia Redman

---

1 What is the misunderstanding about the course?
   a the level
   b the timing
2 How would you describe the student's feelings about the situation?
   a offended
   b frustrated
3 How would you describe the tone of the email?
   a aggressive
   b reasonable

2 Work in pairs. What do you think the college should do in response to the email? Give reasons for your answer.

3 Writing skill linking contrasting ideas

a Work in pairs. Look at the contrasting ideas in each item below. Find the sentences in the email that express these ideas. Then underline the words or phrases that are used to link them.

1 The course should be for beginners. No one else is a beginner.
2 Each lesson starts with a simple idea. It progresses quickly to difficult ideas.
3 The teacher is not at fault. He helps me as much as he can.
4 The other students know a lot. I know nothing.
5 No one is to blame for this. I still feel it is unfair.

b Look again at the sentences in the email with *despite* and *whereas*. How would you rewrite them using *although* and *on the other hand*? Tell your partner.

c Complete these sentences (1–4) with appropriate linking words and phrases from the box.

| on the other hand | but |
| despite the fact that | on the contrary |

1 _____ the brochure says the start date is September 12th, the first real class is a week later, on the 19th.
2 The course is advertised as "practical," _____ you learn a lot of theory as well.
3 The art history course is a two-year program. The art appreciation course, _____ , is only ten weeks long.
4 Training as a fitness instructor is not easy. _____ , it's one of the toughest classes I've ever taken.

4 Imagine you enrolled in one of the other courses listed on page 136. Think of a misunderstanding that occurred with the course. Write an email to the college explaining the misunderstanding and asking for a refund.

5 Exchange emails with a partner. Compare what you have written. Use these questions to check your emails.

- Does the email make clear what the misunderstanding was?
- Is the tone of the email reasonable?
- Has the writer used linking words and phrases correctly?
- Do you think the email will get the response or action the writer wants?

A shaman (or tribal healer) from the Amazon, Paraguay

Before you watch

1 Work in pairs. Look at the photo and the caption. What do you know about shamans? How do you think they treat sick people?

2 Key vocabulary

a Work in pairs. Read the sentences (1–5). The words in **bold** are used in the video. Guess the meaning of the words.

1 We have a nature **reserve** near our house. A lot of people go there to watch birds.
2 At the moment, there is no **cure** for cancer. However, scientists say they are getting close to finding one.
3 They live in an **isolated** part of Scotland two hours from the nearest town.
4 After I broke my arm, it took three months for it to **heal** properly.
5 The yoga class always begins with the teacher leading a **chant**.

b Write the words in **bold** in Exercise 2a next to their definitions (a–e).

a remote and on its own _____
b a word or phrase that is repeated in a rhythmic way, usually by a group of people _____
c become healthy again _____
d an area of land where plants or animals are officially protected _____
e a medicine or treatment that makes an illness or disease go away _____

While you watch

3 ▶ 11.1 Watch the video about medicinal plants. Work in pairs and answer the questions.

1 Where do the medicinal plants come from?
2 Why are these plants now at risk?
3 What are the scientists visiting Paraguay hoping to find?

4 ▶ 11.1 Read these statements (1–7). Then watch the video again and circle the correct options to complete the statements.

1 The plants in the forest could contain cures for diabetes, malaria, and *heart disease / common fevers and colds*.
2 As the plants disappear, the *shamans / potential cures* disappear with them.
3 Paraguay has one of the highest *deforestation / infant mortality* rates in the world.

4 At the village, Gervasio is *using chants / dancing*, perhaps to make a spiritual connection with the forest.
5 Together, they look for a specific type of plant that the scientists want to use in *fever / cancer* research.
6 Gervasio's wife then makes a local *dish / tea* with the plant.
7 The scientists have published *a book / online articles* about Paraguay's medicinal plants.

After you watch

5 Vocabulary in context

a ▶ 11.2 Watch the clips from the video. Choose the correct meaning of the words and phrases.

b Complete these sentences in your own words. Then share your sentences with a partner.

1 I have extensive knowledge of …
2 … is a good source of …
3 A potential disadvantage of drinking too much coffee is …

6 Work in small groups. Make a list of herbs, spices, vitamins, or other remedies commonly used in your country to help treat these medical problems. Add another problem and cure. Then tell each other if you have tried any of these cures and with what success.

Problem	Cure
1 Cold	*vitamin C (orange juice)*
2 Sore throat	
3 Toothache	
4 Stomachache	
5	

7 Work in pairs. Read the statements below. Which do you think are true? Do you have any similar beliefs in your country?

1 Eating fish is good for your brain.
2 Spicy food causes stomach ulcers.
3 Chicken soup helps cure a cold.
4 If you go outside with wet hair, you'll catch a cold.
5 Eating cheese before bed can give you bad dreams.
6 Drinking lemon tea with honey soothes a sore throat.

UNIT 11 REVIEW AND MEMORY BOOSTER

Grammar

1 Circle the correct options to complete this story about a linguist.

When police in Brazil interviewed an immigrant who spoke an unrecognizable language, they called Ziad Fazah, hoping that he ¹ *will / would* be able to help them. Fazah, originally from Lebanon, claimed that he ² *could / managed to* speak 54 different languages. He quickly realized that the man was speaking a dialect used in Afghanistan. With Fazah's help, the man ³ *could / was able to* explain that he had escaped from Afghanistan and was seeking asylum in Brazil.

Fazah's talents were first noticed by the Lebanese government when he was seventeen. They ⁴ *would / were going to* use him as an interpreter, but soon afterward he moved to Brazil with his parents. There, he married a Brazilian and began giving private language lessons. Fazah ⁵ *would remain / would have remained* unknown, but in 2006 his language abilities were tested on a Spanish television show, and he received international attention. Some people questioned his abilities. ⁶ *Was he really able / Did he really manage* to speak fluently in over 50 languages? The evidence was not completely convincing, but even if it is half that number, it is still impressive.

2 Work in pairs. Answer these questions about the story in Exercise 1.

1 Why were the police interviewing the man from Afghanistan?
2 What does the writer conclude about Ziad Fazah's language-speaking abilities?

3 ▶▶ **MB** Work in pairs. Tell your partner something:

1 you could do when you were younger, but can't do now.
2 you were going to do yesterday, but forgot.
3 you couldn't do at first, but managed to do in the end.

I CAN	
talk about past ability	
express the future in the past	

Vocabulary

4 Complete each expression about learning with a verb, a preposition, or an adjective.

1 Learning _____ your mistakes is learning the _____ way, but it works!
2 Don't worry if you don't understand the system at first; you'll soon pick it _____ .
3 There's just too much information to _____ in all at once. Do they expect us to learn it all _____ heart?

5 ▶▶ **MB** Work in pairs. Look at the photos.

1 How are children encouraged to learn in these places?
2 How is this similar to or different from the way you learned at school?

I CAN	
use expressions related to learning	
talk about knowledge and education	

Real life

6 Match sentences 1–4 with sentences a–d that have the same meaning.

1 What do you mean by that?
2 Could you give me an example?
3 Can you speak up a little?
4 I don't really get what you're saying.

a I don't really understand. ____
b For instance? ____
c Can you explain that? ____
d I can't hear you very clearly. ____

7 Think of two things you learned in Unit 11 about learning and memory. Then work in pairs and tell your partner about them. For each statement, your partner should respond with a different expression from Exercise 6.

I CAN	
ask for and get clarification	

Unit 12 Money

Costing US$3 million, the Lamborghini Sesto Elemento brings new meaning to luxury driving.

FEATURES

1 Work in pairs. Look at the photo and the caption. Would you buy this car if money were no issue? What luxuries would or wouldn't you spend money on?

2 ▶ 103 Look at the statement below. Do you agree with it? Listen to two people's responses to it. Work in pairs. Which speaker do you agree with more?

"It doesn't matter if the gap between rich and poor is getting wider as long as everyone's standard of living is rising anyway."

3 ▶ 103 Listen to the speakers again. Complete these phrases about the economy that the speakers use. Then tell your partner what you think each expression means.

1 the standard of ___living___
2 the haves and the have _____
3 the _____ gap
4 people's buying _____
5 the cost of _____
6 quality of _____

4 Work in pairs. Are these statements true or false for your country? What evidence is there of this?

1 The cost of living is higher now than a few years ago.
2 People have a better quality of life now than in the past.

12a Saving for a rainy day

Vocabulary money

1 Complete the sentences (1–6) with the correct form of these verbs. One verb is extra.

borrow	earn	invest	lend
owe	save	spend	

1 According to a recent study, the best-paying jobs in the US are in the medical field. Most surgeons, for example, _____ six-figure salaries.
2 The best thing you can _____ in is a good education.
3 It's OK to ask people to _____ you money if you know you can pay it back.
4 Why do some people _____ money all their lives and never use it?
5 We're told to manage our money carefully, but our government always _____ more money than it has.
6 It is very stressful to always _____ money—to the bank, the credit card company, etc.

2 Complete these sentences with nouns that express the same ideas as in Exercise 1. The first letter is provided.

1 Most surgeons have a very high i_____ .
2 The best i_____ you can make is …
3 Asking for a l_____ is OK if …
4 What's the point of having s_____ if you don't use them?
5 Why does government s_____ always exceed its income?
6 It is very stressful to always have d_____ .

Reading

3 Work in pairs. What do you know about Norway: its landscape, its people, its industry?

4 Read the article. Work in pairs. In what ways is Norway a rich country?

5 Work in pairs. Read the article again. Complete these summaries of the four paragraphs.

1 For a long time, Norway has had a better … than other countries.
2 The two reasons for Norway's success are … and …
3 For Norwegians, being rich means …
4 Norway is saving money for …

6 Work in pairs. Do you think that the Norwegians are right to save their money? Why or why not?

SAVING FOR A RAINY DAY

▶ 104

Come on, Norway; this doesn't even feel like a competition anymore! Consistently listed among the top five happiest countries in the world, Norway offers a quality of life that other countries can only dream of.
5 It is one of the wealthiest countries in the world; only Luxembourg and a couple of others are richer. As well as earning a good salary, Norwegians also get a good education, usually find a job they want—unemployment is just 2.5 percent—and enjoy good health. People say
10 even the prisons are quite comfortable!

Norway hasn't always been a rich country. Just last century, Norwegians were emigrating to the USA in the thousands in search of a better life. The rise in oil prices in the 1970s changed all that (Norway has a lot of oil). But it isn't only
15 Norway's huge oil reserves that account for its success— other less successful economies have even greater resources. It is also due to the Norwegians' strong work ethic. Norwegians are always near the top in global surveys of worker productivity rates.

20 In Oslo, don't expect to see Dubai-style skyscrapers and rows of Ferraris and Porsches. Norway may be rich, but it is modest. In fact, the people of Norway are trying to redefine wealth to mean "having a balanced life." The government has passed laws that emphasize the
25 importance of family and time off, offering subsidized childcare, long vacations, and generous maternity and paternity leave.[1] It has even said that fathers must—by law—take time off to be with their children. It is one of the only countries to do so.

30 At the same time, the country is saving for the future. Every dollar earned from oil is put straight into what is now the world's biggest pension fund—worth over $200 billion. None of this money is spent on infrastructure projects—not even new schools and
35 hospitals. At a time when most other countries just borrow money to finance the pensions of their growing retired population, Norway is sitting pretty.[2]

[1]**leave** (n) /liːv/ time off from work
[2]**sitting pretty** (v) /ˌsɪtɪŋ ˈprɪti/ in a good situation

Grammar focus adverbs: *only, just, even*

> **FOCUS ADVERBS: *ONLY, JUST, EVEN***
>
> **only**
> 1 **Only** Luxembourg and a couple of other countries are richer.
>
> **just**
> 2 **Just** last century, Norwegians were emigrating to the USA.
> 3 Most other countries **just** borrow money to finance the pensions of their growing retired population.
>
> **even**
> 4 People say **even** the prisons are quite comfortable!
> 5 This doesn't **even** feel like a competition anymore!
>
> For more information and practice, see page 178.

7 Look at the grammar box. Which of these statements (a, b, or c) is true of each of the three focus adverbs: *only, just,* and *even*?

a The focus adverb comes directly after the word or phrase it is emphasizing.
b The focus adverb comes directly before the word or phrase it is emphasizing.
c When emphasizing a verb, the focus adverb comes directly after the main verb.

8 Work in pairs. Find and underline other examples of *only, just,* and *even* in the article. What word or phrase does each adverb focus on?

9 Work in pairs. Discuss the meaning of each sentence (1–6). Then match each one with the sentence that follows it (a–f).

1 Only visitors think Norway is expensive. ＿＿
2 Visitors think only Norway is expensive. ＿＿
3 Among Scandinavian countries, I have visited Norway just once. ＿＿
4 Among Scandinavian countries, I have visited just Norway. ＿＿
5 Even fathers are given time off to be with their children. ＿＿
6 Fathers are given time off to be with their children, even when the children are older. ＿＿

a Of course, mothers are given a lot of time off, too.
b I have visited the other countries several times.
c However, all Scandinavian countries are expensive.
d I haven't visited the other countries at all.
e The locals themselves find it reasonable.
f This is in addition to the time they are given off when the children are babies.

10 Put the focus adverbs in parentheses in the correct place in these sentences.

1 No, thanks. I'm/looking. (just)
2 The most difficult problems have a solution. (even)
3 I'm going to brush my teeth, then we can leave. (just)
4 Don't worry. It's money. (only)
5 He's always losing things. He lost his own wedding ring once. (even)
6 It's a suggestion—you don't have to follow it. (only)
7 It's the second time we've met. (only)

11 Pronunciation focus adverbs

a ▶ 105 Listen and check your answers to Exercise 10. Are the focus adverbs stressed?

b Work in pairs. Practice saying the sentences in Exercise 10 in the same way.

Speaking myLife

12 Work in pairs. Place a focus adverb (*only, just, even*) in the correct place in each sentence below. There is sometimes more than one possible answer. Discuss whether these facts are true of your country.

1 Many people work long hours during the week, so they see their children on weekends.
2 People with college degrees are finding it difficult to get jobs these days.
3 For many people, a job is a way to make money, not something they particularly enjoy.
4 The rich are a very small part of the population.
5 The state's welfare program gives financial aid to the poor, but it meets their basic needs.

13 Work in pairs. Write two sentences about your country using focus adverbs. Choose from these topics:

- the cost of living
- work-life balance
- retirement and pensions
- transportation
- employment

*The cost of living is high in our capital city. **Even** basic things like bread and milk are expensive.*

14 Work with another pair. Read your sentences from Exercise 13 to each other. Were your descriptions similar?

12b Get someone else to do it

Vocabulary services

1 Work in pairs. Match the words in box A with the words in box B to make as many services as you can.

A car	carpet	**B** alterations	
child	clothing	cleaning	cutting
computer	dog	installation	care
furniture	hair	painting	planning
house	party	repair	restoration
shoe	window	walking	washing

2 Work in pairs. Discuss these questions about the services in Exercise 1.

1 Which of these things do people generally do themselves?
2 Which of these services might people pay someone else to do?
3 Which services do you think involve the greatest skill?

Listening

3 ▶ 106 Work in pairs. Listen to an interview with an economics professor. Discuss the questions.

1 Which services from Exercise 1 do the speakers mention?
2 Does the professor think people paying for these services is a good thing or a bad thing? Why?

4 ▶ 106 Work in pairs. Listen to the interview again. Discuss the following things.

1 why more people are paying for these services
2 the reaction of the interviewer to the story of the person who hired some help at Christmas
3 what the professor says about the people who provide these services

Wordbuilding *the* + adjective

> **WORDBUILDING** *the* + adjective

We can use *the* + adjective to refer to a group of people. *the rich, the poor, the powerless*

For more practice, see Workbook page 99.

5 Look at the wordbuilding box. Match the groups of people (a–c) with the expressions on the right.

a people who are over 70 ○   ○ the homeless

b people with no jobs   ○   ○ the elderly

c people without housing ○   ○ the unemployed

Grammar causative *have* and *get*

> **CAUSATIVE *HAVE* and *GET***
>
> *have/get* + something + past participle
> 1 *Nowadays, you can **have your car washed** inside and out by professional car washers for as little as $8.*
> 2 *I've even heard of people who **get their Christmas tree put up**.*
>
> *have* + someone + base form of the verb
> 3 *You don't have to be rich to **have a house cleaner clean** your home once a week.*
>
> *get* + someone + infinitive
> 4 *The idea of **getting someone to wash** your car was unthinkable.*

For more information and practice, see page 178.

6 Look at the grammar box. In which sentence(s) (1–4) is:

a someone doing a job for you? _____
b the person doing the job not mentioned? _____
c the person who does the job always mentioned? _____

7 Look at track 106 of the audioscript on page 190. Underline other examples of each type of causative verb.

8 Complete the summary of a survey about paying for services. Use the correct form of the verbs in parentheses.

> We all have tasks that need to get ¹_____ (do) that we would rather not do ourselves. These days, an increasing number of Americans are outsourcing their chores. Nearly half of those surveyed have other people ²_____ (do) their gardening, and a third get someone ³_____ (help) with house cleaning. People are happy to pay for having the house ⁴_____ (clean) regularly, getting the lawn ⁵_____ (mow), and having a handyman ⁶_____ (fix) things that are broken. With online sites, almost any odd job can be outsourced for the right price. It costs around $25 per hour to have a personal assistant ⁷_____ (organize) your affairs, and up to $50 per hour to have children or pets ⁸_____ (look) after. It seems that more households have decided that it is worth spending some money to save time.

9 Look at these things (1–3) that an affluent couple gets other people to do for them. Complete the sentences with causative forms. Use the correct form of the verbs in parentheses.

1 When they had a party last month, someone organized everything for them.
  They _____ everything for them. (get)
2 A personal trainer takes their children to the park to play soccer.
  They _____ their children to the park to play soccer. (have)
3 A driver picks their children up from school every day.
  They _____ from school every day. (have)

10 Look at the services in Exercise 1 again. Using the causative verbs *have* or *get*, write down:

• one thing that you usually get someone else to do.
• one thing that you would never get someone else to do.

Compare your sentences with a partner.

11 Pronunciation /ʃ/, /tʃ/, /ʒ/, and /dʒ/

a ▶ 107 Listen carefully to how the underlined letters are pronounced in the following words. Then practice saying them with a partner.

/ʃ/	/tʃ/	/ʒ/	/dʒ/
carwa<u>sh</u>	<u>ch</u>ores	deci<u>s</u>ion	chan<u>ge</u>
<u>sh</u>elves	ri<u>ch</u>er	gara<u>g</u>e	colle<u>ge</u>
<u>sh</u>opper	wat<u>ch</u>	plea<u>s</u>ure	fri<u>dge</u>

b ▶ 108 Work in pairs. Listen to these words. Discuss which of the four sounds /ʃ/, /tʃ/, /ʒ/, or /dʒ/ is in each word. Then practice saying them.

agent	arrange	cheese	choice
fashion	general	January	machine
sugar	television	usual	

Speaking myLife

12 The letters DIY stand for "do it yourself." Work in pairs. Match the verbs in box A with the nouns in box B to make as many jobs as you can. How many of these are DIY jobs?

A assemble	clean		**B** the roof	some shelves
decorate	hang		a carpet	the kitchen
install	fix		a picture	a bed frame
put up	tile		a faucet	

13 Work in pairs. Look at the apartment in the photo below. Make a list of all the things that you would need to get done before you could live in it. Then decide which things you would do yourself and which things you would get professional help to do. Explain your plans to another pair.

12c Start-up

Reading

1 Work in pairs. Look at the photo on page 147 and answer these questions.

1 What kind of food do you think is sold from this truck?
2 Do you think businesses like this make a lot of money? Why or why not?
3 Do you go to these kinds of take-out food trucks? Why or why not?

2 Read the article and make brief notes on the following. Then compare your notes with a partner.

1 the basic business idea
2 the gap or opportunity in the market
3 advertising
4 why the business is popular

3 Look at the subheadings (A–F) below. Match each subheading with one of the paragraphs (1–6) in the article.

A Spreading the word ____
B Hard times can be good times ____
C Big business ____
D Making yourself attractive ____
E Small beginnings ____
F A social event ____

Vocabulary business words

4 Work in pairs. Find these words or phrases (a–g) related to business in the article. What do you think they mean? Check your answers on page 155.

a trend (paragraph 1)
b recession (paragraph 2)
c set up (paragraph 2)
d upscale (paragraph 3)
e passing fad (paragraph 3)
f buzz (paragraph 4)
g catchy (paragraph 5)

Critical thinking opinion words

5 Writers often use adjectives, adverbs, and adverbial phrases to give their opinion. Find these words or phrases in the article and discuss in pairs what the writer is saying about each situation.

1 Even more significantly (line 6)
   The writer thinks this is very important.
2 Strangely (line 12)
3 even (line 25)
4 impressive (line 43)
5 definitely (line 57)
6 And after all, (lines 59–60)

6 Work in pairs. Overall, how would you sum up the author's opinion of this business idea? Do you agree with him? Why or why not?

Speaking *my*Life

7 Work in small groups. Imagine that you have bought the old railway carriage in the photo below. Discussing each of these points, come up with a business idea for it.

• the service you will offer (e.g., restaurant, vacation accommodations, take-out food and drink, something else?)
• the location (e.g., in a town, the countryside, a beach, a sports venue?)
• the customers (a particular group or the general public?)
• the promotion of the idea (how will you attract customers?)

8 As a group, present your ideas to the class. At the end, vote on which you think is the best business plan.

START-UP

▶ 109

1 It started as a simple business idea. Two friends in Los Angeles thought it might be fun to mix Korean barbecue recipes with Mexican tacos and sell the take-out food from a van. That was in 2008, and the resulting tacos—what
5 founder Roy Choi calls "Los Angeles on a plate"—became an instant success. Even more significantly, their Kogi BBQ food truck started a whole new trend in mobile cuisine.[1]

2 Food trucks and vans have been around for a long time. There are hot dog and hamburger vans selling cheap eats
10 along roadsides and next to construction sites all over California. What Kogi BBQ food did was to bring higher quality food to consumers at a reasonable price. Strangely, the economic recession of 2008 was an excellent opportunity for this kind of business. Choi could set up a business at a
15 fraction[2] of the cost of opening a new restaurant. He could also easily find staff from among the increased number of unemployed workers that had become available. At the same time, consumers—now less willing to spend their money in traditional restaurants—were happy to find that they could
20 still go out and find good food at an affordable price.

3 Today, thousands of upscale food trucks are parked on city streets from San Francisco to Washington, D.C., selling everything from luxurious lobster rolls to handmade ice cream. What seemed at the time to be a passing fad is
25 now a growing, $800-million annual industry. There has even been a Hollywood movie, *Chef*, about the phenomenon.

4 Choi is modest about his part in this revolution. "I picked up on the feeling that food was important," he writes, "not just a meal to fuel yourself to do something else." But it
30 wasn't simply the idea to fuse[3] Korean and Mexican cuisine that brought in the customers. What really put Kogi on the map was its early use of social media. Initially, Kogi's small team didn't have much luck selling their food outside nightclubs on Sunset Boulevard. Then they started
35 exploiting the growing power of social media. Kogi used Twitter to constantly update customers on its changing location. Little by little, a loyal group of plugged-in[4] young followers appeared, tracking Kogi, and they started to create a buzz around the brand. Within a
40 few months, Kogi was attracting hundreds of customers—and serving up to 200 kilos of meat—at several stops every day. *Newsweek* called it "America's first viral eatery." Kogi BBQ now has an impressive 152,000 Twitter followers, four trucks, and a full catering
45 operation.

5 Branding and a catchy name are very important: *Banh in the USA* (Vietnamese sandwiches), *Ragin' Cajun* (Creole food), and *Waff 'n' Roll* (waffles) are some good examples. The trucks themselves are brightly painted
50 and covered with colorful stickers.

6 At 10 p.m. on a cold Saturday night, I join the line outside the Kogi BBQ truck. It's a long line, mostly of young people. Customers take photos of their tacos as they buy them and send the photos to their friends.
55 One couple has driven two hours to be here, and they joke and chat with a local couple who are regulars. There is definitely an important social aspect to this. It may be take-out food, but it's a shared experience, and—from what I can see—a very happy one. And after
60 all, isn't that what eating should be about?

> [1]**cuisine** (n) /kwɪˈziːn/ a style of cooking
> [2]**fraction** (n) /ˈfrækʃ(ə)n/ a small amount (of something)
> [3]**fuse** (v) /fjuːz/ combine (often to make something new)
> [4]**plugged-in** (adj) /ˈplʌɡd ɪn/ technologically connected

12d The bottom line

Real life negotiating

1 Work in pairs. Which of these things have you negotiated for? Are there any other things that you have negotiated for recently? Did you get the deal you hoped for?

- your salary
- a car or other expensive item
- who does the chores at home
- more time to finish a piece of work

2 Read this advice about negotiating. Do you agree with it? How does it relate to your own experience? Discuss with a partner.

"Never get emotionally involved in the thing you are negotiating for. If the other person sees how much you want something, you will be at a disadvantage."

3 ▶ **110** Listen to a woman who is trying to negotiate with a real estate agent for a lease (or contract) on a building. Work in pairs. Answer the questions.

1 What point do they have trouble agreeing on?
2 What does the woman suggest to get around this problem?
3 How does the negotiation end?
4 How important is it to each person to agree on this lease?

4 ▶ **110** Look at the expressions for negotiating. Listen again and complete these expressions with the words you hear.

> ▶ **NEGOTIATING**
>
> A key thing for us is ¹ _____ the lease.
> I was hoping we could ² _____ down.
> If you look at it from our point of view, we're a
> ³ _____ and ...
> Let's face it, five years is a ⁴ _____ .
> Do you think your client would be willing to
> ⁵ _____ a bit on that?
> I'm sure you'll appreciate that my client's
> ⁶ _____ is ...
> To tell you the truth, that's why the rent is
> ⁷ _____ .
> Isn't there some way around that?
> Not that I can think of.
> What did you have in mind?
> If I were in your shoes, I think I'd just
> ⁸ _____ .
> At the end of the day, it has to ⁹ _____
> for you.

5 Work in pairs. Look at the expressions for negotiating again. Which expressions are used for the following?

- to say what the important thing is
- to be direct and clear
- to talk about an obstacle to the agreement
- to ask the other person to see your side

6 Could each person have done better in the negotiation? If so, how? Discuss with your partner.

7 Pronunciation long vowel sounds

a ▶ **111** Listen to the long vowel sounds and repeat the words.

/eɪ/ del<u>ay</u> t<u>a</u>ke   /əʊ/ l<u>ow</u> neg<u>o</u>tiate
/iː/ m<u>e</u>dium d<u>e</u>tailed   /uː/ incl<u>u</u>de sh<u>oe</u>s
/aɪ/ f<u>i</u>nal l<u>i</u>ne

b ▶ **112** Work in pairs. Listen to these phrases and underline the long vowel sound in each phrase. Then practice saying the phrases.

1 A key thing for us is ...
2 I was hoping we could ...
3 Let's face it, ...
4 At the end of the day, ...
5 What did you have in mind?
6 To tell you the truth, ...

8 Work in pairs.

Student A: You are living in a foreign country for eight months and want to buy a car to use while you are there. You see a secondhand car advertised in the newspaper. It seems to be exactly what you are looking for. Look at the information on page 153.

Student B: You have a secondhand car that you want to sell. Look at the information on page 155.

Have a conversation to negotiate the sale of the car.

A: The car is great. It's exactly what I'm looking for.
B: That's good. You'd like to buy it then?
A: Well, ideally, yes, I would. But ...

12e Get to the point

Writing a short report

1 Read this brief report about a training course that someone attended. Work in pairs and answer the questions.

1 What was the aim of the course? Was it successful?
2 What was unusual about the course?

As requested, here is my feedback on the one-day public speaking course at the LeGard School in Paris.

Overall, it was a great experience, although not at all what I had expected. The teachers all have a background in theater and acting. So rather than learning about how to structure a talk or use PowerPoint slides, we concentrated on various drama techniques: specifically, voice control, breathing, posture, and movement. Initially, I was very skeptical about this. However, as the day progressed, the value became clearer. We were asked to use the techniques in short role plays—a family argument, or a friend's dinner party. Normally, I would feel very embarrassed about acting or performing in front of other people, but I didn't; the techniques improved my confidence enormously. Consequently, I now feel much more ready to take on the challenge of public speaking.

To sum up, I would strongly recommend this innovative course as an introduction to public speaking, although a follow-up course on how to write a speech might be necessary.

2 Read the report again and make brief notes about the following. Then compare your notes with a partner.

1 type of course
2 location
3 general impression
4 details of the course
5 positive points
6 what the course lacked
7 recommendation

3 Writing skill **key phrases in report writing**

a Underline words or phrases in the report with these meanings. (They are listed in the order that they appear in the report.)

1 Because I was asked to do this
2 When you look at the whole thing
3 To give precise details
4 At the beginning
5 As a result of this
6 My conclusion is that

b Complete these sentences. Use four of the words or phrases you underlined in the report.

1 _____ , I am sending you a price list for our courses, _____ the courses in report and letter writing.
2 The course is very expensive. _____ , I would not recommend it.
3 _____ , I thought it would be too difficult, but the teacher explained everything very carefully during the lesson.

4 Write a short report (150–180 words) giving feedback on a course you have taken. Include these points:

• the name and length of the course
• the number of participants
• the methods used
• the effectiveness of the course
• your recommendation

5 Exchange reports with a partner. Use these questions to check your partner's report.

• Does the report include all the points listed in Exercise 4?
• Does it use some of the key phrases for report writing?
• What is your overall impression of the course?

12f The Farmery

Plants growing in an urban farm market in
North Carolina, USA

Before you watch

1 Work in pairs. Look at the photo and the title of the video. What new business idea do you think is shown here?

2 Key vocabulary

a Work in pairs. Read the sentences (1–5). The words and phrases in **bold** are used in the video. Guess the meaning of the words and phrases.

1 We have a small **greenhouse** in the backyard where we grow tomatoes.
2 Supermarkets generally experience between five and ten percent **inventory loss** in fruit and vegetables.
3 The company is planning to **consolidate** its business activities at a new site in Arizona.
4 The grape **harvest** takes place every September and needs a lot of extra workers to complete.
5 We walked along the beach, collecting seashells and interesting colored **pebbles**.

b Write the words and phrases in **bold** in Exercise 2a next to their definitions (a–e).

a the cutting and collecting of crops when they are fully grown or ripe _____
b losing items of stock because they are damaged, wasted, or stolen _____
c small round stones _____
d a glass building in which plants or vegetables are grown _____
e combine things in order to make them more effective or easier to deal with _____

While you watch

3 ▶ **12.1, 12.2** Watch Parts 1–2 of the video and check (✓) the things you see. Then work in pairs and compare your answers. Tell your partner what you think Ben Greene's business idea is and what makes it original.

☐ fields
☐ farm animals
☐ crops
☐ farm buildings
☐ a restaurant
☐ a greenhouse
☐ shipping containers
☐ mushrooms
☐ vegetable greens
☐ frogs

4 ▶ **12.1** Watch Part 1 of the video again. Complete the summary with the correct form of these verbs.

| consolidate | grow | hang | lose |
| transport | sell | use | |

Most food grown on farms has to be harvested, packed, and then ¹ _____ to the shops. At every stage, you ² _____ some of the harvest. So Ben Greene's idea was to ³ _____ this whole process into one site. At The Farmery, a structure made from shipping containers and greenhouse parts, Greene ⁴ _____ the food within the building and then ⁵ _____ it in an area at the bottom of the building. The plants grow on living walls that ⁶ _____ off the outside of shipping containers. It's a very different method— Greene ⁷ _____ systems where the plants grow in water. The Farmery focuses on mushrooms, herbs, and salad greens.

5 ▶ **12.2** Read the questions below. Watch Part 2 of the video again and make notes. Then discuss the questions with a partner.

1 What does Ben Greene say he is giving customers with this new way of buying food?
2 How would he like to expand his business?
3 What are the two markets he has identified for food grown in this way?
4 How does Ben Greene hope people will look at food after experiencing The Farmery?
5 Above all, how does he want people to feel when they have visited The Farmery?

After you watch

6 Vocabulary in context

a ▶ **12.3** Watch the clips from the video. Choose the correct meaning of the words and phrases.

b Complete these sentences in your own words. Then share your sentences with a partner.

1 I want to pursue a career in … because …
2 … is a very complex subject.
3 I'm on a mission to …

7 Work in pairs. What do you think of The Farmery? Do you think it would be a good idea in your area? Why or why not?

8 Work in small groups. Below is a list of products that could be made and sold at the same site. Choose one and decide how to make buying it an interesting experience for customers. Present your ideas to the class. Which was the best idea?

- clothes or shoes
- chocolate
- bread or cakes
- furniture

Grammar

1 Put the words in parentheses in the correct order to complete the text.

The internet has changed the economy in more ways ¹_____ (how / just / than) we shop. It has also encouraged us to share more, such as by giving free online advice on how to do things. Whereas before we might have gone straight to a garage ²_____ (to / repaired / our car / have), now we look online first to see if someone can tell us how to fix it. ³_____ (set up / some communities / have / even) internet groups where neighbors lend each other things. If you have a hole in your roof, in the past you would ⁴_____ (paid / to / fix / someone / have) it. But now, you might ask a neighbor if you could borrow a ladder, or you ⁵_____ (even / ask / might / for) their help. We are all winners in this sharing economy because ⁶_____ (help / to / other people / getting) us saves money and builds social connections.

2 Read the text above again. According to the author, what are the benefits of the sharing economy brought about by the internet?

3 Work in pairs. Tell your partner about a) two jobs you would only get someone else to do, and b) something you have just had done.

I CAN
use focus adverbs to add emphasis
use causative *have* and *get*

Vocabulary

4 Match each verb (1–3) with a suitable noun to make phrases. Which of these jobs could you do yourself? Which would you have someone do for you? Tell a partner.

1 assemble ○   ○ a leaky faucet
2 put up ○   ○ a bed frame
3 fix ○   ○ some shelves

5 Complete the definitions (1–4) with four of these words.

earnings	invest	lend	life
living	loan	owe	salary

1 If you have an obligation to pay someone, you _____ them money.
2 Your _____ is the money that you receive from your work or investments.
3 Your quality of _____ refers to your level of health, well-being, and happiness.
4 A(n) _____ is money you borrow to buy something.

6 **>> MB** Work in pairs. Write definitions for these words and phrases: *debt, the income gap, standard of living*.

I CAN
talk about money and the economy

Real life

7 Complete the conversation by matching each of the travel agent's statements (1–4) with the customer's responses (a–d).

1 **TA:** So, how does our proposal look? We've suggested four different hotels in different cities. ____
2 **TA:** Well, you asked for top hotels, and I'm sure you'll appreciate that they aren't cheap. ____
3 **TA:** Exactly. This is a once-in-a-lifetime trip. ____
4 **TA:** I'm not sure about that, but I can check if you like. ____

a **C:** I understand that. Nice hotels are a key thing for us, because it is our honeymoon, at the end of the day.
b **C:** If you could, that would be great. I'm sure there must be a way around this.
c **C:** It looks amazing, but to tell you the truth, it's more money than we were hoping to spend.
d **C:** Would it be cheaper if we stayed in just one hotel for the whole two weeks?

8 **>> MB** Work in pairs. Act out the conversation in Exercise 7. Add one more exchange between the travel agent and the customer to finish the negotiation.

I CAN
negotiate a proposal

UNIT 2b Exercise 10, page 25

Student A

Photo A

Location:	Kenya, Maasai Mara National Reserve
Subject:	A Kenyan chef waits to serve breakfast to tourists on safari in the Maasai Mara National Reserve.
Story:	Tourists in Kenya pay over $300 per day for a hot air balloon safari. Included in the safari is a champagne breakfast.
Emotions/ Ideas:	The luxury that some tourists enjoy.

UNIT 2e Exercise 4, page 29

- Photographer Steve Winter and writer Douglas Chadwick were writing a story on rhinos in Kaziranga National Park in India.
- They drove into the park to start filming.
- A few kilometers into the park, they saw three young rhinos on the road.
- The driver of the jeep stopped the car, and Steve and Douglas got out to film the rhinos.
- The mother of the three rhinos came out of the trees to their left, hit the jeep with her horn, and tried to push it off the road.
- Steve and Douglas got back into the jeep.
- The driver put his foot down, and the jeep moved off.
- The mother rhino chased after them for 200 meters.

UNIT 5a Exercise 1, page 58

Urban features

apartment building	bus station	shopping mall
residential area	pedestrian area	city hall
green space	high-rise building	sports center
luxury apartments	office building	city center
pedestrian zone	railway station	parking lot
shopping center	business center	

UNIT 6b Exercise 11, page 73

Student A

Prepare a list of questions to find out more about the volunteer vacation. Ask about:

- the length of the vacation.
- the kind of work involved.
- the skills and experience required (if any).
- the type of accommodation provided.
- the cost.
- anything else you should know.

UNIT 10b Exercise 13, page 121

Pair A

UNIT 12d Exercise 8, page 148

Student A

You want to buy this car. It is a seven-year-old VW Golf, and the advertised price is $3,000. It is in good condition but has done a lot of miles (100,000). You would like to get it for less, if you can. The problem is you have been looking for a long time and want to get a car quickly so that you can drive to work every day.

UNIT 3c Exercise 8, page 38

Product 4—Solar Wi-Fi Streetlight

The StarSight system consists of a series of pylons that use solar panels to power streetlamps, a Wi-Fi box for wireless internet access, and, if needed, closed-circuit TVs for security surveillance. The result is an integrated system of electricity and communication, plus better street lighting, which has been shown to help reduce crime.

Developed by: Kolam Partnership Ltd.
Launch countries: Nigeria, South Africa, Turkey

UNIT 2b Exercise 10, page 25

Student B

Photo B

Location:	Ontario, Canada
Subject:	Twin girls, Lily and Gillian, born in China, meet each other after a long separation.
Story:	Lily and Gillian were adopted when they were less than one year old by two different families in Canada. The families meet regularly so the girls can spend time together.
Emotions/ Ideas:	Happiness at being reunited; the strong bond there is between twins.

UNIT 3c Exercise 8, page 38

Product 1—Portable Clay Cooler

This pot-in-pot system uses evaporation from a layer of wet sand between two pots to help extend the life of farmers' goods. Tomatoes can last weeks instead of just days. This means more fresh produce at the market and more income for farmers.

Developed by: Mohammed Bah Abba
Launch country: Nigeria

UNIT 6b Exercise 11, page 73

Student B

Program 2

Borneo Flora initiative—volunteers welcome
Do important work cataloging plants in the tropical rain forests of Borneo. This is outdoor work in very hot and humid conditions. Two-month program including one week's initial training. Training will be conducted by expert scientists. You will be living in tents with other volunteers. Practical experience of camping is an advantage.
Cost: $2,300 (including flights)

UNIT 11c Exercise 9, page 134

Quiz

Circle A, B, or C to complete each sentence below so that it is true for you. Then look at the key on page 155 to find out what type of learner you are. Work in pairs and discuss if you agree with this.

1 WHEN I STUDY GRAMMAR, I LEARN BEST BY ...
    A reading clear rules   B writing down examples
    C putting it into practice in conversation
2 IN LESSONS, I PREFER ...
    A discussing   B looking at pictures, maps, diagrams, or videos
    C doing something practical
3 I REMEMBER NEW VOCABULARY BEST WHEN IT IS ACCOMPANIED BY ...
    A a clear definition   B an image   C a demonstration
4 IF I AM DISTRACTED IN CLASS, I USUALLY ...
    A hum or sing to myself   B make little drawings in my book
    C play with a pen or pencil
5 WHEN LEARNING A NEW SKILL, I PREFER ...
    A someone to explain it to me   B someone to demonstrate it
    C just to get on with it myself
6 WHEN I'M NOT SURE HOW TO SPELL A WORD, I ...
    A say the word aloud to myself   B try to visualize it in my mind
    C write down different versions
7 I PREFER TO READ STORIES WITH LOTS OF ...
    A dialog   B descriptive passages   C action or adventure
8 I PROBABLY LEARN MOST WHEN I'M ...
    A listening to other people speak English
    B watching an English movie or documentary
    C trying to use English myself

UNIT 3c Exercise 8, page 38

Product 2—Sugarcane Charcoal

Burning wood and dung—the main fuel sources for many in the developing world—has contributed to deforestation and breathing problems among inhabitants. These briquettes (small bricks) made from crushed sugarcane stalks not only make use of a local resource, they also burn more cleanly and allow residents to start a charcoal business for less than $50.

Developed by: MIT D-Lab
Launch country: Haiti

UNIT 6b Exercise 11, page 73

Student B

> **Program 1**
>
> *Volunteers needed to help to rebuild Joseph's Elementary School in Mali*
>
> - minimum three weeks; maximum twelve weeks
> - physical work—you need to be fit and hardworking
> - no experience needed—volunteers will be trained on the job
> - conditions: living in small rural village; climate is very hot and dry; two days off per week
> - accommodation provided: basic; sharing with other volunteers
>
> Cost: from $1,400 upwards (including flights)
>
> Note: Volunteers can choose to live with a local family instead (additional cost)

UNIT 11c Exercise 9, page 134

Answers to quiz

Mostly A's—This means you have an auditory learning style. In other words, you remember best when you hear things.

Mostly B's—This means you have a visual learning style. In other words, you remember best when you see things.

Mostly C's—This means you have a kinesthetic learning style. In other words, you remember best when you do things or when things are acted out.

UNIT 12c Exercise 4, page 146

Vocabulary—business words

a   trend (n) = a fashion or direction
b   recession (n) = a period of economic decline
c   set up (v) = establish
d   upscale (adj) = high quality and more expensive
e   passing (adj) fad (n) = something that is popular for only a short time
f   buzz (n) = excitement and activity
g   catchy (adj) = easy to remember

UNIT 12d Exercise 8, page 148

Student B

> You want to sell this car. It is a seven-year-old VW Golf, and the advertised price is $3,000. It is in good condition but has done a lot of miles (100,000). You would like to get as close to the asking price as possible. However, it has been advertised for two months, and you would like to sell it soon.

UNIT 3c Exercise 8, page 38

> **Product 3—Water Container**
>
>
>
> In poor rural areas, clean water is often miles away from the people who need it, leaving them vulnerable to diseases found in unclean water. The Q Drum holds 13 gallons (59 liters) in a rolling container that makes it easy to transport safe drinking water—a task that is usually done by women and children.
>
> Developed by: P. J. and J. P. S. Hendrikse
> Launch country: South Africa

UNIT 10b Exercise 13, page 121

Pair B

		¹							
	²l	o	u	³d		⁴f	⁵a	r	
⁶									
⁷v	i	s	i	o	n				
				⁸t	r	a	i	n	
			⁹b	u	¹⁰s	h			
¹¹g	¹²o								
¹³m	e	n	t	i	o	n	¹⁴e	y	e
			¹⁵k	e	y				

GRAMMAR SUMMARY UNIT 1

Present tenses: simple, continuous, and perfect

We use the simple present to express something we see as permanent or unchanging. This can be:

- a fact, e.g., Water **boils** at 100°C.

- a habit, e.g., He **eats** a lot of junk food.

- a routine, e.g., Joanna **calls** her sister every day.

We use the present continuous to express:

- something happening at the time of speaking.
  I'm **waiting** for the train to come—it's late again.

- a temporary situation.
  Juan's **working** for a bank at the moment, but he wants to change careers.

- something happening around the time of speaking.
  She's **trying** to find a new job.

- a currently changing situation.
  The future of some animals **is becoming** less certain.

Remember that we don't use stative verbs (verbs that describe states) with a continuous tense.
  I don't **know** him very well. (not I'm not knowing)

We use the present perfect (simple and continuous) to express a connection between the present and the past. This can be:

- when a past event has an impact on, or relevance in, the present.
  Poor Sam—he's **broken** his leg.

- when something started in the past and continues into the present.
  I've **been** best friends with Ian since we were in college.

▶ Exercises 1 and 2

Present perfect simple and continuous

We use the present perfect simple and continuous to talk about the same time periods. We use the present perfect continuous when we want to emphasize the duration of the event. We use it to talk about:

- past events that have an impact on the present.
  She's tired—she's **been working** all day.

- repeated past events that have an impact on the present.
  A: You look fit and healthy!
  B: Thanks—I've **been exercising** a lot recently.

- prolonged (long) events that started in the past and continue in the present.
  We've **been waiting** for the bus for over an hour!

- repeated events that started in the past and continue in the present.
  I've **been coming** to this café for years.

We often have a choice whether to use the present perfect simple or present perfect continuous. We choose the present perfect continuous when we want to emphasize duration or repetition.
  I've **lived** here for over ten years. (no particular emphasis)
  I've **been living** here for over ten years. (emphasis on how long it has been)

In some cases, there is a bigger difference in meaning.
  I've **written** a lot of emails this morning. (= I've finished writing emails.)
  I've **been writing** emails all morning. (= I may still have more to write.)

▶ Exercise 3

Simple past and present perfect

We use both simple past and present perfect to talk about the past.

We use the simple past to refer to something at a specific time in the past.
  I **lived** with my parents until I was 25.

We use the present perfect to express a connection between the past and the present.
  Aaron's **lost** his phone. (past event that is relevant now)
  I've **lived** with my parents all my life. (event which started in the past and continues)

Time expressions

We normally use adverbs of finished time periods with the simple past. With the present perfect simple or continuous, we normally use adverbs of unfinished time periods. Common time expressions include:

Simple past: *last week, in the past, in 2016, yesterday, a few days ago, when I was a child*
  I started work there **a year ago**.

Present perfect simple: *ever, so far, just, over the past three months, this year, since I was a child, yet, before, already, recently*
  I have never worked abroad **before**.

Present perfect continuous: *just, over the past three months, this year, since I was a child, all morning*
  I've been working here **since last year**.

Some time adverbials can be used with both simple past and present perfect.
  I waited **all morning**.
  I've been waiting **all morning**.

▶ Exercises 4 and 5

Exercises

1a Circle the correct tenses to complete the sentences.

1 More and more people *are becoming / become* vegetarians.
2 A: Who's that?
   B: Mateo. *He's bought / He buys* a new car.
3 They *know / have known* each other for a long time.
4 *I often meet / I'm meeting* my friends on Saturday evenings.
5 *She's staying / She stays* with her parents until she finds an apartment.
6 Martha *is always being / is always* very reliable.
7 *It rains / It's raining* again—we can't go to the park.
8 *I learn / I'm learning* French at the moment.

1b Match the sentences (1–8) from Exercise 1a with the uses below (a–h).

a fact ____
b routine ____
c something happening at the time of speaking ____
d something happening around the time of speaking ____
e a changing situation ____
f a temporary situation ____
g past event with relevance in the present ____
h past event that continues in the present ____

2 Complete the conversation with the simple present, present continuous, or present perfect simple of the verbs in parentheses.

A: You ¹_____ (be) late!
B: I know, sorry! I was talking to Peter.
A: Oh, how is he?
B: He's looking very fit. But I'm not surprised—he ²_____ (go) to the gym every day after work.
A: I ³_____ (not see) him for a long time. Does he still work in his father's company?
B: Yes, but he ⁴_____ (look) for another job. He wants to go and live abroad.
A: Really? I know a lot of people who ⁵_____ (move) abroad recently.
B: Me, too—it's strange.
A: Anyway, I ⁶_____ (be) really hungry. Should we order something to eat?
B: Yes, of course. Oh sorry, my phone ⁷_____ (ring). It might be my boss. I have to answer it … Sorry!

3 Complete the sentences with the present perfect simple or continuous of the verbs in parentheses.

1 I'm really fed up! I _____ (wait) for the train for over an hour!
2 A: Is that a new car?
   B: No. I _____ (have) it for three years now.
3 A: Why are you so red?
   B: I _____ (work) outside in the sun all morning.
4 How long _____ (they / be) married for?
5 My eyes hurt. I _____ (look) at the computer screen for too long.
6 A: Do you want to watch *The Martian*?
   B: No. I _____ (see) it already.

4 Circle the correct time phrases to complete the sentences.

1 I lived there *since 2015 / from 2012 to 2014*.
2 She's eaten out twice *this week / last week*.
3 We met *in 1998 / since 1998*.
4 I've been feeling sick *a few days ago / for a few days*.
5 I've had this watch *since / when* I was a teenager.
6 They've been living in the same house *since / for* twenty years.

5 Complete the emails with the most appropriate form of the verbs in parentheses. Use the simple past, present perfect simple, or present perfect continuous.

Dear Jeanne,
My daughter and I ¹_____ (argue) a lot recently, and it's making me really sad. We mainly argue because she never helps around the house. I come home late from work, and the house is a mess. I ²_____ (try) speaking to her lots of times, but she won't listen. She ³_____ (not speak) to me since our last argument, and that was three days ago! When I was young, I always ⁴_____ (help) my parents at home, but she just doesn't care. What can I do? Clara

Dear Clara,
I'm sorry to hear about your problem. Why does your daughter think she doesn't need to help? Perhaps because you ⁵_____ (not teach) her to respect you when she was little. Now she's almost an adult, and it may be too late. I can only advise you to keep talking and explaining. Tell her: "When I ⁶_____ (work) all day, you need to help me clean up in the evening." Give her reasons, not rules—it might help. Jeanne

GRAMMAR SUMMARY UNIT 2

Narrative past tenses

We use several different tenses when we narrate a story in the past.

We use the **simple past**:

- to describe the main events in sequence, i.e., one event after another.
  *He **got** in the car, **started** the engine, and **drove** away.*

- to describe a general state in the past.
  *It **was** one of the coldest winters in memory.*

We use the **past perfect**:

- when we need to make it clear that one past event happened before another one.
  *When the police arrived, the thieves **had** already **left**.*

- to describe something that happened (or a state that was true) before the main event(s) or story.
  *I couldn't believe it when I saw the plane tickets in his hand. I'**d** always **wanted** to visit Australia!*

We use the **past continuous** to describe an activity in progress in the past. It can be:

- the background to an event within the story.
  *I **was sleeping** when the phone rang.* (event interrupts background activity)
  *It **was raining** when we arrived.* (background activity continues after event)

- the background to the main story.
  *It was 2015, and I **was living** in Paris.*

We use the **past perfect continuous** to describe a longer activity in progress in the past:

- before a main event.
  *It **had been snowing** all night, and my flight was canceled.*

- up to a main event.
  *We'**d been enjoying** a morning on the beach when something strange happened.*

We form the past perfect continuous with *had + been + -ing*.
  *He **had been** study**ing** for weeks for the test.* (+)
  *She **hadn't been** waiting for long.* (−)
  ***Had** you **been** expecting the news?* (?)

We use both past continuous and past perfect continuous to talk about an activity in progress in the past. With the past perfect continuous, there is more emphasis on the duration of the activity.
  *I'**d been walking** all morning, so I had really sore feet.*
  *I **was crossing** the road when I saw him.*

▶ **Exercises 1, 2, and 3**

The passive

Form

We form the passive with the correct form of the verb *be* and the past participle of the main verb. To change the tense, we change the form of *be*.

The photography exhibition	**is** *held every year.*
	has been *held here since 2010.*
	was *held in June.*
	had been *held just days before.*

There are also infinitive (with and without *to*) and *-ing* forms of the passive.
  *I didn't expect **to be criticized** so much.*
  *My article might **be published** in the magazine.*
  *I enjoy **being photographed**.*

We don't normally use the passive with the present perfect continuous or past perfect continuous.

Use

When we use the active form, the focus of the sentence is on the agent (the person or thing that does the action).
  Ansel Adams took this photo.

When we use the passive, the object of the active sentence becomes the subject.
  Ansel Adams took <u>this photo</u>.
  OBJECT
  <u>*This photo*</u> ***was taken*** *by Ansel Adams.*
  SUBJECT

In passive sentences, we often don't mention the agent at all. We do this:

- when the agent is unknown or unimportant, e.g., in news reports.
  *The story **was published** in over thirty languages.*
  *The car **was stolen** in the middle of the night.*

- when we prefer not to directly mention someone by name, e.g., because they did something wrong.
  *I see the kitchen **hasn't been cleaned** again.*

If we want to mention the agent, we introduce it with the preposition *by*.
  *The photo was shared **by over ten million people**.*

We often use the passive to add some follow-up information.
  *The photo of Albert Einstein sticking his tongue out is one of the most famous in history. **It was taken** in 1951 by photographer Arthur Sasse.*

▶ **Exercises 4 and 5**

Exercises

1a Number the sentences in the correct order (1–9) to make a story.

_____ When she arrived at the restaurant, she realized that she'd left her purse at home.

_____ Anu had completely forgotten about her friend's birthday dinner, and now she was late!

_____ In the end, she had a great evening, and everyone really enjoyed themselves.

_____ After paying the taxi driver, she joined her friends, who were all hungry.

_____ Anu was sitting at home when she received a message on her phone.

_____ So, she ran inside the restaurant and asked her friends for some money.

_____ She decided to get a taxi to the restaurant.

_____ They'd been waiting for a long time for her to arrive!

_____ It was from her friend, and it was about the dinner party that evening.

1b Write the underlined verbs from Exercise 1a next to their uses below (a–e).

a   a main event in the story _____

b   something that happened before the main events in the story _____

c   an activity in progress in the past (background to the main story) _____

d   an activity in progress up to a main event in the past _____

e   one event in the story that happened before another event in the story _____

2 Complete the sentences with the past perfect continuous of the verbs in parentheses.

1   The roads were really wet because it _____ (rain) all night.

2   André couldn't concentrate because he _____ (not sleep) well.

3   We _____ (not wait) for long before the train arrived.

4   I _____ (study) hard all morning, so I decided to take a break.

5   _____ (you / look) for a new job for a long time before you found one?

6   He was very happy with his result, because he _____ (try) to pass the exam for years.

7   I had a sore throat because I _____ (sing) all morning.

3 Complete the text with the correct form of the verbs in parentheses.

One day in 2001, Adele Geraghty
¹ _was reading_ (read) a newspaper when she ² _saw_ (see) an ad for a poetry competition. She ³ _decided_ (decide) to email some of her work. Soon after, she ⁴ _received_ (receive) a reply from a university professor named Phil. He said that he ⁵ _had been receiving_ (receive) similar messages from other people all week, but he didn't know why. Adele found out that the newspaper ⁶ _had printed_ (print) Phil's email address by mistake, instead of the email for the poetry competition, so she ⁷ _wrote_ (write) to Phil to tell him. Adele and Phil felt an instant connection and ⁸ _developed_ (develop) a strong friendship, even though Adele lived in the USA, and Phil was 3,000 miles away in the UK. They ⁹ _met_ (meet) for the first time in 2002—exactly one year after they ¹⁰ _he sent_ (send) their first messages— and five years after that, they got married.

4 Work in pairs. How would you rewrite the sentences (or parts of sentences) in _italics_ using the passive?

1   The first book printed in English was a collection of stories about the Trojan Wars, printed in 1473. _You can see it in the British Library in London._

2   One of the most popular songs in 2014 was "Happy." _Pharrell Williams wrote and sang it._

3   The Olympic Games takes place every four years. _In 2024, they will hold it in Paris._

4   In 2006, Edvard Munch's famous painting _The Scream_ was found. _Two years earlier, a thief stole it from a gallery in Oslo._

5   In 1962, three prisoners escaped from the Alcatraz prison island in California. _The police never found them,_ and they are still on the US government's list of wanted fugitives.

5 Complete the sentences with the correct passive form of the verbs in parentheses.

1   Bernhard Schlink wrote _The Reader_ in 1995. It _was made_ (make) into an award-winning film in 2008.

2   Snapchat _has been downloaded_ (download) over 500 million times since it was created.

3   I tried to get the book from the library, but it _had been_ already _taken out_ (take out).

4   Larger cities can _be seen_ (see) easily from the International Space Station.

5   She hopes _to be awarded_ (award) a prize for her latest documentary series.

GRAMMAR SUMMARY UNIT 3

Future forms

Making predictions

We use *will*, *might*, *be going to*, and *be about to* to make predictions.

We use *will* (or *won't*) when we are confident about a prediction. We can add *probably* if we are slightly less certain.

> A: *I'm sure you'll do really well in the exam.*
> B: *Well, I'll probably pass. But there's still a lot of work to do.*

We use *might* (or *might not*) when we are less confident about a prediction.

> *Take an umbrella—it might rain later.*

We use (*not*) *be going to* when we have some evidence for a prediction.

> *Look at the line—we're going to be here forever!*

We use *be about to* + base verb to make a prediction that something will happen very soon.

> *Oh, no! I think the car's about to break down.*

▶ Exercise 1

Plans and arrangements

We use *be going to* and the present continuous to talk about plans and arrangements. There is often little difference between them.

We use *be going to* + base verb to talk about a plan or an intention. We normally use *be going to* when we have decided to do something, but it is still an intention rather than a fixed arrangement.

> *Are you going to watch the tennis match later?*
> *I'm going to visit my cousin in Australia this summer.* (= I have decided to go, but I haven't booked my ticket yet.)

We use the present continuous to talk about a fixed arrangement to do something at a specified time in the future. Often the arrangement involves someone else, or we have already taken some kind of action such as buying a ticket, signing a contract, etc.

> *I'm starting my new job next week.*
> *She's flying to New York on Tuesday.*

We also use the present continuous to find out if people are free.

> *Are you doing anything tonight?* (= Do you want to do something together?)

We can also use *be about to* to talk about something we plan to do very soon, and *might* when we feel less confident about a plan.

> *I'm about to leave work, so I'll be home soon.*
> *I might come tonight, but I'm not sure yet.*

Instant decisions and offers

We use *will*:

- for a decision we make at the time of speaking.
  > A: *Do you want a ride to the movies?*
  > B: *No, thanks. I'll get the bus.*

- to make offers and promises.
  > *I'll send you a message later to confirm.*

▶ Exercises 2 and 3

Future continuous and future perfect

Future continuous: form

We form the future continuous with *will* + *be* + *-ing*.
> *We'll be sitting on a beach this time tomorrow!* (+)
> *We won't be leaving until 5 p.m.* (−)
> *Will you be working when I get home tonight?* (?)

Future continuous: use

We use the future continuous to describe an action in progress at or around a certain time in the future.
> *I'll be watching TV at 8:30 tonight.*

We also use the future continuous to predict events we expect to be in progress at a certain time in the future.
> *In ten years, we'll be using computers in very different ways.*

We often use time phrases (e.g., *this time next week*, *tomorrow at 8 p.m.*, *until*) with the future continuous.
> *This time next week, I'll be taking my final college exam.*

Future perfect: form

We form the future perfect with *will* + *have* + past participle.
> *We'll have arrived by 1 p.m.* (+)
> *We won't have finished the report before Monday.* (−)
> *Will people have stopped using social networks in fifty years' time?* (?)

Future perfect: use

We use the future perfect to describe an action completed before a certain time in the future.
> *I'll have finished my college project by the end of the summer.*

We often use the future perfect with time expressions like *in five years*, *in ten years' time*, *by*, *by the time*, *before*, and *already*.
> *I'll have gone to bed by the time you get home.*

▶ Exercises 4, 5, and 6

Exercises

1 Circle the correct options to complete the sentences.

1 I'm sure that he *might not / won't* be late. He's always on time.
2 He's *going to / about to* be really happy when he sees what I've made for dinner. He loves pizza!
3 They *will / might* be able to come and see us on the weekend, but they aren't sure yet.
4 Get on the train—*it will / it's about* to leave!
5 It *isn't going to / might not* rain today—look, there are no clouds in the sky.

2a Complete the sentences with the correct form of the verbs in parentheses. Use the most logical future form—*will*, *be going to*, or present continuous.

1 I've bought my ticket! I *'m flying* (fly) to Canada next month!
2 A: Would you like some tea or coffee?
   B: I *will have* (have) some coffee, please.
3 We *are going to* (visit) Tom's parents next month, but we haven't decided when exactly.
4 A: I'm really hungry!
   B: I *will make* (make) you a sandwich.
5 They *are eating* (eat) out tonight. They've already booked a table at their favorite restaurant.

2b Match the sentences (1–5) from Exercise 2a with the uses below (a–d).

a a plan or intention *3*
b a fixed arrangement *1 , 5*
c an instant decision *2*
d an offer *4*

3 Complete the conversation using the correct future form of these verbs.

ask	do	go	meet	pick

A: Mike, [1] *are* you *doing* anything tonight?
B: Not really. Why?
A: A few of us [2] *are going* to an exhibition about future technologies. I [3] *'m meeting* the others at 6:30 p.m. outside the museum. Do you want to come?
B: That sounds good. How about going for dinner afterward?
A: That's a good idea. I [4] *will ask* the others if they'd like to join us.
B: Great. Would you be able to give me a ride?
A: Yeah, sure. I [5] *will pick* you up from your office after work.

4 Circle the correct options to complete the text.

Experts say that by 2030, the world's population [1] *will be increasing / will have increased* to 8.5 billion. These extra people [2] *will have used / will be using* a lot more energy, so we'll need to find new energy sources. Solar power is one possible solution, and countries in Africa may have a big role to play in this. For example, Morocco has recently built a huge solar power plant, which [3] *will be starting / will have started* to produce a third of the country's energy within five years. The government hopes that one day, Morocco [4] *will have become / will be becoming* energy-independent, and that they [5] *will be selling / will have sold* energy to other countries around the world. If everything goes as planned, some day in the future, a person living in Europe [6] *will have used / will be using* electricity produced in Africa.

5 Complete the pairs of sentences with the future continuous or future perfect of the verbs in parentheses.

1 This time next week, I *will be sitting* (not sit) in this office. I *will have started* (start) my new job by then.
2 From 12:30 p.m. to 2:30 p.m., she *will be teaching* (teach). The lesson *will not have finished* (not finish) by 2 p.m.
3 In the future, most people *will be driving* (not drive) gas cars. But I don't think we *will have stopped* (stop) using gas completely.
4 A: I *will be passing* (pass) near your house tomorrow at about 4 p.m. Do you want to meet up?
   B: Sorry, but I *will not have gotten* (not get) back from work by then.

6 Read the information in Paula's diary. Complete the sentences below with either the future continuous or the future perfect of the verbs in parentheses. Use negative forms when necessary.

9 a.m.	start work	3–4	phone call with client
10–11	meeting		
12–1	lunch	6–7	go to gym
		7:30	dinner with Greg

1 Paula *will have started* (start) work at 9:30 a.m.
2 Her meeting *will not have finished* (finish) by 10:45 a.m.
3 She *will be having* (have) lunch between 12 and 1 p.m.
4 At 6:30 p.m., Paula *will be working out* (work out) in the gym.
5 She *will have gone* (go) to the gym by the time she has dinner.

GRAMMAR SUMMARY UNIT 4

Determiners

We use determiners before a noun to show which particular person or thing we are talking about.

We use *each*, *every*, *the whole*, *either*, and *neither* with **singular, countable nouns**. We use *each* and *every* to talk about all the members in a group. We prefer *each* when we are thinking about each member of the group separately.

> I've been to **every** museum in this city.
> **Each** gallery has a café and restaurant.

When there are only two things or people, we use *each*, not *every*.

> There were drawings on **each** side of the paper.

We use *the whole* to talk about all of something.

> I was sick, so I missed **the whole** festival.

We use *either* to say "one or the other." The negative form is "neither." It means "not one or the other."

> I'm happy to go to **either** café. They both sound good.
> I applied to two schools, but **neither** application was successful.

We use *all*, *both*, and *most* with **plural nouns**. We use *both* to talk about two things. We use *most* to say "the majority."

> **All** the stores were closed when we arrived.
> **Both** galleries have free entry.
> **Most** people where I work bring lunch from home.

We use *any* and *no* with **singular**, **plural**, and **uncountable nouns**. We can use *any* in a negative sentence or *no* in a positive sentence with the same meaning.

> There isn't **any** snow in the mountains.
> There's **no** snow in the mountains.

We also use *any* to mean "it doesn't matter which."

> Choose **any** seat you want.

We use *all*, *certain*, and *some* with **plural** and **uncountable nouns**. We use *certain* to refer to a particular place, thing, or person without naming it.

> Visitors should leave **all** food at reception.
> **Some** museums in the city are free to visit.
> The gallery is only open on **certain** days of the week.

With many determiners, we add *of* before a pronoun or before the noun phrase beginning with a possessive adjective (*my*, *her*, etc.), an article, or words like *this*, *these*, etc.

> **Some of** Sally's friends are coming tonight.
> Were **any of** the paintings good?
> A: Which **of** these two dresses do you prefer?
> B: Neither **of** them.

▶ **Exercises 1, 2, and 3**

Expressions of quantity

We use expressions of quantity to say how much or how many. Like determiners, the choice of expression depends on the meaning we want to express and whether the noun is countable or uncountable.

A large number/amount: *a lot of, lots of, plenty of, loads of, many, much, a large number of, a large/huge amount of, the majority of*

Neither a large nor a small number: *several, some, enough*

A small number/amount: *not many, not much, a little, a few, few, little, a small number of, a small amount of, a lack of, almost no, hardly any*

Zero amount: *no, not any*

We use *(not) many, (a) few, a (small/large) number of,* and *several* with **plural countable nouns**.

> There are **several** hotels around here.

We use *(not) much, (a) little, a bit of,* and *a large/huge/small amount of* with **uncountable nouns**.

> I had **a bit of** free time, so I went for a walk.

We use *a lot of, lots of, plenty of, loads of, a lack of, (almost) no, (not/hardly) any, some, enough,* and *the majority of* with **both plural and uncountable nouns**.

> There are **lots of** interesting things to see here.
> Don't rush—we've got **plenty of** time.
> There are **hardly any** music venues in this town.
> There's **a lack of** jobs for young people in my country.

In informal, spoken English, we don't normally use *many* or *much* on their own in a positive sentence. We use *a lot of, lots of,* etc., instead. *Many* and *much* are normal in negative sentences and questions.

However, we do use *too many/much* and *so many/much* in positive sentences.

▶ **Exercises 4 and 5**

little and *a little*; *few* and *a few*

There is a difference in meaning between *little* and *a little*, and between *few* and *a few*. We use *a little* and *a few* to mean "some, but not a lot."

> Would you like **a little** milk with your coffee?

We use *little* and *few* to express a more negative meaning. They mean "not much" and "not many."

> There is **little** money to improve public transportation.

We don't normally use *few* and *little* in informal, spoken English. We use *not much/many* instead.

> I don't have **much** time to study.

▶ **Exercise 6**

Exercises

1 Circle the correct determiners to complete the sentences.

1 *Every / All the* people that came to the party said they'd had a great time.
2 Only *certain / each* trains have space for bicycles.
3 *The whole / Most* artists don't earn a lot of money.
4 *Some / Each* singers like to meet their fans after their concerts.
5 She remembered that she hadn't drunk *no / any* coffee that morning.
6 There were *any / no* cars in the parking lot.
7 *Either / Neither* film that we watched over the weekend was very interesting.

2 Circle the correct options to complete the conversation.

A: So, what do you think of our new house?
B: It's really nice! I love how ¹ *each / both* room is painted in a different color.
A: Yes, we wanted ² *every / all* of the rooms to have their own identity.
B: That's a pretty painting on the wall. Where did you get it?
A: We bought it in ³ *an / some* art gallery near our house. It's by a local artist.
B: How nice! I don't have ⁴ *any / no* paintings in my house. I should get some!
A: We put a painting in ⁵ *most / every* room in the house—even the bathroom! And ⁶ *most of / most* them were painted by local artists.

3 Complete the text with these determiners.

any	both	certain
either	most	the whole

The Musée d'Orsay in Paris is one of the most famous art galleries in the world. ¹_____ of the artworks on display are French, from the period 1848 to 1914. ²_____ museum is worth visiting, but ³_____ sections are more popular than others. The most famous works on display are the "impressionist" paintings.

The building itself is also a work of art. Originally a railway station, it became a gallery in 1986. It has two famous clocks from its days as a station. ⁴_____ clocks still show the correct time.

Entrance to the museum is free on the first Sunday of ⁵_____ month. To get there, take the metro to Solférino or the Assemblée Nationale. ⁶_____ stop will leave you a five-minute walk from the museum.

4 Circle the correct quantifiers to complete the sentences.

1 There are *lots of / a large amount of* excellent museums in Madrid.
2 I went to Mexico City on business, so I didn't have *much / many* free time there to go sightseeing.
3 The city council can't build new parks because there is *any / almost no* money available.
4 She doesn't have *no / a huge amount of* money, so she can't afford to live on her own.
5 There are only *a small number of / a little* music venues in the city.

5 Complete the conversation with these quantifiers.

a little	hardly any
several	too much
lots of	

A: So, do you think we should book a trip to Barcelona?
B: Well, I'm not sure. I think I'd rather try somewhere quieter—you know, a place where *hardly any* tourists go. And where there's not ² *too much* pollution.
A: I know what you mean. But there are ³ *lots of* things to do in Barcelona. Museums, shopping, concerts—it says on this website that there are even ⁴ *several* beaches nearby.
B: Really? That sounds fun. Maybe we can do ⁵ *a little* sightseeing in the morning—just an hour or two—and then spend the rest of the day at the beach!
A: OK, let's do it then. I'll book the plane tickets now.

6 Look at sentences 1–4. Circle the best continuation (a or b) for each sentence.

1 There are a few good movies on tonight.
  a We can choose which one we'd like to watch.
  b So we should think of something else to do.

2 There was little traffic on the roads.
  a So she got home a bit later than expected.
  b So she got home a bit earlier than expected.

3 There are few hotels in this part of the city.
  a I'm sure you'll find somewhere good to stay.
  b So you might need to stay somewhere else.

4 We have a little time before our train leaves.
  a Let's go and get some food for the journey.
  b We need to go straight to the station.

GRAMMAR SUMMARY UNIT 5

Verb + infinitive or *-ing*

When we use two verbs together in a sentence, the form of the second verb depends on the first verb.

Verb + infinitive

We use the infinitive after the following verbs:
(can/can't) afford, agree, allow, arrange, ask, begin, choose, continue, decide, expect, fail, help*, hope, intend, learn, manage, need, offer, plan, pretend, promise, refuse, seem, start, threaten, want, would like, would love, would prefer

> She **refused to change** the date of the meeting.
> The government **failed to reduce** unemployment.
> There **seems to be** a problem with my internet connection.

Verb + object + infinitive

We use an object + infinitive after *ask, get, help*, need,* and *tell.*

> We **need the city council to build** more parks.
> How can we **get people to move** to the area?

Note that we can use *ask, help,* and *need* with and without an object.

> She **asked to leave** the room.
> The policeman **asked me to show** some ID.

Verb + object + base form of the verb

We use an object + base form of the verb after *help*, let,* and *make.*

> My boss didn't **let me go** home until 7 p.m.
> The movie really **made us laugh.**

*We can use the infinitive form or the base verb after *help.*
> He **helped me to clean** the apartment. = He **helped me clean** the apartment.

Remember that we also use the base verb after modal verbs.

Verb + -ing

We use the *-ing* form after the following verbs:
adore, avoid, begin, can't help, can't stand, consider, continue, describe, enjoy, finish, imagine, involve, keep, mention, (don't) mind, miss, practice, recommend, risk, spend (time/money), start, suggest

> Can you **imagine living** on the 100th floor of an apartment building?

We also use the *-ing* form after phrasal verbs, e.g., give up, keep on, look into, think about.

> The meeting was over, but he **kept on talking.**

▶ Exercises 1, 2, and 3

Verbs with both *-ing* and the infinitive

After *continue* and *start*, we can use both the *-ing* form and the infinitive, with no change in meaning.

> It **continued to rain** all day. = It **continued raining** all day.
> I've **started to learn** Spanish. = I've **started learning** Spanish.

With *hate, like, love,* and *prefer,* the basic meaning remains the same. However, we normally use the *-ing* form when talking in general about our preferences.

> I **love visiting** new places.
> Max and Sara **hate going** to the movies.

Verbs with two meanings

The form of the verb following *go on, mean, regret, remember, stop,* and *try* changes its meaning.

go on + -ing = continue an action
> My knee was hurting, but I **went on running.**

go on + infinitive = do something different
> After she graduated from college, she **went on to become** an important politician.

mean + -ing = involve
> My train is at 6:30 a.m., which **means getting** up very early.

mean + infinitive = intend
> Sorry—I **meant to call** you, but I forgot.

regret + -ing = feel sorry about something you did or didn't do
> He **regrets quitting** his job.

regret + infinitive = feel sorry that you have to tell someone about a situation (formal)
> We **regret to inform** you that your application was unsuccessful.

remember + -ing = have memories of an earlier event
> I **remember coming** here when I was a child.

remember + infinitive = not forget to do something
> Did you **remember to lock** the door?

stop + -ing = finish doing an action
> She **stopped driving** when her phone rang.

stop + infinitive = finish an action in order to do another action
> We **stopped to get** some gas.

try + -ing = do something to see what happens
> I **tried not drinking** coffee in the morning, but I hated it.

try + infinitive = make an effort, normally unsuccessfully
> I **tried to call** you, but I couldn't get through.

▶ Exercises 4, 5, and 6

Exercises

1 Circle the correct options to complete the sentences.

1 We can't afford *going / to go* on vacation this year.
2 I asked the sales clerk *to help / helping* me.
3 Why do the neighbors keep *making / to make* so much noise?
4 The local council is thinking about *build / building* a new shopping center.
5 My manager made me *to work / work* late yesterday.
6 They'd like *coming / to come* to see our new house.

2 Complete the groups of sentences with the correct form of the verbs in **bold**.

drive
1 He agreed _To drive_ me to the airport.
2 She doesn't enjoy _driving_ in the rain.
3 Mark let me _drive_ his new sports car.

exercise
4 My doctor told me _to exercise_ more often.
5 I make my children _exercise_ with me.
6 He has just finished _exercising_ .

work
7 Do you mind _working_ on weekends?
8 She got him _to work_ for her for free.
9 I might _working_ from home on Friday.

3 Complete the conversation with the correct form of these verbs.

take	expand	write	hire

A: Have you heard they are planning ¹_____ the airport?
B: It's about time! It gets so busy there, and the lines are always really long.
A: But I think we need people ²_____ fewer flights, not more. Think about all the pollution it would create.
B: Well, do you have another suggestion?
A: Maybe they should spend the money on ³_____ more staff instead.
B: That's actually a good idea. You should ⁴_____ to the government and tell them!

4 Look at sentences 1–4. Circle the best explanation (a or b) for each sentence.

1 Lukas stopped to have something to eat.
   a He was full.
   b He was hungry.

2 Remember to meet me at the theater.
   a We met there in the past.
   b We've arranged to meet there in the future.

3 The speaker went on to suggest some solutions.
   a The speaker started to talk about solutions.
   b The speaker had been talking about solutions for a long time.

4 I regret buying that car.
   a I'm sorry to tell you that I bought that car.
   b It wasn't a good idea to buy that car.

5 Circle the correct options to complete the dialogs.

1 A: This is a disaster! I've lost my passport!
   B: Try *to calm down / calming down*. When did you last see it?
2 A: I'm calling to find out if I passed the exam.
   B: Unfortunately, I regret *informing / to inform* you that you did not pass.
3 A: Do you want coffee?
   B: No, thanks—just water. I've stopped *to drink / drinking* coffee in the afternoon.
4 A: You should find a bigger apartment.
   B: You're right. I can't go on *living / to live* here. It's just too small!
5 A: Why didn't you tell me you were leaving your job?
   B: Sorry. I meant *to tell / telling* you, but I forgot.
6 A: This is the café I've been telling you about.
   B: Oh, I remember *to come / coming* here with some friends a few years ago.

6 Complete the announcement with the correct form of these verbs.

eat	go	leave	make
organize	sightsee	talk	

The Faculty of Engineering has decided _to organize_ a two-day study trip to Bogotá, Colombia. On the first day, we will be joined by a local professor, who will give us a brief tour of the city and will then go on ²_to talk_ about the TransMilenio bus system, which revolutionized public transportation in the city in the 2000s. The next day, we will visit Soacha to see a recent development project there. This will mean ³_leaving_ Bogotá early in the morning, but the project sounds fascinating and we feel sure that you will not regret ⁴_making_ the trip there. We will stop in Soacha ⁵_to eat_ lunch, and then we will return to Bogotá, where you will be able to spend some time ⁶_sightsee_ . Please email the faculty administration by next Friday if you intend ⁷_to go_ on the trip.

GRAMMAR SUMMARY UNIT 6

Negative forms

To make **negative statements with** *think*, *believe*, *suppose*, *imagine*, **and** *want*, it's more common to make the first verb in the sentence negative, not the second.

> I **don't think** it's a good idea.

Negative forms of *have to* **and** *can*: *Don't have to* and *can't* have completely different meanings.

> You **can't** cross the street here. (= It is forbidden and dangerous. There will be consequences.)
> You **don't have to** cross the street here. (= You can cross a little farther up the street.)

To make **negative short answers with** *hope*, *expect*, *believe*, *guess*, *suppose*, **and** *be afraid*, we add *not*. *Believe not* is mainly used in more formal contexts.

> A: Do you think Marc is going to be late again?
> B: I **hope not**.

The affirmative equivalent is *so*, e.g., *I'm afraid so*.

Negative imperatives: To make an imperative negative, we use *don't*. The form is the same if you are talking to one person or more than one person.

> **Don't** forget to print your train tickets.

Negative infinitive: To make an infinitive negative, we add *not* before *to*.

> We agreed **not to go** on another beach vacation this year.

Negative suggestions: To make a negative suggestion, we use *let's not*.

> **Let's not** go out tonight—we can just watch a DVD.

▶ **Exercises 1 and 2**

Negative words: *neither*, *none*, *no*
We use *no* directly before a plural or uncountable noun in a sentence with a positive verb.

> There are **no** trains to the airport at this time of night.

We can't use *no* if there is an article or possessive adjective before the noun. Use *none of* instead.

> **None of my friends** remembered my birthday.

None is a pronoun. We use it in place of a noun to say "not one" or "not any."

> There were three stores in the village when I lived here. There are **none** now.

We use *neither* + auxiliary verb + pronoun to agree with a negative statement. It means "also not."

> A: I don't like cold weather.
> B: **Neither do I**.

The affirmative equivalent is *so* (*So do I*).

We can also use pronoun + *neither* with the same meaning.

> A: I don't like this movie.
> B: **Me neither**.

The affirmative equivalent is *too* (*Me too*).

▶ **Exercise 3**

Question forms

We form **direct questions** by inverting the subject and auxiliary verb. In simple present and simple past, where there is no auxiliary verb, we need to add a form of the auxiliary verb *do*.

> **Did you** enjoy your vacation?

We often ask **direct negative questions** (questions with a negative verb form) when we expect or want the other person to agree.

> **Wasn't** it cold this morning? (= You must agree!)

We also use negative questions to show surprise.

> **Didn't** you like the hotel? I thought it was great.

▶ **Exercise 4**

When we want to be polite, we can add a phrase to the beginning of the question to make an **indirect question**.

> **Do you know** what time the tour starts?

The word order after the added phrase is the same as an affirmative statement (with no inversion or auxiliary).

> Could you tell me **where the trail starts**?

We also use phrases like *I'd like to know* and *I was wondering* to introduce an indirect question. These are followed by a period, not a question mark.

> **I'd like to know** how much this car costs.

We can also make indirect questions by adding *surely* to the start of the sentence. We do this when we expect the other person to agree, or to express surprise.

> **Surely** the museum won't be open this late in the day?

▶ **Exercise 5**

We form **tag questions** with an auxiliary verb + pronoun. We put them at the end of a statement. If the statement is positive, we add a negative tag question. If the statement is negative, we add a positive tag question.

> It's cold today, **isn't it**?
> They didn't like the concert, **did they**?

We use the auxiliary from the statement to form the question tag. If there is no auxiliary in the statement, we use a form of *do*.

> It **wasn't** as hot as last year, **was it**?
> You live in Madrid, **don't** you?

We use tag questions:

- to check information, often when we're surprised. When we do this, we use rising intonation in the tag question.
  You don't speak Spanish, **do you?**

- to ask someone to agree. When we do this, we use falling intonation in the tag question.
  We're working tomorrow, **aren't we?**

▶ **Exercise 6**

Exercises

1 Circle the most appropriate negative forms to complete the sentences.

1 A: Do you think it's going to rain later?
  B: I hope *not / no.*
2 *Let's don't / Let's not* wait any longer.
3 He *doesn't think it's / thinks it isn't* a good idea.
4 I expect you *not to be / to be not* late tonight.
5 *No / Don't* speak during the exam.
6 The museum is free today, so you *don't have to / can't* pay to enter.

2 Complete the second sentence in each item (1–6) so it has the same meaning as the first sentence. Use the word or phrase in **bold**.

1 I don't think we should get take-out tonight.
  let's

  _____ get take-out tonight.

2 My opinion is that his story isn't true.
  believe

  _____ his story is true.

3 It's not necessary to book a table before going to the restaurant.
  have to
  You _____ book a table before going to the restaurant.

4 You must not forget to lock the door before you leave.
  don't

  _____ to lock the door before you leave.

5 A: Did I pass my exam?
  B: I'm sorry, but you didn't.
  afraid
  B: I _____ .

6 She doesn't intend to spend too much money on her vacation.
  to
  She's planning _____ too much money on her vacation.

3 Circle the correct options to complete the conversation.

A: What would you like to do today? [1] *None of / None* the stores are open yet, so maybe we should just grab a coffee.
B: But we've just had breakfast. I don't want more coffee.
A: Actually, [2] *either / neither* do I. How about going to the new modern art gallery?
B: Good idea! But there are [3] *no / none* buses that go there directly.

A: Let's walk, then.
B: It's too hot to walk!
A: A taxi, then?
B: OK. I need to go to the bank first, though. I have [4] *no / none of* money left at all!
A: Me [5] *either / neither.*

4 Complete the negative questions (1–5) using the verbs in parentheses. Use the same tense as that used in the responses.

1 A: _____ the restaurant?
  B: No, I didn't. It was terrible. (like)
2 A: _____ it a fun day yesterday?
  B: Yes, it was. I had a great time. (be)
3 A: _____ to the lesson?
  B: No, he isn't. He's sick. (come)
4 A: _____ yet?
  B: No, I haven't. I'm starving! (eat)
5 A: _____ you call to tell them you're OK?
  B: Yes, you're right—I should. (should)

5 Rewrite the direct questions (1–5) as indirect questions.

1 Where is the station?
  Could you tell me _____?
2 When are you leaving?
  Can I ask _____?
3 Where were you yesterday?
  I was wondering _____.
4 Are they going on vacation again? I can't believe it!
  Surely _____?
5 Who's that man over there?
  Do you know _____?

6 Write tag questions for these statements.

1 You're going on a safari this summer,

  _____?

2 He isn't married,

  _____?

3 You woke up very early this morning,

  _____?

4 We're not late for the party,

  _____?

5 She didn't pass her exam,

  _____?

6 You haven't been to my new apartment,

  _____?

7 He has already seen the movie,

  _____?

GRAMMAR SUMMARY UNIT 7

Zero and first conditionals

Zero conditional

We use the zero conditional to talk about facts or things that are generally true. The form is:

If + simple present + simple present
***If** you **punish** a child, you **need** to tell them why.*

We can also use *when* instead of *if*. The meaning is the same.

***When** children misbehave, it's often because they want attention. (= **If** children misbehave, …)*

First conditional

We use the first conditional to talk about a particular possible future event or situation. The form is:

If + simple present + *will/won't* + base verb
***If** he **does** well in high school, he**'ll get** into a good college.*

We can put the clause with *if* first, or we can put the main clause first. When the *if*-clause comes first, we add a comma before the main clause. When the *if*-clause comes second, we don't need a comma.

*They**'ll cancel** the concert **if** it **rains**.*

Unless, as long as

We can use *unless* or *as long as* in place of *if* in conditional sentences. We use *unless* to say *if not*.

*You **won't pass** your exam **unless** you **work** hard. (= If you don't work hard, you won't pass your exam.)*

We use *as long as* to say "if and only if."
*You can play in the park **as long as** you don't get your clothes dirty.*

We never use a future form after *if*, *unless*, or *as long as*.
~~*If the weather will be nice this weekend, we'll go to the beach.*~~
*If the weather **is** nice this weekend, we'll go to the beach.*

▶ **Exercises 1 and 2**

Time linkers

Like *if*, *unless*, and *as long as*, we don't use a future form after the time linkers *when*, *as soon as*, *before*, *after*, *while*, or *until*. We use a present tense, even when we're referring to the future.

*I'll call you **when** I'm getting ready to leave.*
*I'll pick you up **as soon as** I **finish** work.*
*We can eat **before** we **go** out.*
*School starts a day **after** we **get** back from vacation.*
*You can make dinner **while** I'm **taking** a shower.*
*You can't go out **until** you **finish** your homework.*

▶ **Exercise 3**

usually, used to, would, be used to, and *get used to*

usually + simple present

We use *usually* + simple present to talk about a habit or action that happens regularly or is generally true.
*I **usually eat** a sandwich for lunch.*

used to and *would* + base form of the verb

We use *used to* + base verb to talk about a repeated past action, habit, or situation. It is sometimes used in contrast with a present situation.
*I **used to eat** unhealthily, but I'm more careful now. (= repeated past action/habit)*
*My parents **used to own** a restaurant. (= past situation)*

The negative is *didn't use to*. We ask questions with *Did you use to …?*
*I **didn't use to like** vegetables when I was a child.*
***Did** you **use to walk** to school or **catch** the bus?*

We use *would* + base verb to talk about a repeated action or habit in the past. We normally say when the action/habit happened.
*I remember when I was little, my dad **would make** pizza every Saturday night.*

We don't use *would* to talk about a state or situation in the past. We use *used to* or simple past.

▶ **Exercise 4**

be/get used to + noun or *-ing*

We use *be used to* + noun or *-ing* to say that something isn't strange or difficult.
*I start work at 7 a.m. every morning, so I'm **used to getting up** early.*
*I've lived in Minnesota for a long time, so I'm **used to the cold winters**.*

We can also use this form in the past or the negative.
*It was hard to go on a diet because I **wasn't used to eating** healthily. (= It was difficult/strange for me.)*

We use *get used to* + noun or *-ing* when we are learning to adapt to something difficult or unfamiliar, and it is becoming normal.
*I'm **getting used to cooking** for myself now that I live on my own.*
*Driving a car was scary at first, but I soon **got used to it**.*

Note that we always use the *-ing* form or a noun after *be/get used to*, not the base verb.

▶ **Exercises 5 and 6**

Exercises

1 Correct the mistake in each conditional sentence.

1. If you won't buy a ticket before you go, you won't get a seat at the concert.

2. If I was late to my lesson, the teacher gets angry.

3. It's dangerous to drive when it will snow hard.

4. You'll do better in your exams, if you study hard.

5. The soccer match will being canceled if the weather is bad.

2 Rewrite the sentences with **unless** or **as long as.**

1. You won't get the job if you don't practice for your interview. (unless)
   _____
   _____

2. You can borrow my car, but only if you promise to be careful. (as long as)
   _____
   _____

3. You can borrow my umbrella only if you remember to return it. (as long as)
   _____
   _____

4. If you don't practice every day, you won't get better at playing the piano. (unless)
   _____
   _____

3 Match the sentence beginnings (1–5) with the endings (a–e). Then complete the sentences with the correct form of the verbs in parentheses.

1. Please call me
2. I'll wait with you at the station
3. While you're cleaning the house,
4. You'll never be able to run the marathon
5. I always get a headache

a. until your train _____ (arrive). ____
b. when I _____ (not drink) enough water. ____
c. I _____ (take) the dog out for a walk. ____
d. unless you _____ (start) training. ____
e. as soon as you ___*get*___ (get) this message. _*1*_

4 Rewrite the sentences (1–5) with **used to** or **would**.

1. When I was living with my parents, I cooked with my mom a lot. (would)
   _____
   _____

2. We lived downtown until two years ago. (used to)
   _____
   _____

3. When they were little, their grandma took them to the movies once a month. (would)
   _____
   _____

4. Did you have a best friend at school? (used to)
   _____
   _____

5. For years, I visited my aunt in Vancouver every summer. (would)
   _____
   _____

5 Rewrite the sentences (1–4) with the correct form of *be/get used to* + *-ing*.

1. It's normal for me to make speeches in front of a lot of people.
   I _____ in front of a lot of people.
2. It's starting to feel normal for me to commute to work every day.
   I _____ to work every day.
3. It wasn't normal for him to eat out so often.
   He _____ out so often.
4. It was hard, but I learned to live on my own.
   It was hard, but I _____ on my own.

6 Complete the text with these verbs. Use the correct form of *used to* + base verb or *be/get used to* + *-ing*. Note they can be affirmative or negative.

do	dream	live	see	take

When I was a kid, I always [1]_____ of living abroad. So I was really happy when I moved to Hong Kong three years ago for work. When I first arrived, it was a bit of a culture shock for me. I'm from a small town, so I [2]_____ so many tall buildings and skyscrapers. I also had to [3]_____ in a very small apartment and paying a lot of rent. In my own country, I lived a five-minute walk from my office. But I [4]_____ the train to work here—the trains are very punctual and frequent. Living abroad can be difficult, but I think everyone can do it—you soon [5]_____ things in a different way.

GRAMMAR SUMMARY UNIT 8

Second, third, and mixed conditionals

Second and third conditionals

We use the second conditional to describe a situation in the present or future. It suggests that the situation and result are unreal or imagined. The form is: *if* + simple past, *would* + base verb.

> *If I **had** a lot of money, I**'d travel** around the world.* (+)
> *If the traffic **weren't** so bad, I **wouldn't mind** driving.* (−)
> ***Would** you **be** able to come to the wedding **if** we **changed** the date?* (?)

We use the third conditional to describe an unreal or imagined situation and result in the past. The form is: *if* + past perfect, *would have* + past participle.

> *If I**'d worked** harder at school, I **would have become** a doctor.* (+)
> *If I **hadn't had** such an inspiring teacher, I **wouldn't have gone** to college.* (−)
> *If you **had been** able to travel more, where **would** you **have visited**?* (?)

As with first conditionals, we can put the clause with *if* first, or we can put the main clause first. When the *if*-clause comes first, we add a comma before the main clause. When the *if*-clause comes second, we don't need a comma.

> *I **would have applied** for the job **if** the pay **had been** better.*

▶ **Exercise 1**

Mixed conditionals

We can also use a combination of second and third conditionals. We use a mixed second and third conditional to describe an unreal situation in the present with an imagined result in the past.

> *If I **had** more money, I**'d have booked** a better hotel.*

We use a mixed third and second conditional to describe an unreal situation in the past with an imagined result in the present.

> *If you**'d gone** to bed earlier, you **wouldn't be** so tired now.*

We can use *were* instead of *was* after *if* to talk about an unreal/imagined present or future situation. When we do this, it sounds more formal.

> *If I **were** wealthy, I **would have bought** the house.*

The phrase "if I were you" is fixed. We don't normally say "if I was you," even in informal situations.

▶ **Exercises 2 and 3**

wish and *if only*

Form and use

We use *wish* and *if only* to talk about unreal or imagined situations that we would like to be true or to come true. The basic meaning of *wish* and *if only* is the same, but *if only* is stronger.

We use *wish* / *if only* + past tense to talk about a situation in the present.

> *I **wish** it **was** summer. I'm tired of this cold weather!*

We use *wish* / *if only* + *could* + base verb to talk about an ability or possibility we would like to have in the present.

> *If only I **could play** a musical instrument. It would be a lot of fun.*
> *I **wish** we **could stay** for lunch. But we've got other plans.*

As with conditionals, we can also use *were* instead of *was*. It sounds more formal.

> *I **wish** Martin **weren't** always so busy.*

▶ **Exercise 4**

We use *wish* / *if only* + past perfect to talk about a situation in the past that we want to be different.

> *If only our plane **had arrived** on time. Now we're stuck here in the airport!*

We use *wish* / *if only* + someone + *would* + base verb to talk about a situation in the present that we want somebody else to act to change. We often use this structure when we are dissatisfied with the situation or when we are complaining.

> *I **wish you wouldn't complain** so much.*
> *I **wish** Sarah **would listen** to other people more.*

We sometimes use *wish* / *if only* + *would* + base verb with things, as well as people.

> *I **wish** it **would stop** raining.*
> *I **wish my phone wouldn't** always **stop** working just when I need it!*

We don't normally use *wish* to talk about the future. We use *hope* instead.

> *We **hope** that we'll see you again soon.*
> (not ~~We wish that we'll see you again soon.~~)

▶ **Exercises 5 and 6**

Exercises

1 Complete the sentences with the verbs in parentheses to make second or third conditionals. Use the context to help you decide which form to use.

1 I'm so busy at the moment. If I _____ (have) more time, I _____ (take) up a new hobby.

2 She felt cold when she left the house that morning. She _____ (wear) a warmer coat if she _____ (know) how cold it was.

3 He can't afford to go on vacation this summer. He _____ (go) to Thailand if he _____ (have) enough money.

4 You look very pale these days. If you _____ (spend) more time outside, you _____ (not be) so pale.

5 He failed his driving test. He _____ (do) better if he _____ (practice) more.

2 Match the sentence beginnings (1–6) with the endings (a–f) to make mixed conditionals. Then decide whether each sentence describes:

i an unreal situation in the past with an imagined result in the present.

ii an unreal situation in the present with an imagined result in the past.

1 If public transportation was more efficient,
2 If you hadn't decided to become a doctor,
3 They would have bought a bigger house
4 He wouldn't feel so hungry now
5 We'd be able to get into our car
6 If she liked playing soccer,

a what job would you do instead? _____
b if they had more money. _____
c if you hadn't lost the keys! _____
d I would have come here by bus. _____
e she would have joined our team. _____
f if he'd eaten more in the morning. _____

3 Complete the sentences (1–5) to make mixed conditionals, using the verbs in parentheses.

1 If I _____ (not leave) so late, I _____ (not be) in such a rush now.

2 He _____ (come) to the theater with us tomorrow if he _____ already _____ (not / see) the play.

3 If they _____ (live) closer to me, I _____ (go) to their party.

4 My life _____ (be) very different now if I _____ (not meet) my husband all those years ago.

5 If she _____ (not be) so busy at the moment, she _____ (help) us move last weekend.

4 Complete the sentences with the correct form of the verbs in parentheses.

1 It's cold today. I wish it _____ (be) warmer!

2 I wish I _____ (not have to) work on the weekend.

3 If only he _____ (live) closer to me.

4 I wish I _____ (can) play the guitar.

5 The bus is so crowded. If only there _____ (not be) so many people!

5 Circle the correct options to complete the conversation.

A: How did your exams go?

B: OK, I hope. I just wish [1] *I'd had / I had* more time to study before the exams! But it's difficult to study and work at the same time.

A: Yes, that must be tiring! What do you do?

B: I work in a restaurant. I enjoy it, but I just wish I [2] *wouldn't have to / didn't have to* work on the weekends. I sometimes wish that I [3] *had taken / took* a year off before coming to college to work and save some money.

A: But do you like your major? You're studying biology, aren't you?

B: Yes, that's right. It's good, but there are very few women in my year. I often wish there [4] *were / had been* more of us.

A: Yes, I'm sure. So, where are you going now?

B: I'm going home. I need to clean the house. I love my roommates, but I wish they [5] *hadn't made / wouldn't make* so much mess all the time!

6 Complete each sentence (1–4) with the correct form of one of these verbs. Note they can be affirmative or negative.

learn	leave	stop	shout

1 If only that dog _____ barking at night. He keeps waking me up!

2 I wish I _____ how to drive a car when I was younger.

3 He wishes his boss _____ at him so often.

4 Someone stole my bag from my car last night. If only I _____ it there overnight.

GRAMMAR SUMMARY UNIT 9

Verb patterns with reporting verbs

Form and use

We can use different verbs to report speech and thoughts. The patterns we use change, depending on the verb.

Verb + infinitive

We use the infinitive after *agree, offer, promise, refuse, swear,* and *threaten.*

> Jack **offered to take** a photograph of me.
> I **refused to leave** the building.
> He **swore to tell** the truth.

Verb + object + infinitive

We use object + infinitive after *advise, ask, beg, convince, encourage, invite, persuade, recommend, urge,* and *warn.*

> Julia **asked me to drive** her to the airport.
> I don't like concerts, but Max **convinced me to come.**

Verb + -ing

We use -ing after *admit, deny, recommend,* and *suggest.*

> They **denied taking** the money.
> Luke **suggested going** to the park.

Verb + preposition + -ing

We use -ing after verb + preposition combinations, e.g., *apologize for, complain about, confess to, insist on,* and *object to.*

> You should **apologize for being** so rude.
> Sara **insisted on eating** at home.

Verb + object + preposition + -ing

With some other verb + preposition combinations, we place an object between the verb and preposition, e.g., *accuse … of, blame … for, criticize … for, congratulate … on, praise … for, thank … for.*

> Anna always **accuses me of being** lazy.
> Lars **praised his son for winning** the competition.

Note that when we use reporting verbs, we often have to make changes to pronouns, time expressions, etc.

> *"You've broken **my** phone!"* → **She blamed me** for breaking **her** phone.
> *"I'll be back **tomorrow**."* → **She promised to be back the next day**.

Some reporting verbs can also be followed by *that* + clause. When we use a reporting verb + *that*, we often make a change to the tense.

> *"We'll be late."* → I warned you **that** we **would** be late.

▶ **Exercises 1, 2, and 3**

Passive reporting verbs

Form and use

We sometimes use passive verbs to report feelings, beliefs, opinions, and rumors, especially in journalism or other formal contexts. We often do this when we don't know or don't want to say who made the statement.

There are two patterns:

* *it* + passive verb + *that* + subject
  It is thought that the prime minister will make an important announcement later today.

* subject + passive verb + infinitive
  A man aged 95 is reported to be a lottery winner for the third time.

To report a past action in the present perfect or simple past with the second pattern, we use a perfect infinitive (an infinitive form with *have* + past participle).

> Three people are said **to have been rescued** from a house fire.

To report an action in the future or in progress now with the second pattern, we use a continuous infinitive (an infinitive form with *be* + *-ing*).

> The company is said **to be looking** for a new manager.

We commonly use the following verbs with both patterns: *believe, confirm, expect, know, report, say, think,* and *understand.*

> **A 22-year-old man is known to have stopped** the global spread of the computer virus.
> **It is known that a 22-year-old man stopped** the global spread of the computer virus.

▶ **Exercises 4, 5, and 6**

Exercises

1 Match the sentence beginnings (1–5) with the endings (a–e).

1 He asked me
2 She admitted
3 They complained about
4 Do you promise
5 I congratulated her on

a having to work on the weekend. ____
b to help him, but I'm too busy. ____
c passing her driving test. ____
d not to be late to the meeting? ____
e taking the money from my wallet. ____

2 Complete the second sentence in each item (1–4) so it has the same meaning as the first sentence. Use the verb in **bold**.

1 She said it was a good idea to visit the museum.
   recommend
   She _____ the museum.

2 "I'm going to leave without you if you don't hurry up."
   threaten
   He _____ without me if I didn't hurry up.

3 She said sorry because she was late.
   apologize
   She _____ late.

4 I told her that she should see a doctor.
   advise
   I _____ a doctor.

3 Complete the text with the correct form of these verbs.

| do | recycle | introduce |
| start | stop | watch |

The town of Modbury in Devon, England, was the first town in Europe to stop using plastic bags. The story started in 2007 after Rebecca Hosking, a wildlife camerawoman, invited local shop owners [1]_____ a documentary about the damage plastic bags cause to the environment. The owners were so shocked that they promised [2]_____ giving plastic bags to customers. They agreed [3]_____ all their bags and encouraged their customers [4]_____ the same. Soon, Modbury became plastic bag-free, and not long after, the UK government decided [5]_____ a charge for all plastic bags in supermarkets. The residents have praised Rebecca Hosking for [6]_____ this revolution, which has generated interest around the world.

4 Correct the mistake in each sentence.

1 It is believe that two prisoners have escaped.

2 The director is expected resign.

3 The photos are thought to been taken in 1990.

4 She is said to write a book at the moment.

5 Circle the correct options to complete the sentences.

1 The team is expected *to arrive / to have arrived* later today.
2 The man is said *to be finding / to have found* a priceless painting in his attic.
3 More people than ever are believed *to have lived / to be living* with their parents because they cannot afford to buy a home.
4 Eating more vegetables and fruit is known *to be / to being* good for your health.
5 The accident is thought *to have been caused / to be causing* by bad weather.

6 Rewrite the underlined phrases with passive reporting structures. Use the prompts and verbs below (1–4).

A: Have you seen that Main Street is closed? I wonder what's happening.
B: It's for the carnival. It's going to be a big event this year. Apparently, [1] the local council has spent a lot of money on it.
A: Oh, of course. Did you go last year?
B: No, I didn't. But I heard that [2] it was really crowded and badly organized. But someone told me that this year, [3] the organizers have made some improvements. And there are going to be more police on the streets.
A: That's good.
B: Should we go and take a look? I'm sure I heard somewhere that [4] some stalls are offering free food on the first day.
A: Free food? Let's go!

1 The local council _____
   _____ (believe).
2 Last year's carnival _____
   _____ (say).
3 It _____
   _____ (think).
4 Some stalls _____
   _____ (expect).

GRAMMAR SUMMARY UNIT 10

the function to describe

Articles: *a/an*, *the*, or zero article?

We use the **indefinite article** (*a/an*) with a singular countable noun. We use it:

- to talk about a non-specific person or thing.
  *I need to buy **a** new car.*

- to say a person or thing is one of many.
  *I think Tereshkova is **a** very interesting astronaut.*

- when we first mention something.
  *One evening, **a** man and **a** woman rang my doorbell.*

- in the structure *as + a(n) +* noun.
  ***As a child**, she loved basketball.*

We also use the indefinite article: to say what somebody does (e.g., *He's a student*); or to talk about frequency (e.g., *twice a month*).

We use the **definite article** (*the*) with a singular or plural countable noun or an uncountable noun. We use it:

- to talk about a specific person/people or thing(s).
  ***The** prime minister gave a speech in Paris today.*

- when we refer back to a person/people or thing(s) already mentioned.
  One evening, a man and a woman rang my doorbell.
  ***The** man introduced himself.*

- before a superlative adjective.
  *That's **the** best movie I've seen this year.*

We also use the definite article: when there is only one of something (e.g., *the moon*); with some countries (e.g., *the US*); with an organization (e.g., *the navy*); with some time periods (e.g., *the 1930s*); with inventions (e.g., *the saxophone*); to talk about parts of a country/area (e.g., *the north of Germany*); with places in a town/city (e.g., *the stores*); with the names of oceans and rivers (e.g., *the Nile*).

We use the **zero article (no article)** with a plural countable noun or an uncountable noun. We use it:

- with uncountable or plural nouns to talk about people or things in a general way.
  *I think **nurses** should be paid more.*

- before certain generally familiar places (school, work, hospital, college).
  *My older brother is studying medicine at **college**.*

We also use the zero article: with the names of most countries; with subjects of study (e.g., *math*); with days and months; with meals (e.g., *breakfast*); in phrases like *this month, last week, next year*; with the names of sports; with the names of lakes; in many phrases with "home" (e.g., *go home*).

▶ **Exercises 1, 2, and 3**

Relative clauses

We use **defining relative clauses** to give essential information in order to identify someone or something. The choice of relative pronoun depends on the type of noun.

- For things, we use *that*.
  *Is this the book **that** you told me about?*

- For people, we use *who*.
  *I know three people **who** study at this college.*

- For possession, we use *whose*.
  *I know someone **whose** mother was a famous actor.*

Note that *whose* can also be used for things.

We can use *what* before a subject and verb to say "the thing(s) that."
  *That's exactly **what** I wanted.*

We can leave out *that* and *who* when they are the object of the verb in the relative clause, but not when they are the subject.
  *I enjoyed the movie (**that**) you recommended.*
  *That's the scientist **who** won the Nobel Prize.*

When we form relative clauses with a preposition, we normally put the preposition at the end of the clause, except in very formal usage. Note that *who* becomes *whom* after a preposition.
  *I'm the person (**who**) you wrote **to**.*
  *I am the person **to whom** you wrote. (formal)*

We also make relative clauses with the relative adverbs **where** and **when**. *Where* means the same as (the more formal) *in which*.
  *This is the restaurant **where** I had my birthday dinner.*

▶ **Exercises 4 and 5**

Non-defining relative clauses contain extra, non-essential information. We can understand which thing, person, place, etc., is being mentioned without the relative clause.
  *My brother, **who lives in New York**, is coming to visit next month. (It's clear as I only have one brother.)*

We use *who* for people and *which* for things. We never use *that* in non-defining clauses. Note that we can use *whose* in both defining and non-defining clauses.

In non-defining relative clauses, we use a comma before the relative clause. If the clause is in the middle of the sentence, we also put a comma at the end of it.

Some non-defining clauses refer to the whole of the main clause. We often use clauses like this to give opinions or to make a comment.
  *They've canceled the concert, **which is disappointing**.*

▶ **Exercise 6**

Exercises

1 Correct the mistake in each sentence.

1 She hasn't found the job yet.

2 I'd like to live in the Paris.

3 As an doctor, she really understands how important your diet is.

4 That's probably worst movie I've ever seen.

2 Read the conversation. Add seven missing articles in the correct places.

A: Thanks for inviting me to your party. Your friends are all so nice!

B: Thanks for coming! Did you manage to speak to everyone?

A: Yes, I think so. I had a long conversation about gardening with man … I can't remember his name … Oh, it's man over there.

B: That's Thomas—he's my neighbor. And he does have amazing garden.

A: Yes, he showed me picture of it on his phone.

B: And did he tell you about Everest?

A: Everest? No, what about it?

B: Well, Thomas is actually famous mountaineer! He's climbed mountains all over the world, including Everest!

A: Wow! That's amazing! Does he still go climbing?

B: Yes, he does. And he takes tour groups up mountains three or four times year. He also gives talks about it all around world.

3 Complete the text with *the*, *a*, or zero article (–).

It seemed like another normal flight for Captain Chesley Sullenberger and Jeffrey Skiles, flying from New York City to North Carolina in [1]_____ USA, on [2]_____ January 15, 2009. But three minutes after take-off, [3]_____ plane hit a flock of geese. The geese damaged both engines, which stopped working. [4]_____ pilots had to make a quick decision about where to make the emergency landing. Sullenberger realized they didn't have time to go back to the airport, so he decided to land the plane on [5]_____ Hudson River. Incredibly, Captain Sullenberger landed the aircraft safely. Within minutes, boats came to help, and all the passengers and crew were rescued. Sullenberger became [6]_____ hero, famous all over the world. He was later hired as [7]_____ safety expert, and thanks to him, [8]_____ new measures for airline safety have been introduced. In 2016, [9]_____ movie about his life was made, starring Tom Hanks.

4a Complete the sentences with appropriate relative pronouns or adverbs.

1 This is the laptop _that / which_ I bought last week.

2 Isn't this the restaurant _where_ we had a really bad meal a few years ago?

3 They thanked the police officers _who_ caught the criminal.

4 The students weren't told _what_ would be on the exam.

5 We stayed in a hotel _which / where_ has a huge swimming pool.

6 Is that your friend _whose_ party we went to last month?

4b Work in pairs. In which of the sentences in Exercise 4a can the relative pronoun be omitted?

5 Rewrite the sentences so they are more informal. Leave out the relative pronoun when possible.

1 That's the woman ~~with whom~~ I played tennis _with_ last week.

_____

2 Are you the person ~~to whom~~ I spoke when I called earlier? _who_ _to_

_____

3 This is the kind of music ~~to which~~ I always listen when I'm driving. _(that)_

_____

6 Combine the sentences in each item (1–4) to make non-defining relative clauses.

1 We live in Salto. It's in the northwest of Uruguay.

We live in Salto, which is in the
Northwest of Uruguay

2 My friend Louis has just started a new job. He lives in Vermont.

My friend Louis, who lives in Vermont,
has just started a new job

3 The museum was closed when we went there. That was disappointing. _which was_
disappointing

_____

4 DDT Bank has serious financial problems. ~~It~~ _which_ employs over 20,000 people.

DDT Bank, which employs over 20,000 people,
has serious financial problems.

GRAMMAR SUMMARY UNIT 11

could, was able to, managed to, and succeeded in

We use *could, was able to, managed to*, and *succeeded in* to talk about ability and possibility in the past.

General ability

We use *could* and *couldn't* + base verb to describe a general ability to do something in the past.

> Jacky **could run** really fast when she was a teenager.
> I **couldn't speak** French until I went to study in Paris.

We also use *was/were able to* for the same meaning. It is more formal than *could/couldn't*.

> Jacky **was able to run** really fast when she was a teenager.
> I **wasn't able to speak** French until I went to study in Paris.

Success/failure in a specific task

We cannot use *could* to talk about success in a specific task in the past. We use *was/were able + to* + base verb, *managed + to* + base verb, or *succeeded in + -ing* instead.

> I **was able to get / managed to get / succeeded in getting** tickets for the concert! I bought the last three tickets available.

We normally use *managed to* + base verb and *succeeded in + -ing* when the task was difficult. We tend to use *succeeded in* (and *was/were able to*) in more formal contexts.

In informal contexts, we often use the simple past to talk about success in a specific task in the past, especially if we don't want to suggest it was difficult.

> I **got** tickets for the concert. There were plenty left.

Note that we DO use *couldn't* to describe failure in a specific task in the past.

> We **couldn't find** a karate class, so we decided to take judo instead.

Possibility/opportunity in the past

We also use *could* and *was/were able to* to say we had a possibility or opportunity to do something in the past.

> I really loved the class because we **could / were able to practice** all the theory we had studied.

▶ **Exercises 1, 2, and 3**

Future in the past

was/were going to and was/were about to (+ base verb)

We use *was/were going to* and *was/were about to* (+ base verb) to say that we intended to do something but didn't.

> I **was going to watch** the baseball game, but I had too much work to do.
> Tania **was about to sit down** when she heard her baby cry.

We also use *was/were going to* and *was/were about to* after verbs like *say, know, promise*, and *think*. When used like this, it is not clear whether the described action happened or not.

> We thought **they were going to finish** the work by the end of the month. (It could mean they finished the work or that they're still doing it.)
> He said **he was going to arrive** at 7 p.m. (It could mean he did arrive at 7 p.m. as expected or that he actually arrived at 9 p.m.)

would (+ base verb) and would have (+ past participle)

We use *would* + base verb to talk about the future in the past when we report thoughts, ideas, expectations, etc., after verbs like *say, know, promise*, and *think*. We use this structure to describe both events that happened and those that didn't.

> He promised he **would help** me, but then he disappeared!
> I knew we **would be** late. (= and we were)

We use *would have* + past participle to talk about something that didn't happen in the past.

> I **would have called** you, but I thought you were busy.

was/were supposed to (+ base verb)

We use *was/were supposed to* + base verb to describe something that we expected to happen but didn't.

> Where have you been? You **were supposed to be** here at noon!

▶ **Exercises 4, 5, and 6**

Exercises

1 Work in pairs. In which of these sentences can the underlined phrase be replaced with *could* or *couldn't*?

1 She <u>was able to</u> pass her exam last week, even though she didn't study for it.
2 Sorry, but I <u>didn't manage to</u> go to the supermarket.
3 He <u>was able to</u> sing beautifully when he was a child.
4 We <u>weren't able to</u> visit the museum because it was closed.
5 I <u>managed to</u> book a flight to Los Angeles for just $48.

2 Read the sentences. Cross out the incorrect option(s).

1 She *was able to / managed to / succeeded in* get the job that she really wanted.
2 I *couldn't / didn't manage / wasn't able* find the way to the castle.
3 We *succeeded in / managed to / were able to* finishing the project on time.
4 Anna *managed to / could / was able to* get a discount on her new car.
5 They *didn't succeed in / couldn't / weren't able to* come to the meeting.
6 I *managed to / was able to / could* eat chocolate whenever I wanted when I was little.

3 Match the sentence beginnings (1–4) with the endings (a–d). Then complete the sentences with the correct form of the verbs in parentheses.

1 My leg was hurting, but I still managed
2 Our hotel was great because we could
3 The company succeeded in
4 Our house is big, but we managed

a _____ (eat) at the restaurant for free. ____
b _____ (paint) it in just two days. ____
c _____ (increase) its profits considerably. ____
d _____ (run) ten kilometers. ____

4 Circle the correct options to complete the conversation.

A: Here you are, finally! I ¹ *was about to go / would go* home.
B: Sorry I'm late. I ² *would have called / would call* you, but ... well, to be honest, I just forgot!
A: I thought so. You're so forgetful! And yesterday you promised you ³ *wouldn't have been / wouldn't be* late this time!
B: I know, I know. I'm so sorry!
A: Maybe you should do something to improve your memory.

B: I actually downloaded an app on my phone last week that said it ⁴ *would have improved / would improve* my memory within five days.
A: And what happened?
B: Well, I used it on the first day, and it seemed quite good. Then I ⁵ *was / were* supposed to use it every day for ten minutes. But then ...
A: Let me guess—you forgot?
B: Of course!

5 Complete the sentences (1–4) with these phrases.

| were going to | was supposed to |
| would have | wouldn't |

1 We _____ make an offer on the house, but then we saw another house that we liked even more.
2 You promised you _____ lie to me ever again!
3 The package _____ arrive an hour ago, but it's still not here.
4 A: I'm soaking! It's pouring rain out there.
B: Why didn't you call me? I _____ picked you up!

6 Complete the second sentence in each item (1–4) so it has the same meaning as the first sentence. Use the word in bold.

1 Just moments before Jaime went to bed, his doorbell rang.
about
Jaime _____ to bed when his doorbell rang.

2 He expected it to be a nice day today, but it was cloudy.
supposed
It _____ a nice day today, but it was cloudy.

3 You said these words to me: "I'll never borrow your car again without asking."
would
You promised you _____ my car again without asking.

4 I didn't buy you a present because I didn't know it was your birthday.
would
I _____ you a present, but I didn't know it was your birthday.

GRAMMAR SUMMARY UNIT 12

Focus adverbs: *only*, *just*, *even*

Use

We use the focus adverbs *only*, *just*, and *even* to focus on or draw attention to particular information in a clause. The focus adverb comes directly before the word or phrase it is emphasizing.

We use *only*:

- to emphasize that a number, size, age, etc., is small or smaller than we expected.
  *Our flights cost **only** $90.*

- to emphasize that something is true only for a single person/thing or a limited number of people/things.
  ***Only** customers can park here.*

- to say that something is unimportant.
  *Don't be offended—I was **only** joking.*

- with *not* to say that more than one thing is true.
  *I'm **not only** interested in money; I also want to find a job that is interesting.*

We use *just*:

- to emphasize that a number, size, age, etc., is small or smaller than we expected.
  *She left the job after **just** six weeks.*

- to emphasize that something happened recently or will be finished soon.
  *They've **just** arrived home.*

- to mean "simply."
  *There's a good bus service in my town, but I normally **just** walk wherever I want to go.*

- with *not* to say that more than one thing is true.
  *They're **not just** friends—they're married!*

Note that we can sometimes use both *only* and *just* without any change of meaning.

We use *even*:

- to introduce something surprising.
  ***Even** I enjoyed the concert, and I don't like rock music!*

- with *not* to emphasize that something isn't true or doesn't happen.
  *The city was so busy that we could**n't even** find a room in the worst hotels.*

- in a comparison, to say that although something is good, bad, big, etc., another thing is better, worse, bigger, etc.
  *Her latest movie is **even** better than her last one.*

Form

Position of focus adverbs

We can put *only*, *even*, and *just* in different places in a sentence. If the focus of the adverb is on the subject, we put it at the beginning of the sentence.
  ***Even** summer is quite cool in this part of the world.*

If the focus of the adverb is on another part of the sentence, we normally put it in the middle of the sentence, before the main verb or after auxiliary verbs (*have*, *do*, *be*) and modal verbs.
  *My phone can't make long-distance calls. It can **only** make local calls.*
  *I'm **just** getting ready. I won't be long.*

▶ Exercises 1, 2, and 3

Causative *have* and *get*

Form and use

We use *have* and *get* in different ways to say that we cause something to happen or cause somebody to do something.

have/get + something + past participle

We use *have/get* + something + past participle when we pay somebody to do something for us. We don't say who does the job. *Get something done* is more informal than *have something done*.
  *She **got her hair cut** yesterday.*
  *I'm **having my computer fixed** this morning.*

We also use *have/get* + something + past participle to say that we experienced something bad.
  *Maria **had/got her phone stolen** last night.* (She didn't want this to happen.)

have + someone + base form of the verb

We use *have* + someone + base verb when we ask or tell somebody to do something for us. We normally use this structure when we have some kind of power over the other person, because he or she is our employee, child, etc. It is quite formal.
  *José **had his lawyer write** a new contract.*

We always say who did the action with this structure.

get + someone + infinitive

We also use *get* + someone + infinitive when we ask or tell somebody to do something for us. We use this structure in any context (not just with people we have power over). It is informal.
  *We **got our teacher to explain** the grammar again.*

We always say who did the action with this structure.

▶ Exercises 4 and 5

Exercises

1 Read the sentences. Circle the best options to complete the explanations below.

1 He stayed at the party for only twenty minutes.
I *think / don't think* this is a long time.
2 Even Martino came to the exhibition.
I'm *surprised / not surprised* he came.
3 The drive to the airport took just half an hour.
This is *more / less* than I expected.
4 Miki's not only a musician.
Miki does *other things, too / just this*.
5 You look even more tired than yesterday.
You *looked / didn't look* tired yesterday.

2 Circle the correct options to complete the conversation.

A: What are you reading?
B: An article about a man who retired when he was [1] *only / even* 35 years old.
A: Wow! He must be really rich. Did he work for a big bank or something?
B: That's the interesting thing. He had a regular job, and he didn't earn a lot. He was [2] *even / just* very careful about spending money, and so he saved 75% of his salary every year. Once he had saved enough money, he retired.
A: How did he save that much money?
B: Well, he made lots of small changes. For example, he sold his car and bought a bike. If you ride your bike everywhere, you don't [3] *even / just* get around more cheaply, you also get free exercise!
A: That's true. Anything else?
B: Another thing was that he never ate out. He had dinner parties at home instead. Often, he told his friends to bring a dish each, so that made it [4] *only / even* cheaper.
A: That's smart. So what's he doing now?
B: Well, he [5] *just / only* moved to Brazil last month.

3 Complete the sentences with *even*, *just*, or *only*. Sometimes more than one focus adverb is possible.

1 Tickets for the concert are available for a very low price—$5.
Tickets for the concert are available for _____ $5.
2 It's going to rain tomorrow and for several days after that.
It's not _____ going to rain tomorrow, but also in the following days.
3 I'm going to leave in thirty seconds.
I'm _____ about to leave.
4 I passed all my exams. I'm surprised I passed my math exam.
I _____ passed my math exam.

5 The pizza I had last week was good. This pizza is better than that last one.
This pizza is _____ better than the one I had last week.
6 I find it strange you're wearing your sunglasses. It isn't sunny.
Why are you wearing sunglasses? It isn't _____ sunny.

4 Circle the correct options to complete the sentences.

1 We had our house *repainted / to repaint / repaint* last week.
2 The teacher had the students *stayed / to stay / stay* after class because of their bad behavior.
3 I'll get them *brought / to bring / bring* us the check.
4 They had a mechanic *checked / to check / check* their car because it was making strange noises.
5 I had a dress *made / to make / make* in Milan for the wedding.
6 We got a company *installed / to install / install* our new carpet.

5 Complete the text with the correct forms of these phrases.

clean your house	deliver the ingredients
do the cooking	send an information pack
find the perfect gift	

Life Solutions is here to make your life easier by doing the little jobs that you don't have time for. No time to clean? We'll find a cleaning company and have [1]_____ for you. Need to buy a present for a friend or relative? Just give us the details, and we'll get one of our highly trained advisors [2]_____ . Friends coming for dinner? We'll plan the menu and get [3]_____ to you. You can even have one of our chefs [4]_____ for you—before your friends arrive, of course! For further details, just call or email and we'll have [5]_____ to you immediately!

Unit 1

▶ 1

Speaker 1

It's kind of odd because we work in the same building, but for different companies. His office is on the 4th floor and mine is on the 5th, and occasionally, we bump into each other in the elevator. It's strange seeing someone you're so close to in a different context. We've been married for seven years, and our wedding anniversary is next week.

Speaker 2

We were really good friends at school, and then in our early twenties we traveled together, but we rarely see each other now. John lives in the suburbs with his wife—she's a friend of my sister's—and I still live in the city. The funny thing is, it doesn't matter how little we see each other—we're still great friends.

Speaker 3

We've always gotten along very well at work, but we never see each other outside the office. He's one of those people that can always make you laugh, which is really important in a stressful work environment. He's very good at his job, too, and I'm always asking for his help with stuff.

▶ 2

This week, we're looking at the subject of animal friendships. We know that animals often cooperate in their own social groups, helping each other to hunt or raise their young. Some highly intelligent animals—like elephants—go even further than this, and sometimes help other animals of the same species who are not in their own family group. But cooperation between animals of different species is unusual, so that's why the story of Suryia, the orangutan, has attracted a lot of interest.

Suryia lives with his keepers at The Institute of Greatly Endangered and Rare Species in Myrtle Beach, South Carolina, which is a kind of sanctuary for rare animals. Recently, this orangutan has been spending time with a local dog—an unlikely friend. Most dogs avoid apes because they are scared of them, but these two have formed a strong bond. Each day, the dog—named Roscoe—comes into the compound and looks for Suryia. When he finds him, they carry on like long-lost friends, hugging and playing together. They've been doing this every day since they first met, and over four million viewers have watched them since their video was posted on YouTube. The founder of the institute, Dr. Antle, explains: "It's clear they are having the time of their lives. Suryia is really playful, but what's more striking is how considerate he is. His understanding of the dog's character is growing day by day. For example, he has noticed that the dog is often hungry, and so he regularly shares his monkey biscuits with him. Orangutans are very generous creatures. If you give one a piece of candy, often they will break it in half and hand one piece back to you."

So how does Dr. Antle explain the fact that their relationship has a lot of the characteristics of what we call "friendship"? He says that the two animals have recognized a basic social need in each other that we don't normally associate with animals. "Animals need fun and interaction, just like us, and these two are not getting this from other animals in their group."

▶ 4

1 I have noticed a similar apathy among other people his age.
2 Jarvis has been saying this for a couple of years.

▶ 6

G = Greta, T = Tom

G: Hi, Tom! This is a surprise. How are you?

T: Oh, hi, Greta. I'm doing fine, thanks.

G: Oh, that's good to hear. I haven't seen you for a really long time. What have you been up to?

T: Actually, I've been working abroad for the last eight months.

G: Really? Anywhere exciting?

T: Yeah, in India. I have a contract to do some teacher training there.

G: Well, it obviously suits you. You're looking very tanned and relaxed.

T: Thanks—it's been a lot of fun. And you? You're looking good, too. How are things?

G: Oh, you know, busy as ever. I've been studying for my law exams.

T: Oh yes, of course—I remember. Is the course going OK?

G: Well, you know, it's a lot of work. But it's going well, generally.

T: Good. And what about Amanda? I haven't seen her in a long time either. How's she doing?

G: Yeah, she's doing well. We still meet up from time to time. She was asking about you the other day, actually.

T: Oh, well, I'm only back for a few days, but please give her my best wishes when you see her next.

G: I will.

T: And the next time I'm back, maybe we can all get together for a drink.

G: That'd be great. How long will you be away for?

T: Well, I have to do another two months over there. Then I'll be back home for a while, I hope.

G: OK. Well, give me a call when you get back. You have my number, right?

T: Yeah, if it's still the same one.

G: Yeah, it is. I'll look forward to that. Anyway, I need to get back to school now—but it was really nice to see you. Hope you have a good trip back.

T: Thanks. Well, it was great to see you too, Greta. Take care … and good luck with your exams.

▶ 7

5 Busy as ever.
6 I'm in kind of a hurry.
7 That'd be great.
8 Give her my best wishes.

Unit 2

▶ 8

P = Presenter, M = Mark Mowlam

P: Take a bestselling book with a great storyline and add a great cast, an experienced director, and a large budget. And what do you get? A box office success, you would think. Think again. Successful books don't always make good movies. Some movie adaptations have worked, others haven't. So what's the secret? That was the question I put earlier to film critic Mark Mowlam, who recently wrote about the making of *The Hobbit*.

M: Well, the key is to make a movie that remains true to the spirit of the book and that captures the heart of the story, even if it doesn't include every detail. Peter Jackson's *The Hobbit* is a fantastic example of this. The writer of the book, J.R.R. Tolkien, created a very original imaginary world. Jackson had to somehow reproduce this in a way that satisfied the millions of people who had read the book and loved it. I think he did a fantastic job. For a start, it's a beautifully filmed movie. Jackson used the varied scenery of his native New Zealand for the movie's locations: the green countryside where Bilbo, the Hobbit, lives; and the dark, scary mountains that Bilbo has to travel to. The result is a movie that is visually stunning. It also feels like the book. Sometimes the story is very fast-moving and gripping; at other times, it goes more slowly and gently.

▶ 11

become—became—become
begin—began—begun

drink—drank—drunk
forget—forgot—forgotten
shine—shone—shone
sing—sang—sung
go—went—gone
win—won—won

▶ 12

Mr. Charles Everson and his wife Linda were driving home one Sunday when a cow fell from the sky and landed on the hood of their van. The cow—which had escaped from a local farm—had been grazing all morning near the edge of a cliff, when it slipped and plunged seventy meters to the road below. The Eversons weren't hurt, but the cow wasn't so lucky—it had to be put to sleep.

▶ 13

As the sixteenth miner, Daniel Herrera, came out, it was love at first sight for Melanie. He had a beautiful smile, and she knew he had a good heart. So she contacted him on Facebook, and they started writing to each other. Daniel wasn't married and was living with his mother. After some months, they began speaking on the phone, and Melanie helped Daniel to overcome the trauma he had experienced. In 2012, she flew to Chile to meet Daniel. He fell in love with her, too, and in 2014 they got married.

▶ 14

I = Interviewer, O = Olaf Paulsen

I: Olaf, for a long time you didn't call yourself a photographer, because it was still just a hobby rather than a full-time paid job.

O: Yes, that's true—although whenever I traveled with my camera, I kind of treated it like a job. I acted like I had been paid by a magazine or newspaper to get some great photos to go with a story.

I: Well, that's what I wanted to ask you about, because more recently you've been called a "visual storyteller" rather than a photographer. Can you explain what people mean by that?

O: For me, a good photographer *is* a storyteller. Visual storytelling means using an image—or a series of images—to communicate what is *really* happening in a place or to a person. A good photo immediately engages the viewer emotionally. It pulls you into the story behind the image.

I: And we see images used everywhere now to tell stories and to express ideas—not just photos, but icons, video animations, infographics, and so on.

O: Absolutely. Visual storytelling is definitely a phenomenon of our time.

As you say, a lot of factual information is presented visually now. Obviously, in the past, photos were used in magazines, in newspapers, or on TV to bring stories to life. The difference now is that it is not just the media companies that are in control of this. Stories can be shared by anyone from anywhere in the world, simply by uploading a photo or sharing a link to an infographic or a striking image. So it's an amazing time for anyone who takes photographs—because it doesn't matter if the photo is taken with a professional camera or just an ordinary mobile phone; you have a way of reaching thousands of people with it very quickly.

I: And do you have any examples of visual storytelling that you particularly like?

O: Umm, there was all the good work that John Stanmeyer did in helping to bring the migrant crisis to the world's attention: for example, his photos of lifejackets left on the beach by refugees who risked crossing the sea to get to Greece. But it doesn't have to be about big stories like that. There was a wonderful photo I saw the other day—I don't remember the name of the photographer—but it's of some boys laughing at a joke they've just heard. The joy of the moment, their youthful delight, is captured wonderfully in the picture. It sums up an emotion in a way that words cannot do.

▶ 18

Conversation 1

A: The bus broke down on the highway, so we were all left waiting until help could arrive.

B: What did you do?

A: Luckily, another bus came within about fifteen minutes, and we all transferred to that one.

B: That must have been a relief.

Conversation 2

A: My pants got caught on the door handle, and as I walked away, they ripped.

B: Oh, no!

A: I had to walk right across the restaurant back to our table with my hands over the hole.

B: How embarrassing!

Conversation 3

A: I bent my house key trying to force it into the door lock, and when I tried to straighten the key, it snapped.

B: How did you get in?

A: I went to the neighbors' house to ask for their help, but they weren't at

home. So I just had to wait until my roommate came home.

B: Yeah, a similar thing happened to me once.

Conversation 4

A: The elevator got stuck between the eighteenth and nineteenth floors, and two people completely panicked.

B: What a nightmare!

A: It was. Then the lights in the elevator went off, and one of them started screaming.

B: Yeah, I think I would have done the same thing.

Conversation 5

A: The tires on my bike were all worn out, and when I hit a bump in the road, one of them popped.

B: Poor you!

A: I fell off and cut my hand. Thank goodness there were no cars behind me.

B: That was lucky.

Conversation 6

A: My computer froze while I was working.

B: Really? Do you know why?

A: No. I thought I'd lost about four hours' work. But when I rebooted, I searched for some of the key words in my document, and I found a temporary file that had most of the document in it.

B: That was good thinking.

Unit 3

▶ 21

1

I expect that most of my generation will live to be around a hundred years old. There are already more than 72,000 people in the US who are over a hundred. It's predicted that by the year 2050, that number will have risen to about 400,000, thanks to advances in medicine.

2

I think in the future, people will be interacting with intelligent machines even more than they do now. I read an article about things called chatbots—these are programs that can hold intelligent conversations with people on the internet. These programs already exist, and some experts predict that the future will bring even more chatbot innovation.

3

I think science will be able to find a solution to global warming. By the middle of this century, I think humans will have discovered ways to control the weather. If you think about it, the benefits, commercial and otherwise, are so great—for agriculture, for stopping natural disasters, and so on—that it's only a matter of time before someone works out a way.

1 eight billion
2 an internet site
3 a twenty-first birthday
4 great poverty
5 another reality

▶ 25

1
A: What are you doing this weekend?
B: I'm not sure, but we might go to the beach if the weather stays nice.
A: Sounds good. I'm just going to stay at home and relax.

2
A: I'm going to buy a wedding dress on Saturday. Jen and I are traveling up to Seattle to choose one.
B: How exciting! Are you going to show it to anyone else before the wedding?
A: I'll let you see it, if you want.

3
A: Will you help me move this table? It won't take long.
B: Sure. I'll just finish writing this email first.

4
A: Have you started your new job yet?
B: No, but I'm about to start. Next Monday is my first day.
A: Good luck. I'm sure you'll be fine.

▶ 26

I = Interviewer, E = Expert
I: Welcome to today's edition of three-minute science. This morning, we're going to take a closer look at 3D printing. It's a technology that most people have heard of, but not everyone understands. So, here we go. Firstly, what is a 3D printer?
E: Well, "3D printing" means three-dimensional printing. So a 3D printer is a machine that can make different kinds of three-dimensional objects—coffee cups, sunglasses, replacement car parts—not just printing on paper. And it uses different materials, like plastic, metal, glass, concrete, even chocolate.
I: And why is it called a printer?
E: Because it makes things in thin slices, building them up layer by layer. Imagine an ordinary ink-jet printer that prints letters on a page. If you let it go over each letter again and again, soon you'd build a letter that comes up from the page in 3D.
I: Is that the only similarity to an ink-jet printer?
E: No. You also connect a 3D printer to a computer—just like an ordinary printer. You create the design for an object on the computer, and then you just press "print."

I: How do the layers of printed objects stick together?
E: A 3D printer uses a range of materials, like plastic or metal or wood. Each layer comes out as a liquid or paste, or as powder. Some materials just naturally set; others are bonded together using heat or light.
I: And what are its advantages over traditional construction?
E: It means you can make individual things cheaply. You can already make standard products in a factory cheaply, but customized products are very expensive. In the future, anyone with a 3D printer will be able to make what they want. There's a Dutch architect who's printing a house next to a canal in Amsterdam. He thinks that in the future, his firm will be building a lot of houses this way, using customized designs that they create with the client.
I: What's the most amazing thing a 3D printer can print?
E: Perhaps the most interesting area is the printing of human body parts made of real cells and electronic components. Some printed body parts—like new 3D-printed ears—already exist, but I expect twenty years from now scientists will be making all kinds of body parts.
I: And what are its disadvantages?
E: 3D printers are still expensive, and they don't mass-produce things, so the cost of each item you print is high. But in ten years' time, the cost will have come down a lot.
I: And, lastly, where will 3D printing be fifteen years from now?
E: A lot of people will already have bought their own 3D printers by then, and we will be making parts for things at home that have broken or can't easily be replaced: a light switch, your favorite bottle opener, or an old phone charger. And, as with any technology, in time we will all have forgotten what life was like before 3D printers existed.

▶ 28

R = Receptionist, G = Guest
1
R: Hello, ma'am. Is everything OK with your room?
G1: Actually, no, it isn't. The window won't close, and there's a lot of noise coming from the street. I keep shutting it, but it just opens again.
R: Have you tried turning the handle at the side of the window to close it?
G1: Handle? No, I didn't know there was one.

R: Yes, if you look on the right-hand side near the bottom, there's a handle that opens and shuts the window.
G1: Oh, sorry, I didn't see that. I'll give that a try then. Thanks.
R: Not at all, ma'am. My pleasure.

2
R: Yes, can I help you?
G2: Umm, yes. I'm in room 768 on the seventh floor. I have the Wi-Fi password, but I can't seem to connect to the internet.
R: Are you using the guest Wi-Fi?
G2: Yes.
R: I'm sorry. Sometimes the connection isn't so good up there. I'm afraid there's not much I can do about it, but you're welcome to come down here to the lobby where there's a stronger signal.

3
G3: Excuse me, I need some help.
R: Of course. How can I help?
G3: I've locked my wallet and passport in the safe in my room, but now I can't remember the code I used. Can you tell me how to open the safe?
R: I believe we have an override code, but I'll need to get the manager for that.
G3: Could you possibly do that now? I'm going out for the evening.
R: OK. One moment, please … I'm afraid she's not answering, but I'll keep trying. When I speak to her, I'll ask her to call your room immediately.

Unit 4

▶ 31

A: People are full of surprises, aren't they? There's a teacher that I work with who's a really shy person. She never really stands out in a group. I worked with her for about two years, and then I found out that on most weekends, she becomes a street performer.
B: What kind of street performer?
A: Well, it turns out she's some kind of acrobat. She was brought up in a circus. On weekends, she still meets up with friends and puts on shows of circus skills in public places, like a busy shopping street. She doesn't do it for money—at least, I don't think so—just for fun. It's not at all what you imagine when you meet her, because she doesn't seem that outgoing.
B: That's interesting. It reminds me a bit of my neighbor. He's an accountant and is really into baseball and other sports. But he also writes poetry. He does it on the train when he's commuting to work—because it takes about an

hour each way to and from work. I don't think many people have read his poems because he's kind of private, but he showed me one the other day. He'd written it when his little boy was sick. It was very touching, actually, and beautifully written.

▶ 33

I = Interviewer, W = Will

I: OK, Will, I know as an artist yourself, you have strong feelings about what art is and isn't. So, I'm going to give you some statements about what various people say art should be, and I want to know which you agree with. OK?

W: OK.

I: So, here's the first one: "All art should contain something pleasing for the viewer."

W: No, not necessarily—the artist's intention might be to make you feel uncomfortable, not to give you a warm feeling.

I: OK. What about this? "Art should involve some hard work on the part of the artist."

W: That's more interesting, but the answer is still "not necessarily"—Monet did some paintings in five minutes.

I: Well, then that links to the next statement: "To be an artist, you need to possess certain technical skills."

W: Well, you often hear people say things like "My three-year-old daughter could have done that," meaning there's no technical skill involved. But an artwork doesn't have to be technically difficult; it could just be a clever idea.

I: OK. "Art should make a social or a political point; without either, it's not true art."

W: No, certainly not. Is the Mona Lisa political? I don't think so.

I: What about this one? "The viewer shouldn't have to make any effort to understand a work of art."

W: No, I disagree with that. The artist has made an effort to produce something, so the viewer should make an effort to understand it.

I: OK. And lastly, "There is no such thing as bad art."

W: Yes, I agree. My role is to present an idea in visual form. Your role is to give yourself time to look at it. Then you can say either "Yes, I really like that," or "No, that doesn't do anything for me." But you can't say "That's not art" or "It's bad art."

▶ 34

A visitor to Australia once noted that "Nature has done everything for Sydney, man nothing; man has done everything for Melbourne, nature nothing." This sums up the essential difference between Australia's two largest cities. Melbourne is Australia's second city, but it has plenty of first-class qualities, from a buzzing arts scene to its enormous range of restaurants. It may have a few grey days, and a muddy river instead of a beautiful harbor, but don't let that worry you. A lack of natural attractions has meant that Melbourne has had to create its own man-made pleasures … and in doing so, it has become Australia's cultural capital. There are hardly any forms of artistic expression that you can't find here. Theater, music, street sculpture, fashion all thrive—alongside a cosmopolitan mix of cafés, restaurants, and pubs.

What's great about Melbourne for visitors is how accessible all these arts are. As well as traditional museums and galleries like the National Gallery of Victoria, and concert halls like Hamer Hall, there are an enormous number of smaller art spaces and venues that cater to every kind of taste. Art is something that the majority of locals enjoy. In fact, for most inhabitants of Melbourne, a visit to the theater or an art exhibition is a routine event. Several festivals take place during the winter months, including the International Film Festival in July, and the Fringe Festival in September—which has a lot of interesting comedy, dance, and theater acts.

And if the locals appreciate their art, they absolutely love their sports. Lots of people around the world know about the Australian Formula 1 Grand Prix and the Australian Open Tennis, which attracts over half a million spectators to Melbourne in a carnival atmosphere. But few people will be familiar with the sports Melburnians themselves follow. Cricket and Australian rules football enjoy a huge amount of support here. If you have a little time to spare, a visit to see either is well worth it, just for the atmosphere. If you're looking to participate rather than just watch, why not try a bit of surfing or swimming? Riding a bike, jogging, or visiting one of Melbourne's many gyms are other possibilities. All this information is on our website at *thetravelshow.org*, so do take a look.

▶ 37

J = Jake, T = Tom

J: Hey, Tom. How was *The Lion King*?

T: It was really good—and I'm not a fan of musicals generally. Do you like them?

J: Not really, no. So what was so good about *The Lion King*?

T: Well, the visual effects are absolutely stunning, the opening scene particularly. All the animals—giraffes, wildebeests, zebras, antelopes—come onto the stage together to set the scene at the beginning, and the costumes are incredible. They're difficult to describe—you can see the people in the costumes, but they seem to move like real animals. Everyone in the audience was spellbound.

J: Wow. And is the story the same as in the Disney movie? Because in that movie, there were some rather annoying characters, like that bird who was supposed to be there for comic effect—what was its name?

T: Zazu. Yeah, I know what you mean. That kind of Disney character gets on my nerves, too. But I didn't notice that with this production. It's more adult than the movie, so it's a bit different. As I say, it was excellent.

J: And what about the music? Did you like it?

T: I loved it! It has a really cool African vibe to it. The songs were written by Elton John, interestingly, and I have a lot of respect for him.

J: Oh, OK. Well, I might check it out then. Are the tickets reasonable?

T: They're not cheap. I can't stand the high prices they charge for most musicals these days—it just seems wrong. But actually, I didn't mind for this one. I thought it was money well spent.

Unit 5

▶ 40

When it's complete, the Belo Monte dam in northern Brazil will be the fourth largest hydroelectric power project in the world. It will generate huge amounts of electricity that will benefit people all over the country. It will also enhance Brazil's reputation as a major producer of renewable energy. Renewable energy already accounts for nearly half of the energy Brazil consumes. As with any such development, there are arguments for and against the dam. In its favor is the fact that the country needs electricity as its population expands, and this is the cheapest way to get it. Its construction has also created 19,000 new jobs, which has boosted the local economy. However, about 400 square kilometers of rain forest have been cleared to make way for the dam and its reservoir. Environmentalists are worried that the huge diversity of plants and animals that thrives here will be lost. Also, eighteen different tribal communities in the area will lose their land and many of their traditional jobs, like hunting and fishing. Supporters of the project say that even though these people have had to move, in the long term, the dam will improve their lives.

▶ 42

I = Interviewer, J = Journalist

I: I know you like exotic places. Have you been to the Indian subcontinent?

J: Yes, I was in India just recently.

I: Were you?

J: Yes, in Kerala in the southwest. Actually, I had intended to go on to visit other parts of India, but Kerala was so fascinating that I stayed there.

I: Were you on vacation?

J: Well, it was meant to be a vacation, but actually it turned into kind of a work trip.

I: Oh dear.

J: Oh, no. I don't regret changing my plans. I became so interested in the place that I started to write an article about it for the newspaper I work for.

I: Really? Is it a travel article?

J: Not really. It's more sociological, I guess. I'm trying to show what a remarkable place Kerala is in the developing world. You see, it's a small state with a big population. The average income is only about $300 a year, and usually that would mean people having a fairly poor quality of life. But in fact, Kerala is a kind of model of social development. The population is **highly literate** and **well-educated**, and they seem **reasonably well off**—compared to other parts of India, anyway. People in Kerala are healthy, and they live almost as long as Americans or Europeans. Infant mortality is also very low. And women, who've always traditionally been the head of the household, continue to be very active—and equal—members of society.

I: That's interesting. I remember going to Kerala with my wife in the 1990s. My memories of it are just as a very tranquil and beautiful place, with lovely beaches and lagoons.

J: Well, of course, those are the parts that tourists like to spend time visiting. But "tranquil" is not necessarily the adjective I would use. Trivandrum, the main city, is absolutely hectic. I stopped there to visit an Indian journalist I know. According to her, people in Trivandrum are **politically active** and **very well-informed** about the country. They never stop debating, and there are often strikes or parades of demonstrators. Some medical students started protesting when I was there. They went on protesting for four days.

I: Well, that doesn't sound great.

J: No, but it is. It's a sign of a successful society. The thing is that the whole system seems to work. That's because, first, Keralites are **naturally tolerant** people. You find Hindus, Muslims, and Christians all living peacefully alongside each other, and you could also include foreigners in that mix—they're treated no differently than anyone else. And secondly, the government has invested a lot in health and education, and continues to invest a lot. The land is also incredibly fertile and well-organized. Small farmers cultivate every inch of the land and none is wasted, which I regret to say isn't always the case in some developing countries.

I: Well, it sounds like it'll be an interesting article. Remember to send me a copy when it's published.

J: Of course I will.

▶ 43

1	state—weight	5	main—plane	
2	low—though	6	stopped—opt	
3	head—said	7	none—fun	
4	course—force	8	waste—faced	

▶ 45

C = Councilor

C: Hello, everybody. Thanks for coming today. We do appreciate it because we need to hear from as many residents as possible before we come to a decision on the future of the skate park. As you know, there have been a number of complaints about noise coming from the park, and noise disturbance is something that we at the council take very seriously. So we'd like to hear your views, and any suggestions you might have for a way forward.

▶ 46

C = Councilor, M = First man,
M2 = Second man, W = First woman,
W2 = Second woman

C: So we'd like to hear your views, and any suggestions you might have for a way forward. Yes—the woman in the blue top. Would you like to introduce yourself and start us off?

W: Well, yes. I live about fifty meters from the skate park—our yard backs up to it. I'm sure that no one, me included, wants to spoil other people's fun. But the thing is that the constant noise coming from these skateboard ramps all day—from ten in the morning to sometimes as late as ten at night—it's spoiling *our* enjoyment of our own yard. Sometimes we can't even hear each other speak!

M: Sorry, but I think that's a bit of an exaggeration. We can all hear each other fine now, and we're right next to the skate park.

M2: For me, the noise is just one factor. And actually, I'm not too bothered by the sound of people having fun. I'm more concerned that the park has become a spot for young people to gather in the evenings. I worry that it's not safe for them.

W: No, that's a very good point. I think it's just a matter of time before we are here again talking about a more serious problem—like drugs or crime.

W2: I think we're forgetting that this is healthy exercise these kids are having. They're not at home watching TV or playing video games. They're outside doing something active. And quite honestly, if that involves making a little noise, then that's something I can live with.

M: Thanks for that—I agree completely. I don't think most of you have really thought about the impact if you close this park down. A lot of kids will be left with nothing to do, or they'll have to find public spaces where they can skateboard that aren't safe. The whole thing just doesn't make any sense to me.

Unit 6

▶ 48

I only get three weeks' vacation a year, so I always choose the places I go to carefully. I try to go to places with dramatic scenery, or to unusual places. It can take time to get to these places, but, personally, I think it's worth it. I saw this hotel on the cover of a travel magazine and thought, "Yes, I have to go there!" It's called the Aescher Guesthouse, and it's in the most beautiful setting, overlooking a Swiss Alpine valley. To get there from Zurich, you have to take two different trains, a cable car, and then it's a walk down through some caves to the hotel. But when you get there, you won't regret it. The views are amazing, and the food is also fantastic. The only downsides are that it's not cheap, and also—because it's so out of the way—sometimes there's no water, so you can't always take a shower when you want one. I spent two days there hiking in the mountains. Some of the other guests went paragliding off the mountainside, which looked incredible. But that's not my kind of thing—I'm not great with heights!

▶ 50

P = Presenter, K = Katie Samuel

P: Have you ever thought about doing some building work during your vacations? Or helping to take care of animals on a wildlife reserve? It seems these days, a lot more working adults are opting for volunteer vacations. With us today is Katie Samuel, author of *Good Travel*, a guide to volunteering vacations. Katie, I can see this might be attractive to some, but don't most people just want to head off to the beach and relax while on vacation?

K: Well, I think that depends on how your volunteer vacation is organized. The good companies are certainly aware that this should be a rewarding travel experience, not just a work trip.

P: But it's not really a vacation as we know it, is it?

K: Again, that depends on your definition. For me, a good vacation is a cultural experience where each side—traveler and host—gives something and takes something. A good example is a program near the Tsavo National Park in Kenya, where volunteers help local people to find ways of making a living that don't involve poaching or killing local wildlife. So they help them to plant crops or develop ideas for tourist businesses. In return, the locals take the volunteers for bush walks—like mini-safaris—and teach them about local wildlife.

P: But the volunteers pay for the trip, don't they?

K: Yes, of course. They have to pay for their own airfares and living expenses, plus something to cover the cost of organizing the trip.

P: OK. And can you tell us what qualifications or skills these organizations are looking for, usually? I mean, surely they don't want people without experience just turning up to teach or build or whatever?

K: Actually, for the most part, volunteers can be trained to do the work. There are a few projects for professional nurses or teachers, but mostly, training is given. At the Cultural Restoration Tourism Project (CRTP), which restores cultural heritage sites around the world, volunteers are placed with local architects and artists. At the moment, they're restoring a 300-year-old monastery in Nepal, and the volunteers are being trained in wall painting by a world-famous painter.

P: Wow! So is it possible that people could come back with a skill they didn't have before they went on vacation?

K: Absolutely—though it might not be a skill you'll ever use again. Helping to bottle-feed a lion cub—that's a project

in Zambia—is unlikely to be of direct use to you back in your New York office. But we all benefit more widely from new experiences, don't we?

P: Of course. So do you know where listeners can find upcoming volunteer vacation possibilities? Some websites, perhaps?

▶ **52**

1   Surely he doesn't intend to give up his well-paid job in order to travel?
2   Can you tell me which travel company you used?
3   Didn't it rain a lot when you were in England?
4   You've been to America, haven't you?
5   Do you know if this bus goes downtown?

▶ **54**

M = Mike, J = Jeff

M: Hi, I'm interested in helping to repair trails on the Continental Divide Trail this summer. I can work for just a few days, can't I?

J: Absolutely. You can work anywhere from two days to two months.

M: That's great. I have about a week in June. Volunteers usually pay something to take part, don't they?

J: No, actually. It's free.

M: Sorry—free? Surely I have to pay for my accommodation, don't I?

J: No, it's completely free. You just have to register by filling out a form and sending it to us.

M: I couldn't find a form online. It's not on your website, is it?

J: You have to collect the form from our office, or I can email it to you.

M: Great. And where on the trail can I work?

J: New Mexico, Montana, Wyoming, …

M: You don't have something in Colorado, do you?

J: Yes, we do. We have spaces in Winfield, Colorado, and a few in Mount Elbert.

M: And can you tell me how long the training is?

J: There's no training beforehand. We train you as you work. But we are looking for a chef at the moment. You don't have any cooking experience, do you?

M: No, I'm afraid not. I really just want to work for a few days helping to build trails.

▶ **56**

M = Malcolm, P = Paul

M: Hi, Paul. This is Malcolm. You emailed me about staying at my place next Thursday for a couple of nights.

P: Oh, hi, Malcolm. Thanks for getting back to me. Is that still OK?

M: That's all fine. I just thought I'd give you a call to explain how to get to my place, because it's a bit complicated. How are you getting here, first of all?

P: I'm coming in by train sometime in the afternoon.

M: OK. I wanted to pick you up, but my car will be at the garage that day.

P: Oh, that's kind of you, but I can make my own way.

M: OK. Well, I'm usually at work till about five thirty, so feel free to come over any time after six.

P: That sounds perfect. And how do I get to your place from the center of town?

M: Well, you could just get a taxi, but it's about eleven kilometers from the center of town, so it won't be cheap. Alternatively, you can hop on a bus to Stoney Creek. Look out for the sports arena on your right and get off there. It's only a twenty-minute ride. From there, Cherry Heights is another fifteen minutes on foot, straight up King St. Once you reach the crossroads at Gray Road, the easiest thing is to give me a call, and I'll come out and meet you.

P: So, bus to Stoney Creek, walk up King St to Cherry Heights, and call you from there?

M: Yup. Call me when you get to the crossroads at Gray Road.

P: OK, got it. That sounds great. If I get held up in any way, I'll let you know. But otherwise, expect a call around six thirty.

M: Great. See you next Thursday then. Bye.

P: Bye.

Unit 7

▶ **58**

I'm from New York, so I'm used to the subway, but there are some things about the Tokyo subway that were definitely new to me. First, don't use your phone. If someone calls, it's OK to answer quickly—you know, say "I'm sorry, I'm on the train," and then hang up. But in general, people are really quiet and private, so don't ever talk loudly. Some rules of behavior are the same as in New York, like giving up your seat to an old person and not eating hot food. And if you have a large backpack, you should put it on a shelf so it's not in people's way. But some other customs seem pretty odd. The one that got me the first time was when someone next to me fell asleep and put their head on my shoulder. It seems there's nothing wrong with that—I've seen it happen to a few people now. You'll also often see people wearing face masks when they have a cold. That's because coughing, sneezing, or using a tissue in public is considered rude. What else? Oh yeah, when you get on a train during rush hour, you'll find there are people—they're called *Oshiya*—who are employed to push you, like, physically, into the crowded car.

▶ 60

On the whole, most of us eat a pretty balanced diet—a mixture of fruits, vegetables, grains, meat, fish, eggs, and dairy. Diet fashions come and go—the protein diet, the grapefruit diet, the starving-two-days-a-week diet, and so on—but, for the most part, we are used to eating a range of foods. It's true that in poorer regions of the world, people eat less meat and more grains and vegetables, and in richer parts more meat and sugary foods … and more fatty food. But everyone at least aims to have some kind of balance. And that's why I was so intrigued to read recently about the traditional diet of the indigenous people of northern Alaska, who are collectively known as Alaska Natives.

Historically, Alaska Natives didn't use to have a so-called balanced diet at all. Because of sub-zero temperatures and a lack of plant life, they had to survive on what they could hunt and fish close to home. They would hunt seal and walrus and reindeer, and then they'd cook the meat in seal oil. Sometimes they'd eat frozen fish, and when times were really hard in winter, they used to eat whale skin and blubber, which, I'm told, is like chewing car tires.

But how could a diet of just meat and fat possibly be healthy? Well, according to Harold Draper, an expert in nutrition, there's no such thing as essential foods—only essential nutrients. And there's not only one way to get those nutrients. In the West, we have gotten used to eating certain foods in order to get each nutrient. For example, we usually eat fruit to get more vitamin C, and dairy products for calcium and vitamin D. But during the long winters, the Alaska Natives found the nutrients and vitamins they needed from their diet of fish and wild animal meat. As for the large amount of fat they consumed, it was a healthier kind of fat, not the saturated fats that cause people in the West so many health problems these days. In fact, heart conditions among people on a traditional Alaska Native diet used to be about half the number in the wider population of North America. I say

"used to" because nowadays, a lot of the indigenous population live close to towns and eat more processed food—pizza, fries, and soda—and unfortunately with this has come a rise in obesity, diabetes, and heart conditions.

▶ 63

1   Fruit and vegetables: apple, raspberries, cucumber, lettuce
2   Dairy products: cheese, butter
3   Breakfast cereals: muesli
4   Sauces: mustard, ketchup
5   Meat and seafood: beef, lamb, tuna

▶ 65

M = Marie, E = Esther

M: I know of henna painting as a custom at Indian weddings, but you came across it in Turkey, didn't you?

E: Yes, in eastern Turkey when I was traveling there. It takes place a few nights before the wedding.

M: Was it kind of like a bachelorette party?

E: Well, in the sense that it marks the last evening that a bride spends as a single woman—with her female family and friends—I suppose it is kind of like that. What happens is, typically, the women from both families get together with the bride, to celebrate with music, song, and dance. But it's not just a party. It's an occasion for sadness too, because it symbolizes the end of life as a single person and the start of another stage.

▶ 66

M = Marie, E = Esther

M: So what happens exactly?

E: Well, the ceremony begins with the preparation of the henna. It's traditional for this to be done by the daughter of a couple who have had a successful marriage themselves. Then, after the bride's head has been covered with a red veil, her hands and feet are decorated with henna. After that, a gold coin is put into the remaining henna. While this is happening, the guests start to sing, umm, separation songs—these are kind of sad, as you can imagine. The party continues well into the night. Then, on the morning of the wedding, a child presents the hennaed coin to the groom as a symbol of future prosperity and good fortune.

▶ 67

M = Marie, E = Esther

M: I know of henna painting as a custom at Indian weddings, but you came across it in Turkey, didn't you?

E: Yes, in eastern Turkey when I was traveling there. It takes place a few nights before the wedding.

M: Was it kind of like a bachelorette party?

E: Well, in the sense that it marks the last evening that a bride spends as a single woman—with her female family and friends—I suppose it is kind of like that. What happens is, typically, the women from both families get together with the bride, to celebrate with music, song, and dance. But it's not just a party. It's an occasion for sadness too, because it symbolizes the end of life as a single person and the start of another stage.

M: So what happens exactly?

E: Well, the ceremony begins with the preparation of the henna. It's traditional for this to be done by the daughter of a couple who have had a successful marriage themselves. Then, after the bride's head has been covered with a red veil, her hands and feet are decorated with henna. After that, a gold coin is put into the remaining henna. While this is happening, the guests start to sing, umm, separation songs—these are kind of sad, as you can imagine. The party continues well into the night. Then, on the morning of the wedding, a child presents the hennaed coin to the groom as a symbol of future prosperity and good fortune.

Unit 8

▶ 70

This mural's been on the wall of a local store in my neighborhood for years. Anyone can write on it. You just have to pick up a piece of chalk and complete the sentence "Before I die, I want to …" This "bucket list" wall isn't the only one of its kind: There are quite a few other walls like it in other cities around the world. The idea was started by a woman in New Orleans, and then it spread.

Sometimes I sit and watch people as they're thinking about what to write on the wall, thinking about the dreams they'd like to come true. Some are goals that are easy to achieve, like "I want to plant a tree"; some just make me laugh, like "I want to fix my kitchen faucet." But others are more personal—people wanting to live up to other people's expectations of them. "I want to be a good parent" was one I found touching. The same things keep coming up, too. A lot of people have an ambition to travel and to learn another language. But, overall, there is an amazing variety of wishes on the wall. I guess some people will fulfill their ambitions and some won't, but this wall shows that most of us are trying to make sense of our direction in life.

▶ 72

1 If the rent were cheaper, I'd take the apartment.
2 What would you have done if you'd been me?
3 So sorry! If I'd known you were here, I'd have asked Jo to get you a coffee.
4 If she had stayed in college, she'd now be a fully qualified journalist.

▶ 73

The National Geographic Explorers' words are spoken by actors.

1 **Albert Lin, Scientist and explorer**
It's got to be invisibility, right? Like, because if you could be invisible, you could see the entire world in the craziest way.
2 **Laly Lichtenfeld, Big cat conservationist**
I'd like to be able to fly. It'd help me see the bigger picture.
3 **Andrés Ruzo, Geologist**
I wish I had the ability to make people magically understand me. You know how frustrating it is, when you wish other people would get what you're trying to say and they just don't. You think, "Goodness, I wish they'd stop looking at me in that confused way!"
4 **Alizé Carrère, Geographer**
If I had a superpower, it would be to be invisible, so people couldn't see me.
5 **Andrew Thompson, Biologist**
Teleporting would be pretty cool. I could travel any place I wanted to. I wish I'd had that power earlier in my career. It would have saved me a lot of air miles. I could also use it to transport things I'd forgotten to take with me on my travels.
6 **Catherine Workman, Conservation biologist**
I would definitely be invisible. I'd go to the White House and listen in on all their conversations.
7 **Neil deGrasse Tyson, Astrophysicist**
I wish I could read other people's minds. But I would like to be able to turn that power on and off—sometimes you just don't want to know what other people are thinking! Also, I'd want to read not just people's minds, but the minds of animals too, like dogs. I've always wondered what dogs are thinking.
8 **Ricky Qi, Filmmaker**
Sometimes I think, "If only I could turn anything into any kind of food I wanted." That would be the most awesome superpower.

▶ 74

1 wish   4 shin
2 shop   5 watch
3 catch   6 choose

▶ 76

1
A: Would you like to drive or should I?
B: I'd rather you drove, if you don't mind. I'm feeling kind of tired.
A: No, that's fine. Actually, I prefer driving to being a passenger.

2
A: What would you like for dinner? I could cook some pasta, or we could get some take-out Indian food.
B: Well, if you don't mind cooking, pasta sounds great. I like simple food more than spicy food.

3
A: So what would you like to do tomorrow? We could just take a walk around the old town. Or, if you prefer, we could go to a museum.
B: To be honest, I'd rather not go to a museum. I think the weather's going to be sunny tomorrow, and it seems a pity to be indoors on a nice day.
A: OK. Great. We'll take a walk then.

4
A: What do you feel like doing this weekend? We're thinking either we could go and see the new Matt Damon movie, or there's a music festival in the park, but I'm not sure who's playing. What do you think?
B: Well, if it were up to me, I'd say let's go to the festival in the park. It doesn't matter if the music isn't very good. I think that would probably be more fun.
A: OK. I'd prefer to do that, too.

Unit 9

▶ 78

N= Newsreader, M = Martha Cash

N: And in China, hundreds of parents of first-year students at the University of Wuhan have been sleeping on the floor of the university's gym, so that they can be near their children in their first anxious days at college. As Martha Cash, our China correspondent, reports.
M: For China's many middle-class parents, getting their children—and often it's an only child—into college is an extremely important step in building a better future for their families. Many parents put all their savings into achieving this goal. But being accepted to college is not the end of the story. The parents want to help their child settle into their new college life, and to follow the child's progress through university. The University of Wuhan recognizes this, and it also recognizes that many Chinese families are not particularly well off. Staying in a local hotel during their children's first days at college is not an option for them. So the university offers free accommodation to parents—up to five hundred at a time—in the form of mats in the university gym. As an expression of parental concern, it's certainly impressive.

▶ 80

1
And finally … A refugee in Germany has been called a hero after he handed in €150,000 in cash to the police. He found the money hidden in a wardrobe. In spite of having little money himself, the 25-year-old Syrian—who is believed to have been in Germany for less than a year—decided the right thing to do was to give the money back. The wardrobe was a gift from a charity to help the man furnish his apartment. Local police are now said to be looking for the money's true owner, but they praised the man for his honesty. As well as gaining the respect of the nation, the man will receive a financial reward, since, under German law, he is entitled to three percent of the money found—in this case, around €4,500.

2
And finally … In Naples, Italy, 250 chefs have collaborated to set a Guinness World Record for the world's longest pizza. Measuring 1.8 kilometers long, it took the chefs eleven hours to make. According to Guinness, the pizza makers used 2,000 kilograms of flour, 1,600 kilograms of tomatoes, 2,000 kilograms of mozzarella cheese, and 200 liters of olive oil. Afterwards, everyone in the crowd got a slice to eat, and the rest was given to people in need. The city of Naples has long been synonymous with pizza. It is thought that the first Margherita pizza was baked in Naples in 1889.

3
And finally … A Latvian scientist based in the UK is reported to be close to finding drugs that will help people live to ages of a hundred and beyond. What is more, he is confident that he himself will live to at least 150. Dr. Zhavoronkov is working with US pharmaceutical company The Life Extension Foundation, which hopes to soon be selling a range of products that will slow down the aging process. To reduce the high cost of new drug trials, Dr. Zhavoronkov has been testing the drugs on himself. Now aged 37, he claims to feel much younger than he did a few years ago.

▶ 82

Conversation 1
J = Jess, P = Phil
J: Hi, Phil. How are things?
P: Not bad. But work has been really stressful lately.
J: Yeah, I know what you mean. By the way, did you hear about Liam?

Apparently, he's been promoted.

P: Liam? But he's only been here a year!

J: I know. But according to Sarah, he's been given the job of area manager.

P: Area manager? I don't believe it! He's not even that good at his current job.

J: Well, Sarah also reckons that he's going to get a huge pay raise—something like double his current salary.

P: Yeah, well, I'd take that with a grain of salt. I don't think the company has that kind of money to throw around at the moment.

Conversation 2

F = Freddie, C = Caitlin

F: Hi, Caitlin. Hey, you know Dr. Harris at the local clinic?

C: Yes.

F: Well, someone told me that he was fired from his job yesterday. It seems that he's not even a real doctor.

C: What? Who told you that?

F: Tara.

C: Hmm, I wouldn't take too much notice of what Tara says. She tends to exaggerate things.

F: No, I'm pretty sure it's true. Apparently, Dr. Harris—if that's even his real name—has gone from one hospital to another across the country using a fake résumé.

C: Oh my goodness, that's terrible.

F: I know. But actually, that doesn't surprise me. You do hear of things like that happening.

C: Maybe, but I *would* be very surprised. Dr. Harris seemed like a genuine guy to me.

Unit 10

▶ 85

Both the mahout and the elephant start their training at a young age. A mahout generally begins to learn his trade when he's about ten years old. At this age, he is given a baby elephant to look after— they will remain bonded to each other throughout their lives. The job of a mahout is traditionally a family trade, with knowledge of how to care for an elephant passed down from one generation to the next. There are no formal qualifications for the job, but you need to be extremely patient. An elephant will learn as many as 65 commands in its life, depending on what work it's expected to do—some elephants carry logs and other heavy objects, others are trained to carry people. The mahout has to teach his elephant all these commands. He must also develop an understanding of his elephant, so that he knows when it's sick or tired or unhappy. This is something that only comes with

time and experience. It's a very physical job and extremely hard work. The elephant must be fed and bathed every day, and watched carefully in case it tries to run away.

▶ 86

This is a photo of the astronaut Buzz Aldrin, taken by the first man on the moon, Neil Armstrong, in 1969. You can see Armstrong taking the photo in the reflection on Aldrin's helmet. It was Armstrong who famously said "That's one small step for man, one giant leap for mankind" when he first stepped onto the moon. Actually, what he really said was "That's one small step for a man, one giant leap for mankind," but no one heard the "a" because of radio interference.

▶ 89

Daniel Kish, **who** has been blind since he was a year old, taught himself to "see" using the technique of echolocation. As he moves around, Kish clicks his tongue and then listens for the echo **that** comes back. If the echo is loud, then he knows that an object is near; if the echo is not so loud, he knows the object is farther away. He has become so skilled at using this technique that he can do many things **that** blind people cannot ordinarily do. By clicking his tongue two or three times a second, he can ride a bicycle, go hiking in the countryside, and play ball games.

Echolocation is a skill **that** is also used in the animal world, **where** it is often key to survival. The best-known example is bats. This has led to Kish being called "the real-life Batman"—a description he welcomes. Just like bats, Kish can tell from the quality of an echo not only how far away an object is, but also its size and its density. A wooden fence, for example, **whose** surface is softer than brick or metal, gives a "warmer" echo than a brick wall. So what can Kish actually "see"? Up close, at about five meters, he can recognize cars and bushes. Houses come into focus at about fifty meters.

Kish now spends a lot of his time training other blind people in his technique, **which** he calls FlashSonar. He says that many blind people already use echolocation in a passive way, but **what** they don't know is how to use it actively. The average person can develop good echolocation skills in about a month if they train for a couple of hours a day. Kish is also looking at the possibility of training fully-sighted people, like firefighters, to use this skill in situations **in which** their vision is limited, like in a smoke-filled building. He is amused by the

nickname **for which** he is now famous, but, mostly, he just loves **what** he is doing and sees great potential for it.

▶ 91

S = Sarah, P = Phil

S: So, you're 24 years old, you graduated a year ago, and you're looking for work with a charity. What attracted you to Shelterbox?

P: Well, I'm familiar with your work because I have a friend who volunteered for you last year—packing boxes—and I think it's a fantastic concept. But mainly, I'm very interested in the idea of working in different countries.

S: I see. And what makes you think you'd be suited to that? I see you studied economics at Harvard. Don't you think that's a rather different world?

P: Yes, it's true that I specialized in economics. But actually, I'm good at coping with difficult environments. I spent three months helping to build a school in Chennai in India last summer. And the year before that, I trekked across the Mojave Desert. So I think I'd be suited to the work.

S: OK. But you'd also be spending a good part of the time here in the office doing paperwork.

P: Yeah, that's also fine. I was expecting that. What kind of paperwork is involved?

S: Well, each trip involves a lot of preparation and a certain amount of follow-up, too. Keeping spreadsheets, writing reports. Are you OK doing that kind of thing?

P: Yeah, I'm pretty good with computers. I'm comfortable with all the usual programs—Excel, Word, some financial software.

S: OK. There's just one thing that's worrying me, though. You're clearly a bright person, and you have a good degree. How do we know that you won't just do this job for a few months and then go and get a better-paying job with a bank or consultancy business?

P: That's a good question. It's actually what a lot of my friends from college have done, but I'll tell you why that's not for me. Firstly, I'm serious about wanting to help people in need. Secondly, I think I need to become more knowledgeable about the world, before I use my economics degree to do something else. If you put your faith in me, I will be absolutely committed to doing the best job that I can!

1	clothes	5	folk
2	lengths	6	surface
3	February	7	island
4	receipt	8	thorough

Unit 11

94

I love this museum. We went to Indianapolis specially to visit it, because we'd heard such great things about it. My kids, who are seven and nine, loved the interactive display of dinosaurs—they could really engage with it. My husband and I learned a lot, too. There was a whole section on Asia—part of the "Take me there" section on foreign cultures. It had so many things I was completely unaware of, like Chinese herbal medicine. The other thing I really liked was the "Children making a difference" section. It included stories of children who had difficult childhoods but have succeeded—like kids who faced prejudice or discrimination. Their stories really inspired me. I'm definitely going to take my kids back to this museum when they're old enough to really get these stories. I think the mixture of visual displays, hands-on stuff, and real-life stories is a great way to acquire knowledge. I guess if I have any criticism of the museum, it's that it's too big—there's too much to take in.

96

You were about to make a comment in a meeting, and then your mind went blank. You were supposed to send a friend a birthday card, but then you forgot. You recognized someone in the street and would have spoken to them, but you didn't because you couldn't remember their name. You promised to mail a letter for someone, and two days later you found it in your pocket. You were going to write down a great idea you had, but when you found a pen and paper, the idea had gone. I could go on, but I won't because I'm sure everyone recognizes these common failures of memory. Do these situations sound familiar to you? Have any of these things happened to you?

97

Everyone thinks they would like to remember more, but, actually, would it make us any happier?

I want to tell you the story of a 41-year-old woman from California known in medical literature as "AJ," who remembers almost every day of her life since the age of eleven.

She remembers that at 12:34 p.m. on Sunday, August 3rd, 1986, a young man she was attracted to called her on the telephone. She remembers that on March 28th, 1992, she had lunch with her father at the Beverly Hills Hotel. It's a bit like it is for the rest of us when certain smells bring back strong memories. AJ's memory is stimulated in the most intense way by dates.

You'd think that being able to recall facts and knowledge in this way would make us more confident and wiser. But in fact, for AJ, having an incredible memory can be distressing. It is as much a burden as it is a benefit. That's because most people's memories are selective: We remember mostly important things, and mostly good things. AJ remembers every detail, good or bad, important or not. So when we blame our poor memories for forgetting to send a birthday card, actually we should be grateful also for all the things that our memories hide because they don't need to be remembered or thought about.

Technology also helps us. We don't need to remember the precise content of an email or the exact time of a meeting anymore, because it's stored in our computers or our mobile phones. Interestingly, the growth of this technology—which psychologists call our external memory—is having an effect on what and how much we remember. Even our memories of happy events, like parties or holidays, get stored in photo albums on our computers. So our internal memories are probably worse than those of people a hundred years ago. Medical science is trying to address the problem of poor memory, and this is what I want to talk about next.

98

(This track is repeated from tracks 96 and 97.)

99

1 I was going to invite Sarah, but I asked Kate instead.
2 She was supposed to be in Cairo this week, but she's sick, so she couldn't go.
3 He would have sent me the original, but he couldn't find it, so he sent me a copy.
4 We were supposed to arrive there by ten o'clock, but the train didn't get in until eleven.
5 He was about to announce his retirement, but now he thinks he'll stay until next year.

101

L = Liz, A = Ahmad

L: Hello, Rousham Adult Education College. Liz speaking.
A: Hi there. My name's Ahmad, and I'm interested in taking a class at your college—umm, the history of art course.
L: Is that the two-year A-level course?
A: Sorry, what do you mean by "A-level"?
L: The A-level art history course is a two-year pre-university course with examinations at the end of each year.
A: Oh, no, no, no, I don't want to take any exams. It's just for interest.
L: OK. In that case, we have a ten-week art appreciation course.
A: Sorry. Can you speak up a little? I can't hear you very well.
L: Yes, we have a ten-week art appreciation course.
A: Can you explain what the course involves?
L: It's a two-hour class once a week and, basically, it teaches you how to look at art, so that you can appreciate it better.
A: Sorry, I don't understand. Are you saying that it doesn't really deal with the history of art?
L: Umm, there's some history of art involved, but it's mainly learning about the techniques that artists use and what their paintings mean.
A: Could you give me an example of the kind of thing students do in the class?
L: Typically, students look at works of art and comment on them. Then they're told more about the artist, what he or she was trying to achieve, and then they look at the work again, to see if they see it differently.
A: OK. It sounds quite interesting. What was the class called again?
L: Art appreciation.
A: And when is it?
L: Every Tuesday—during the term, that is—from 7 p.m. to 9 p.m., starting on … one minute … yeah, starting on April 5th. The cost is $198, unless you're a registered student.
A: Sorry, I didn't catch the start date. Did you say May 5th?
L: No, April 5th.
A: OK. Well, thanks. I'll think about it, but it sounds interesting.
L: No worries. Bye!

Unit 12

103

Speaker 1

No, it does matter, absolutely. Because you end up with a divided society instead of a united one—the haves and the have nots, as some people call it. Japan has a much smaller income gap between rich and poor than the US, for example. That's partly because most bosses in Japan don't take huge salaries. They understand that that would be socially irresponsible. It would create feelings of envy and resentment among people who are worse off. The result is that Japan actually has a much more united society than some Western countries, where there are big differences in pay between top and bottom.

Speaker 2

Well, I think it's OK if the rich are getting richer—as long as everyone else's standard of living is rising, too. In other words, if people who aren't earning so much can nevertheless see that their buying power is increasing. Of course, that depends on their wages going up faster than the cost of living. But actually, I think it's how people *see* things that's important. If they think their quality of life is good, then they won't mind if the rich have a better standard of living. On the other hand, if they think they're getting a bad deal and that the rich aren't contributing, then they'll complain.

▶ **105**

1 No, thanks. I'm just looking.
2 Even the most difficult problems have a solution.
3 I'm just going to brush my teeth, then we can leave.
4 Don't worry. It's only money.
5 He's always losing things. He even lost his own wedding ring once.
6 It's only a suggestion—you don't have to follow it.
7 It's only the second time we've met.

▶ **106**

I = Interviewer, D = David Stiles

I: Are we all getting lazier or has economic development just meant that there's now someone available to do any job you want? Forty years ago, the idea of getting someone to hand wash your car was unthinkable—except to the very rich. Either you washed it yourself at home on a Sunday morning, or you took it down to the automatic carwash at your local garage. Nowadays, you can have it washed inside and out by professional car washers for as little as $8. David Stiles, Professor of Economics at Cranford Institute, is here with us to try to explain this phenomenon. What's changed, Professor?

D: Well, first of all, hello and thank you for inviting me onto your program. So, the short answer to your question is "economic development." As society gets richer, people have more money available to buy services, and to get other people to do things that they themselves don't particularly want to do or feel they're not good at doing— like installing a carpet or painting their house.

I: And I suppose it has to do with time, too. We all lead such busy lives.

D: Yes, that's true. It saves time and, of course, the big positive is that it creates a lot of employment. You don't have to be especially rich to have a house cleaner clean your home once a week, or to get your windows cleaned every couple of months. But I think you made a valid point at the beginning about people getting lazier. There are some rich people who take things to the extreme. I'm thinking of people who, for example, employ personal shoppers or who have someone walk their dog every day. When they have a party, they probably get a professional party planner to organize the party. I've even heard of people who get their Christmas tree put up, and then have someone else decorate it for them.

I: That's a bit extreme. Decorating the Christmas tree is supposed to be a fun activity for the family.

D: Well, I tend to agree with you, but I don't think the people who provide the services are necessarily complaining. That's how the economy works. People—particularly the wealthy—pay to have things done for them, and the people who provide the services benefit from that.

▶ **110**

LA = Leasing agent, C = Customer

LA: So, you took a look at the offices. What do you think?

C: Yeah, I think they're absolutely perfect for our needs.

LA: That's great. You'd like to take them then?

C: Well, ideally, yes, I would. But …

LA: But?

C: Well, a key thing for us is the length of the lease.

LA: It's a five-year lease. I think that was in the information I sent you.

C: Yes, that's right. But actually, I was hoping we could negotiate that down because, if you look at it from our point of view, we're a young business and we don't really know how things are going to go over the next few years. Let's face it, five years is a long time. Do you think your client would be willing to move a bit on that?

LA: I doubt it. I'm sure you'll appreciate that my client's main concern is for someone to rent the property for as long as possible. It gives them security. To tell you the truth, that's why the rent is so low. I can ask my client, but I'm not sure we'll get a positive response.

C: Hmm … Isn't there some way around that, maybe?

LA: Not that I can think of. What did you have in mind?

C: Well, perhaps we could sign a five-year lease but with a get-out clause after, say, three years.

LA: I'm afraid that won't work. We do actually have other people interested in the premises, so I'm pretty sure someone will take it on a five-year lease. If I were in your shoes and I found the terms of the lease difficult, I think I'd just walk away. At the end of the day, it has to feel right for you.

C: But it *does* feel right for me. Hang on a minute. I'm just going to call my business partner and see what he thinks.

LA: OK, no problem.

NATIONAL GEOGRAPHIC LEARNING

Life Student's Book 5, **2nd Edition**
Paul Dummett, John Hughes, Helen Stephenson

Vice President, Editorial Director:
  John McHugh

Publisher: Andrew Robinson

Senior Development Editor: Derek Mackrell

Associate Development Editor: Yvonne Tan

Editorial Assistant: Dawne Law

Director of Global Marketing: Ian Martin

Senior Product Marketing Manager:
  Caitlin Thomas

Media Researcher: Rebecca Ray,
  Leila Hishmeh

Senior IP Analyst: Alexandra Ricciardi

IP Project Manager: Carissa Poweleit

Senior Director, Production:
  Michael Burggren

Production Manager: Daisy Sosa

Content Project Manager: Beth McNally

Manufacturing Planner:
  Mary Beth Hennebury

Art Director: Brenda Carmichael

Cover Design: Lisa Trager

Text Design: emc design ltd.

Compositor: Doubleodesign Ireland, Ltd

American Adaptation: Kasia McNabb

For product information and technology assistance, contact us at
Cengage Learning Customer & Sales Support, cengage.com/contact

For permission to use material from this text or product,
submit all requests online at **cengage.com/permissions**
Further permissions questions can be emailed to
permissionrequest@cengage.com

Student Book + App: 978-1-337-90566-4
Student Book + App + My Life Online: 978-1-337-90572-5

National Geographic Learning
20 Channel Center Street
Boston, MA 02210
USA

National Geographic Learning, a Cengage Learning Company, has a mission to bring the world to the classroom and the classroom to life. With our English language programs, students learn about their world by experiencing it. Through our partnerships with National Geographic and TED Talks, they develop the language and skills they need to be successful global citizens and leaders.

Locate your local office at **international.cengage.com/region**

Visit National Geographic Learning online at **NGL.Cengage.com/ELT**
Visit our corporate website at **www.cengage.com**

CREDITS
Although every effort has been made to contact copyright holders before publication, this has not always been possible. If notified, the publisher will undertake to rectify any errors or omissions at the earliest opportunity.
Text: p10/p180 Adapted from: "When Suryia the orangutan meets a hound dog by the river, the two carry on like long lost friends," www.nationalgeographic.com; p12 Adapted from "Can the Selfie Generation Unplug and Get Into Parks?" by Timothy Egan with Casey Egan, National Geographic, October 2016; p27 Adapted from: "Guardians of the Fairy Tale: The Brothers Grimm" by Thomas O'Neill, www.nationalgeographic.com; p34 Adapted from: "Seven Billion," www.nationalgeographic.com; p49 Source: Australiacouncil.gov.au; p51 Sources: "4 reasons we love sad songs: Unexpected rewards of melancholy music" by A. Pawlowski, October 28, 2014; "Why We Can't Stop Listening to Sad Songs" by Jen Kim, October 26, 2015; "Why Your Brain Craves Music" by Michael D. Lemonick, April 15, 2013; p58 Source: "Dubai" by Afshin Molavi, January 2007, http://ngm.nationalgeographic.com/; p63 Adapted from: "Teenage Brains" by Drew Dobbs and "The development of fairness—egalitarian children grow into meritocratic teens" by Ed Yong, www.nationalgeographic.com; p87 Sources: "Universals and cultural variation in turn-taking in conversation" by Tanya Stivers et al., April 2, 2009; "Cultural Variations in Personal Space: Theory, Methods, and Evidence" by Mark Baldassare and Susan Feller, Ethos 3.4, October 28, 2009; "The Incredible Thing We Do During Conversations" by Ed Yong, January 4, 2016; p94 Source: "The Secret History of the Women Who Got Us Beyond the Moon" by Simon Worrall, National Geographic, May 8, 2016; p96/p187 Source: "What superpower do you wish you had?", http://www.nationalgeographic.com. Reproduced by permission; p99 Source: "Madagascar's Pierced Heart" by Robert Draper, http://ngm.nationalgeographic.com/; p105 Source: utstudentsandnews.blogspot.co.uk; p106 Source: "A life revealed" by Cathy Newman, April 2002, www.ngm.nationalgeographic.com; p123: "The King Herself" by Chip Brown, www.ngm.nationalgeographic.com. Reproduced by permission; p130 Source: "Innovation in education for work: The Lumiar schools, Sao Paolo, Brazil" by Leonie Shanks, Innovation Unit, October 2012; p135: "Animal minds" by Virginia Morell, March 2008, www.ngm.nationalgeographic.com. Reproduced by permission; p147: "How One Korean Taco Truck Launched an $800 Million Industry" by David Brindley, www.ngm.nationalgeographic.com. Reproduced by permission.
Cover: © JOSEP LAGO/AFP/Getty Images.
Photos: 6–7 ©National Geographic Maps. DATA SOURCES: Shaded relief and bathymetry: GTOPO30, USGS EROS Data Center, 2000. FTOPO1/Amante and Eakins, 2009. Land cover: Natural Earth. naturalearthdata.com. Population Density: LandScan 2012 Global Population Database. Developed by Oak Ridge National Laboratory (ORNL), July 2013. Distributed by East View Geospatial: geospatial.com and East View Information Services: eastview.com/online/landscan. Original copyright year: 2015; 6 (t) © danielcastromaia/Shutterstock.com; 6 (m) © Carsten Peter/National Geographic Creative; 6 (b) © Michael Nichols/National Geographic Creative; 7 (t) imageBROKER/Alamy Stock Photo; 7 (bl) © Aleksandr Lukjanov; 7 (br) © sippakorn/Shutterstock.com; 8 (tl) © Shivji Joshi; 8 (tm) © pikselstock/Shutterstock.com;

Printed in China by CTPS
Print Number: 01 Print Year: 2018

8 (tr) © Jing Wei; 8 (mtl) © Alejandra Brun/AFP/Getty Images; 8 (mtm) © StockLapse/Getty Images; 8 (mtr) © Peter Boehi; 8 (mbl) © Harrison Liu; 8 (mbm) Randy Duchaine/Alamy Stock Photo; 8 (mbr) © Stringer China/Reuters; 8 (bl) © Jody MacDonald/National Geographic Creative; 8 (bm) © David R. Frazier Photolibrary, Inc./Alamy Stock Photo; 8 (br) © DlightSwitch/Barcroft Media/Getty Images; 9 © Shivji Joshi; 10 © Stevi Calandra/National Geographic Channel/National Geographic Creative; 12 © Corey Arnold/National Geographic Creative; 15 © Bob Krist/Getty Images; 16 David R. Frazier Photolibrary, Inc./Alamy Stock Photo; 17 © hadynyah/iStockphoto; 18 © Tetra Images/Getty Images; 21 © pikselstock/Shutterstock.com; 22 AF archive/Alamy Stock Photo; 24 (t) © Abdulrahman Alhinai; 24 (b) © John Stanmeyer/National Geographic Creative; 25 (l) Ariadne Van Zandbergen/Alamy Stock Photo; 25 (r) National Geographic Creative/Alamy Stock Photo; 27 imageBROKER/Alamy Stock Photo; 28 © Stockbyte/Getty Images; 29 © Ralph Loesche/Shutterstock.com; 30 © Carsten Peter/National Geographic Creative; 32 National Geographic Creative/Alamy Stock Photo; 33 © Jing Wei; 34 © Randy Olson/National Geographic Creative; 36 DUS architects, 3D Print Canal House, ongoing project, Amsterdam; 37 Alexander Tolstykh/Alamy Stock Photo; 38 (all) © Renee Comet/National Geographic Creative; 39 age fotostock/Alamy Stock Photo; 40 © Joe Raedle/Getty Images; 42 © BSIP/Getty Images; 43 B Christopher/Alamy Stock Photo; 44 Sueddeutsche Zeitung Photo/Alamy Stock Photo; 45 © Alejandra Brun/AFP/Getty Images; 46 © Alexandre Orion, Ossario, 2016 Urban Intervention Created by Selective Cleaning; 48 Travelscape Images/Alamy Stock Photo; 51 © Bancomer; 52 © Leonard Adam/Getty Images; 53 © Lee Snider Photo Images/Shutterstock.com; 54 Richard Ellis/Alamy Stock Photo; 56 (left col) © Jeff J Mitchell/Getty Images; 56 (right col: l) © Alejandra Brun/AFP/Getty Images; 56 (right col: r) © Alexandre Orion; 57 © StockLapse/Getty Images; 58 © DigitalGlobe/ScapeWare3d/Getty Images; 60 (l) Frans Lanting Studio/Alamy Stock Photo; 60 (r) © Michael Melford/National Geographic Creative; 63 © Kitra Cahana/Getty Images; 64 © lzf/Shutterstock.com; 66 imageBROKER/Alamy Stock Photo; 68 © YAY Media AS/Alamy Stock Photo; 69 © Peter Boehi; 70 © Chris Johns/National Geographic Creative; 72 Wead/Alamy Stock Photo; 73 Danita Delimont/Alamy Stock Photo; 75 (t) © Ian Trower/Age Fotostock/Photolibrary Group/Getty Images; 75 (m) © Richard Nowitz/National Geographic Creative; 75 (b) © Sextantio Press; 76 © Keenpress/National Geographic Creative; 78 © Aleksandr Lukjanov; 79 © Mariusz Kluzniak/Getty Images; 80 (left col) © Manfred Gottschalk/Getty Images; 80 (right col: l) © Peter Boehi; 80 (right col: r) © Ian Trower/Age Fotostock/Photolibrary Group/Getty Images; 81 © Harrison Liu; 82 © Charles Eshelman/FilmMagic/Getty Images; 84 © Yva Momatiuk and John Eastcott/National Geographic Creative; 87 © Tom Merton/OJO Images/Getty Images; 88 © James L. Stanfield/National Geographic Creative; 89 ZUMA Press, Inc./Alamy Stock Photo; 90 © danielcastromaia/Shutterstock.com; 91 (tl) Roberto Nistri/Alamy Stock Photo; 91 (tr) © nhungboon/Shutterstock.com; 91 (ml) © corlaffra/Shutterstock.com; 91 (mr) Papilio/Alamy Stock Photo; 91 (bl) © Mark Bridger/Shutterstock.com; 91 (br) © chaipanya/Shutterstock.com; 92 RosalreneBetancourt 10/Alamy Stock Photo; 93 Randy Duchaine/Alamy Stock Photo; 94 NASA Archive/Alamy Stock Photo; 96 (tl) © Albert Yu-Min Lin/National Geographic Creative; 96 (tr) Courtesy of Laly Lichtenfeld; 96 (mtl) © Andres Ruzo/National Geographic Creative; 96 (mtr) © Alize Carrere/National Geographic Creative; 96 (mbl) © Andrew Thompson; 96 (mbr) © Jen Shook; 96 (bl) © Rick Kern/WireImage/Getty Images; 96 (br) © Ricky Qi; 99 © Nazzu/Shutterstock.com; 100 Ashok Tholpady/Alamy Stock Photo; 102 © sippakorn/Shutterstock.com; 104 © oversnap/Getty Images; 105 © Stringer China/Reuters; 106 dpa picture alliance/Alamy Stock Photo; 108 © Mario Laporta/AFP/Getty Images; 111 © Cate Gillon/Getty Images; 113 © 1000 Words/Shutterstock.com; 114 © Jason Edwards/National Geographic Creative; 116 (left col) © Kyodo News/Getty Images; 116 (right col: l) dpa picture alliance/Alamy Stock Photo; 116 (right col: r) © Cate Gillon/Getty Images; 117 © Jody MacDonald/National Geographic Creative; 118 © NASA; 120 © Marco Grob/National Geographic Creative; 123 (t, b) © Kenneth Garrett/National Geographic Creative; 124 © Shelterbox; 126 © Photo-Loci/Alamy Stock Photo; 128 © Bjoern Bertheau; 129 © David R. Frazier Photolibrary, Inc./Alamy Stock Photo; 130 © Paulo Friedman; 132 © Christopher Pledger/eyevine/Redux; 135 © cheetahok/Shutterstock.com; 138 © Michael Nichols/National Geographic Creative; 140 (l) © David R. Frazier Photolibrary, Inc./Alamy Stock Photo; 140 (r) © Paulo Friedman; 141 © DlightSwitch/Barcroft Media/Getty Images; 142 © Luka Tambaca/National Geographic Creative; 144 Peter Horree/Alamy Stock Photo; 145 © giuseppe carbone/Shutterstock.com; 146 Phil Wills/Alamy Stock Photo; 147 © Gerd Ludwig/National Geographic Creative; 149 © Dougal Waters/Getty Images; 150 © The Farmery (TheFarmery.com); 152 © Lynn Koenig/Getty Images; 153 (t) Motoring Picture Library/Alamy Stock Photo; 153 (b) © Renee Comet/National Geographic Creative; 154 (t, b) © Renee Comet/National Geographic Creative; 155 (l) Motoring Picture Library/Alamy Stock Photo; 155 (r) © Renee Comet/National Geographic Creative.
Illustrations: 31 David Russell.

ACKNOWLEDGEMENTS
The *Life* publishing team would like to thank the following teachers and students who provided invaluable and detailed feedback on the first edition:
Armik Adamians, Colombo Americano, Cali; Carlos Alberto Aguirre, Universidad Madero, Puebla; Anabel Aikin, La Escuela Oficial de Idiomas de Coslada, Madrid; Pamela Alvarez, Colegio Eccleston, Lanús; Manuel Antonio, CEL – Unicamp, São Paulo; Bob Ashcroft, Shonan Koka University; Linda Azzopardi, Clubclass; Éricka Bauchwitz, Universidad Madero, Puebla; Paola Biancolini, Università Cattolica del Sacro Cuore, Milan; Laura Bottiglieri, Universidad Nacional de Salta; Richard Brookes, Brookes Talen, Aalsmeer; Maria Cante, Universidad Madero, Puebla; Carmín Castillo, Universidad Madero, Puebla; Ana Laura Chacón, Universidad Madero, Puebla; Somchao Chatnaridom, Suratthani Rajabhat University, Surat Thani; Adrian Cini, British Study Centres, London; Andrew Clarke, Centre of English Studies, Dublin; Mariano Cordoni, Centro Universitario de Idiomas, Buenos Aires; Monica Cuellar, Universidad La Gran Colombia; Jacqui Davis-Bowen, St Giles International; Nuria Mendoza Dominguez, Universidad Nebrija, Madrid; Robin Duncan, ITC London; Christine Eade, Libera Università Internazionale degli Studi Sociali Guido Carli, Rome; Leopoldo Pinzon Escobar, Universidad Catolica; Joanne Evans, Linguarama, Berlin; Juan David Figueroa, Colombo Americano, Cali; Emmanuel Flores, Universidad del Valle de Puebla; Sally Fryer, University of Sheffield, Sheffield; Antonio David Berbel García, Escuela Oficial de Idiomas de Almería; Lia Gargioni, Feltrinelli Secondary School, Milan; Roberta Giugni, Galileo Galilei Secondary School, Legnano; Monica Gomez, Universidad Pontificia Bolivariana; Doctor Erwin Gonzales, Centro de Idiomas Universidad Nacional San Agustin; Ivonne Gonzalez, Universidad de La Sabana; J Gouman, Pieter Zandt Scholengemeenschap, Kampen; Cherryll Harrison, UNINT, Rome; Lottie Harrison, International House Recoleta; Marjo Heij, CSG Prins Maurits, Middelharnis; María del Pilar Hernández, Universidad Madero, Puebla; Luz Stella Hernandez, Universidad de La Sabana; Rogelio Herrera, Colombo Americano, Cali; Amy Huang, Language Canada, Taipei; Huang Huei-Jiun, Pu Tai Senior High School; Nelson Jaramillo, Colombo Americano, Cali; Jacek Kaczmarek, Xiehe YouDe High School, Taipei; Thurgadevi Kalay, Kaplan, Singapore; Noreen Kane, Centre of English Studies, Dublin; Billy Kao, Jinwen University of Science and Technology; Shih-Fan Kao, Jinwen University of Science and Technology, Taipei; Youmay Kao, Mackay Junior College of Medicine, Nursing, and Management, Taipei; Fleur Kelder, Vechtstede College, Weesp; Dr Sarinya Khattiya, Chiang Mai University; Lucy Khoo, Kaplan, Singapore; Karen Koh, Kaplan, Singapore; Susan Langerfeld, Liceo Scientifico Statale Augusto Righi, Rome; Hilary Lawler, Centre of English Studies, Dublin; Eva Lendi, Kantonsschule Zürich Nord, Zürich; Evon Lo, Jinwen University of Science and Technology; Peter Loftus, Centre of English Studies, Dublin; José Luiz, Inglês com Tecnologia, Cruzeiro; Christopher MacGuire, UC Language Center; Eric Maher, Centre of English Studies, Dublin; Nick Malewski, ITC London; Claudia Maribell Loo, Universidad Madero, Puebla; Malcolm Marr, ITC London; Graciela Martin, ICANA (Belgrano); Erik Meek, CS Vincent van Gogh, Assen; Marlene Merkt, Kantonsschule Zürich Nord, Zürich; David Moran, Qatar University, Doha; Rosella Morini, Feltrinelli Secondary School, Milan; Judith Mundell, Quarenghi Adult Learning Centre, Milan; Cinthya Nestor, Universidad Madero, Puebla; Peter O'Connor, Musashino University, Tokyo; Cliona O'Neill, Trinity School, Rome; María José Colón Orellana, Escola Oficial d'Idiomes de Terrassa, Barcelona; Viviana Ortega, Universidad Mayor, Santiago; Luc Peeters, Kyoto Sangyo University, Kyoto; Sanja Brekalo Pelin, La Escuela Oficial de Idiomas de Coslada, Madrid; Itzel Carolina Pérez, Universidad Madero, Puebla; Sutthima Peung, Rajamangala University of Technology Rattanakosin; Marina Pezzuoli, Liceo Scientifico Amedeo Avogadro, Rome; Andrew Pharis, Aichi Gakuin University, Nagoya; Hugh Podmore, St Giles International; Carolina Porras, Universidad de La Sabana; Brigit Portilla, Colombo Americano, Cali; Soudaben Pradeep, Kaplan; Judith Puertas, Colombo Americano, Cali; Takako Ramsden, Kyoto Sangyo University, Kyoto; Sophie Rebel-Dijkstra, Aeres Hogeschool; Zita Reszler, Nottingham Language Academy, Nottingham; Sophia Rizzo, St Giles International; Gloria Stella Quintero Riveros, Universidad Catolica; Cecilia Rosas, Euroidiomas; Eleonora Salas, IICANA Centro, Córdoba; Victoria Samaniego, La Escuela Oficial de Idiomas de Pozuelo de Alarcón, Madrid; Jeanette Sandre, Universidad Madero, Puebla; Bruno Scafati, ARICANA; Anya Shaw, International House Belgrano; Anne Smith, UNINT, Rome & University of Rome Tor Vergata; Suzannah Spencer-George, British Study Centres, Bournemouth; Students of Cultura Inglesa, São Paulo; Makiko Takeda, Aichi Gakuin University, Nagoya; Jilly Taylor, British Study Centres, London; Juliana Trisno, Kaplan, Singapore; Ruey Miin Tsao, National Cheng Kung University, Tainan City; Michelle Uitterhoeve, Vechtstede College, Weesp; Anna Maria Usai, Liceo Spallanzani, Rome; Carolina Valdiri, Colombo Americano, Cali; Gina Vasquez, Colombo Americano, Cali; Andreas Vikran, NET School of English, Milan; Mimi Watts, Università Cattolica del Sacro Cuore, Milan; Helen Ward, Oxford; Yvonne Wee, Kaplan Higher Education Academy, Singapore; Christopher Wood, Meijo University; Yanina Zagarrio, ARICANA.